WORKING AT STORMONT

Also by John A Oliver

ULSTER TODAY AND TOMORROW

Working at Stormont

MEMOIRS

by

JOHN ANDREW OLIVER

Published in association with the
Institute of Irish Studies
The Queen's University of Belfast,
and the Royal Town Planning Institute
Northern Section Irish Branch

DUBLIN
INSTITUTE OF PUBLIC ADMINISTRATION
1978

© 1978 John Andrew Oliver

FIRST PUBLISHED 1978 BY THE

INSTITUTE OF PUBLIC ADMINISTRATION

59 LANSDOWNE ROAD, DUBLIN 4

ISBN 0 902173 83 9

NOTE: These are the author's personal memoirs, recording his personal views and impressions. They should not be taken as having any official authority.

SET IN 11 POINT LINOTYPE BASKERVILLE LEADED ONE POINT

PRINTED IN NORTHERN IRELAND BY W & G BAIRD LIMITED, ANTRIM

CONTENTS

LIST OF ILLUSTRATIONS

INTRODUCTION

I wish to tell how I tried to do my job and to earn my pay during forty years in the Northern Ireland civil service.

So far as I know nothing comparable has ever been written before. Apart from a few articles dealing with specific topics in a severely objective manner and published in learned journals, there has been no attempt made to set down in black and white the firsthand experience of an administrative civil servant at Stormont. This is understandable, for civil servants are by tradition anonymous, their work is confidential and they are trained to eschew controversy. Even in the small Ulster community, where everyone knows everyone and where civil servants are surrounded by relatives, friends, neighbours and interest groups that know them personally, civil servants still maintain such a discreet silence about their work, indeed such a shell of reticence, that few people have any idea of what 'they actually do all day up there at Stormont'. Besides, it is the job of ministers to do the talking. Constitutionally and politically ministers are in charge and, what is more, are answerable for the work of their ministries and for all that is done in their names. It is for ministers to explain, to justify, to accept blame, to take credit.

Why then should I set out to overcome so many restrictions and why should the Department of Finance have so readily agreed to my publishing this book?

I found one day that I was twice as old as my boss. In other words, as a result of some political changes a new minister had come to my department in the person of a young man of around thirty years of age, fresh, youthful in outlook and of the same generation as my sons. I was over sixty. On looking further around from that time onward I saw that I was older than any minister in our whole administration and, what is more relevant, my experience in public work stretched back a great deal further than the experience of any of them. This caused me to think about the past and to consider whether I did not have a duty to place on record the story of the events, the changes and the forces at work in the long period since I joined the service in 1937. The province has had many ups and downs and has been through further upsets since 1968. All these have attracted publicity and comment bearing almost entirely on religion, violence and party politics. It is a matter of bitter regret to many Ulster men and women that in this welter of talk the world seems to have lost sight of the beautiful place that Ulster is, the decency and friendliness of the great bulk of her people and— what is relevant to my position—the splendid record of solid achievement by countless people in the whole field of public ad- ministration. Ulster is no administrative backwater; it is a well-run country with something to teach the rest of the world.

Let me put my personal position into perspective. My experience is neither unique nor even special. There are amongst my col- leagues some with longer service, some with greater knowledge of finance and of industrial promotion, some with greater skill in handling the official machine and many with greater artistry in writing. It just happens that over an unbroken period of almost forty years I (an Ulsterman with family roots deep in Ulster soil) have been continuously engaged as an administrative officer, in re- sponsible central positions, close to ministers, on work that im- pinged directly on the lives of ordinary men and women and that was constantly affected by politics. I thought at first of writing a textbook on the Northern Ireland administration but I soon de- cided that I was not the man to do it. I have been too close to the problems and the occasions I am describing. The writing of an ob- jective and comprehensive textbook would call for the skills of a more detached observer. I hope that he will come forward one day. Instead, I am going to try to compile a memoir of experiences shared with many colleagues; and on that thread I shall string some events of importance and some lessons learned. I shall tell my story in the first person even at the risk of seeming egotistical, which no civil servant wants to do. When a civil servant goes so far as to publish his memoirs he must steel himself to reveal something of his upbringing, education and experience because these com- bine to make the administrator and therefore form part of the proper study of public administration. One consequence of this form of treatment is that I have to be selective in my choice of topics, because in my personal experience I naturally saw only a fraction of the whole story. Another problem concerns the use of the plural form. Government work is a team affair; few can manage to do much on their own and all are bound up together. After a lifetime in the practice of the art I find it hard to break myself from the habit of writing 'We were trying to do such and such' or 'this was one of our failures'. In using the plural form I may seem to be involving my former colleagues and of course they may have no wish to associate themselves with all of the statements. In order to get over this difficulty let us tactfully leave it that where the references are favourable, others may claim the credit; where they are unfavourable, the plural is merely a figure of speech, one of the oddities of an old buffer trying to relive the past.

Another reason for taking the personal and individual approach is the concern which the administrator has for the individual person. Contrary to the general impression of some sort of mechanical apparatus it is in fact individual men and women who prepare bills for parliament and the various schemes just as it is individual men and women who are eventually affected by them. The personal approach adopted here may therefore serve as a reminder of the personal element in administration.

But, apart from providing a narrative thread, my personal position and my personal fortunes and misfortunes are of no importance. The reader is invited to substitute for me any of the senior administrative people at Stormont because, give or take some details, their story would bear out my story and would probably be even more illuminating.

In presuming to write about the civil service I am acutely aware of the fact that I can speak at first hand of only a small section of it, namely the administrative section that is concerned with policy and legislation. All my time has been spent in carpeted offices in the splendid environs of Parliament Buildings and the Stormont estate. I have never been a clerical officer. I have never trudged from door to door in Strabane or Newry as a visiting officer for social security nor prosecuted at petty sessions. I have never been an agricultural inspector examining cattle on a wet and windy farm. Without attempting to speak for all those men and women I simply acknowledge the essential part they play in our work and I readily associate myself with them when I come to write, as I shall do repeatedly, of the qualities of hard work, courage and persistence which abound in the service. Their story ought one day to be written, too.

This book will contain no startling revelations about politics or politicians. The relationships between someone in my position and his minister are entirely confidential and must always remain so. While therefore I shall be trying to describe the quality of those relationships and shall be giving many examples—real examples from real life—I shall be adhering most strictly to the code of absolute confidentiality. Wild donkeys would not drag from me one single indiscretion. Mind you, in saying that, I am not taking up any pious attitude. The Official Secrets Act would probably prevent me—or put me in gaol; but vastly more powerful than any act of parliament is the tradition, the practice, the total way of life that guards the confidential treatment of internal government business as a real trust.

My aims therefore are to set down an account of some of the main trends in public administration here, to describe them as seen by an official and to fill an undoubted gap—in British literature generally—by trying to convey in immediate, personal and candid terms what it is actually like to be involved and to carry administrative responsibility.

My methods will be three-fold. First, I shall describe the events in the sequence of time: prewar, wartime, postwar reconstruction, the troubles, the end of the Stormont Parliament, direct rule, the end of direct rule, the Constitution Act of 1973, the power-sharing executive, Sunningdale and the Council of Ireland, direct rule mark II and mark III and the Constitutional Convention. Second, I shall examine the subject from a totally different aspect, from the aspect of the day-to-day work, the working conditions, the pay, the living conditions, methods, constraints and satisfactions. Third, I shall try to draw some threads together at the end in terms of people, sources and the quality of service.

It is just possible that this account may prove to have useful by-products. To the extent that it is read in schools, colleges and universities it may stimulate young men and women to think about the service and to take it up as a career. They are certainly going to be needed. And although I am thinking primarily of young people in Ulster, there is a wide open door for recruits from outside the province as well, for one of our undoubted strengths has been, right since 1921, the seminal admixture in the service of traditions, religions and cultures. Younger readers need not jump to the conclusion that since memoirs deal with the past, the whole subject is over and done with. Far from it. The problems at the centre of affairs will stay very much the same and (give or take a computer or two) the methods of dealing with them described in this book are not likely to change very greatly. And no matter what political or constitutional upheavals lie in store for us, Ulster will still have to be administered somehow. The second by-product may lie in the contribution which a personal, truthful story of life and work can make to the material of social history. Truthful the story will certainly be. I shall abide by the truth as I see it, knowing full well of course that truth is many-sided and that others may have seen events in a different light. And memory can play tricks. And, as King Henry V said (on another famous battlefield):

> Old men forget: yet all shall be forgot,
> But he'll remember with advantages
> What feats he did that day.

Three warnings in one.

With all those qualifications I assure the reader that this will be a truthful account of life as one ordinary man has seen it in the service of Ulster.

Part I

THE YEARS OF SERVICE

Chapter 1

MADE IN ULSTER

Ulster readers will have a good idea of what I mean when I say that my family, on all sides, was a typical big presbyterian family of tenant farmers in north Derry. Other readers deserve a fuller explanation.

My people had come over from Scotland in the early years of the seventeenth century and had settled in the area between Coleraine and Limavady in what is now county Londonderry. By dint of hard work (for genealogical research in Ireland is notoriously difficult) I have been able to trace all the main strands.

The Olivers came with Sir Robert McLellane and 127 of his countrymen from Kirkcudbright. They lived for a time around the town of Limavady and eventually, in 1692, at Derrybeg, a fertile townland bearing oak trees, apple orchards and cornfields a mile or so to the east of the town. At local government gatherings I like to remind the audience that John Oliver was the first town clerk of Newtownlimavady as long ago as 26 June 1660 and that he managed to hold the job through the reigns of Charles II, James II, William and Mary, and Anne, giving it up only on 5 April 1715. From then on there was an unbroken succession of John, Andrew and James Olivers at Derrybeg right down to the 1920s. They were presbyterian dissenters and tenant farmers. Now and then they produced a school teacher, a presbyterian minister or a small shopkeeper but they were never landed, titled or prominent people. Like many similar families they repeatedly sent sons and daughters to settle in America. From what I have been able to find out the Olivers managed to obtain an education in generation after generation and to keep up a fair level of writing, reading and culture. For example I have seen the signature of a John Oliver on the will of the Reverend Thomas Fulton who took up his charge in Dunboe (Castlerock) as early as 1656 and there is much well-attested evidence of Andrew and James Oliver busying themselves with public affairs throughout the eighteenth century. Although Presbyterians throughout, the Olivers appear to have done much work for the episcopal parish acting as overseers and applotters. Limavady, or Newtownlimavady, was of course one of the planned new towns of the Ulster plantation and seems to have had, very early on, the rudiments of an accounting system for I have found John Oliver being appointed on 14 February 1702 as 'Applotter of what public money shall be levied for this present year.'

On my mother's side the Sherrards lived in Magilligan a few miles to the north of 'Newtown', as it was called, and a much poorer area. This is a most unusual neighbourhood, a sandy peninsula jutting out between Lough Foyle and the Atlantic, geologically a raised beach and totally without trees or hedges. It was so flat and bare that the ordnance survey selected it as the base for their original trigonometrical survey of Ireland and the two baseline terminal points have been preserved. Partly because of its position and partly because of the sheer difficulty of reaching it over the hills and along the beach from Downhill, Magilligan remained for generations inaccessible, isolated and cut off from most influences. Although in a county that was otherwise 'planted' by the London companies in the early seventeenth century, Magilligan was never granted to any of those companies—the Clothworkers, the Skinners, the Fishmongers and so on. It retained its distinctive quality, remote and untouched, a blend of catholic and presbyterian, of Irish and Scottish, of gael and planter, well into the twentieth century and provided a static social and intellectual atmosphere against which it is interesting to test the evolving issues treated in the early chapters of these memoirs.

Dissenters and tenant farmers again, the Sherrards or Shearers (who came over from Argyle) developed a large family connection in the area and represented roughly the same standard of living, education and attainment as the Olivers. For readers outside Ulster it is necessary to explain that there is no social class to which people like these can be conveniently allocated. A glance at the old homestead and at the thin poor soil as it runs through the fingers might suggest that the Sherrards must have been amongst the lowest helots in society. And yet in 1783 we find Hugh Sherrard in company with Connolly McCausland (one of the landed gentry) appointed 'to provide water pipes at one shilling a foot, with seven pence a foot to be charged on the length of each dwelling house including entries.' A few years later in 1814, we find Joseph Sherrard heading a list of men founding the new presbyterian meeting house of Magilligan.

The Morrells, another branch, farmed at Ballywildrick, Articlave, and were in a bigger way of business. They were Huguenot in origin and adhered to the Reformed Presbyterian Church. They took an active part in local boards and indeed in regional administration right down to the power-sharing executive government of 1974 and beyond. They have extremely wide family connections throughout Ulster.

The fourth grandparent was Rosanna McMullan from another farming family at Glebe, Castlerock, with extensions east to Coleraine and west into Magilligan.

Of all those four main groups our immediate family knew most about the Sherrards in Magilligan and spent most time with them from 1910 or so till 1939. We became deeply attached not only to them personally but also to their friends and neighbours and to the area as a whole. There were many personal and church links with Scotland as it is possible to look across the sea to the island of Islay and the Paps of Jura. It was after all across this short stretch of water that St. Columba sailed on his way to Iona. Even the dialect in Magilligan is strongly Scottish. One of my uncles was something of a minor authority on Robert Burns and could quote from memory long passages from 'It was a' for our Rightful King' and 'The De'il's awa' the Exciseman.' But by far the most powerful influence on the Sherrards and on us all as children was that of the Presbyterian Church itself. This was presbyterianism in a pretty severe and puritan form. The doctrine was calvinist and the morality stern. The meeting house was a bare, unadorned and barn-shaped structure of black basalt, where long sermons of great ferocity were preached, the metrical psalms sung in slow time and musical accompaniment spurned. A precentor gave the note with a tuning fork. Even in the workaday world of milking or winding a hay rope the strains of the twenty-third psalm or the Old Hundredth could be heard across the farmyard. The influence was extremely powerful and in my own case has lasted the whole of my life. Though I abandoned all formal church connections while I was a young man, the deeper influences of the Scottish presbyterian tradition, the moral teaching, the spartan habits, the early rising, the plain food, the walking of long distances, the saving for a rainy day, have never entirely left me.

By the time I was born in 1913 our family had moved to Belfast with the general movement into the growing industrial city. There were seven of us, first four girls, then myself and two young brothers, a warm and closely knit family if ever there was one. With spouses and offspring there are now sixty-four of us and we

keep in touch with a further couple of hundred relatives throughout Ulster and beyond. The primary school we went to, St. Jude's,
succeeded in firing us with a desire for learning. My father, Robert
John Oliver, born in 1869, had a considerable influence on our
development. A highly intelligent and vigorous man who never
fulfilled his true potential, he was widely-read and widely-travel-
led. His was the world of H G Wells, Conan Doyle, Arnold Ben-
nett and *Blackwood's Magazine* and he loved attending the lecture
halls of those days. From his modest position in the linen department of Robinson and Cleaver's, one of the leading export houses
of the time, he enjoyed friendship with customers across the world
and corresponded with them in flowery but moving prose and large
clear handwriting. In politics he was a home ruler and a supporter
of J B and W S Armour of north Antrim; he favoured a united
Ireland within the British Empire. He had no use whatever for the
new parliament of Northern Ireland then being set up in Belfast,
constantly disparaging its leaders in colourful language. Nothing
that they could do was right in his eyes. No one that I have known
since, in any political circle, was more scathing about jobs for the
boys,' 'feathering their own nests' and all the other vulnerable aspects of a new expanding political establishment. Even when his
friend and relative Senator John A Long of Limavady became
parliamentary secretary to Sir James Craig (the first prime minister) I recall his pungent denunciation of the whole process of
'manufcturing jobs for hangers-on of the ruling clique.' The effect
of this colourful if critical home background must have been to in-
tensify my childhood understanding of all that was happening
around us in the early twenties.

   After primary school I had the extreme good fortune to be sent
to Inst, that is to say, The Royal Belfast Academical Institution, the
leading boys' day grammar school in the centre of Belfast and one
of the best schools in the British Isles. Here was a large school,
established in 1810, developed from the outset on strictly non-
sectarian lines; the majority of boys were Protestant but there were
always some Catholics and a steady stream of talented Jewish boys
came as well. The atmosphere encouraged the cultivation of ideals
with little emphasis on examinations and a great deal on hard
learning for its own sake, Latin, grammar, debate, argument and
civic awareness. Weak on science and mathematics I leant towards
literature and languages along with history and above all geography which I unashamedly loved. What I had in comparison with
other boys was enthusiasm. Anything I decided to take up, I pursued with zest, energy and pleasure. Embarrassing and tiresome to

other people, I am sure, this enthusiastic approach was to me the spice of life. It was not a matter of will-power or determination. I just could not help it; nor have I ever since. Reflecting on the whole affair now I value greatly the opportunity which the rudimentary Belfast city scholarship system of 1926 gave this little boy to mix, in a rigorously demanding academic atmosphere with others from every geographical, social, religious and political sector of Belfast and twenty miles or so around.

At the Queen's University of Belfast I made the mistake of choosing modern languages as my main subjects. I was not a true linguist—apart from everything else I had no ear for sounds—and I was much keener on my subsidiary subjects: geography, economics and political science. The plain fact was that French and German did not stretch many of us. It has been pleasant and convenient ever since to have those two languages (and the help that they provide in picking up other languages) but if I could have my university life over again I should not choose 'Mod. Lang.' Study of languages did, nevertheless, give opportunities for travel which were unusual in the 1930s: a stimulating summer in Paris, half a year in Königsberg (away out beyond the Polish Corridor in East Prussia), a term at the Zimmern School of International Studies in Geneva and then a full year at Bonn am Rhein with much else besides. In 1936, in the midst of all this headlong activity, I rashly and without advice or preparation sat for the marathon first division examinations run by the British Civil Service Commission in London. I failed badly. After calming down a bit I entered for the competition a second time and managed to pull it off. Although I had led a most active life at Queen's, taking part in countless activities, especially debating in the Literific (the Literary and Scientific Society, older than the university or the preceding Queen's College), taking part in student union and students representative council affairs and editing *The New Northman* as well as (simultaneously!) its deadly rival, *The Queensman*, I cannot truthfully say that I got all the benefit from Queen's that I might have. In a way I envied the medicals who were particularly strong and already part of a much bigger world of medicine, hospitals and life in general. Engineering, the new faculty of agriculture, and the faculty of law, growing rapidly with the arrival of a legislature and high court in Belfast, all seemed enviable to me. The large preponderance of girls in the French and German classes was a constant if happy distraction for someone from a boys' school. My disappointment cannot be laid at the door of Professor Douglas Savory nor of

Professor Gilbert Waterhouse, both good teachers and men of
stature. I simply was not in tune with them and I dissipated my
efforts far too widely. Career guidance did not exist as a formal
exercise and there was nothing remotely comparable with the
Trinity College Dublin tradition of steering young men into the
public services. Many of the students and junior staff in arts regarded the Northern Ireland Parliament as some sort of upstart,
reactionary institution which no self-respecting graduate could
bring himself to serve. The year I graduated, 1936, saw the
National Council for Civil Liberties in action, with Professor R M
Henry and Professor Alexander Macbeath prominent as radical
critics of the new regime. Despite all this discouragement I persisted in trying for the public service as a career.

Should it be the Northern Ireland Civil Service? Or should I go
for Whitehall, the Indian or the Foreign and Consular Service?
After arguing this out with my friends during long country walks
(as solemn young men used to do in those days) I made up my mind
firmly in favour of going for Stormont. The reasons, as I remember, were the very considerable attraction of a well-paid permanent
job at home in a time of economic slump and the prospect of good
living and working conditions, together with a dash of patriotism
and idealism. Another reason, apparent in retrospect, was the fact
that I had travelled and lived abroad so much in the previous five
years that the appetite for travel had been satisfied for the time
being and the attraction of life in Ireland began to seem greater.
Although Queen's was unsympathetic to the thought of Stormont
as a career, Inst was not. The issue did not arise in quite the same
form with eighteen-year-old schoolboys as with graduates of twenty-
two entering the higher reaches of the public service; nevertheless
a great many Instonians were going into the new service and many
have done so since, not only as clerks but as lawyers, accountants,
engineers, architects and so on. They have occupied some of the
most senior and influential positions including in 1976 the position
of head of the civil service of Northern Ireland. The matter almost
became an embarrassment when the Constitutional Convention
was being set up in the spring of 1975, as five of the key senior appointments connected directly or indirectly with the convention
went to Instonians. The influence of the many Instonians on the
Stormont scene would make a worthwhile study in itself.

And so, in October 1937, I entered along with David Holden of
Sussex, Rossall and Cambridge. The head of the service, W B
Spender, did Holden the honour of going down by car and meeting

him off the Liverpool ferry boat—a charming practice which later heads did not keep up. While this old-world courtesy was being honoured on the Donegall Quay I walked to the office from my home nearby but in my excitement arrived much too early.

Chapter 2

IMPRESSIONS OF A NEW RECRUIT

The service which I entered in 1937 was small, dignified, efficient; it worked in what we would regard now as a leisurely fashion, displayed professionalism only in patches and had room for many quirks of practice and personality.

There had, from the time of the split (as we euphemsitically refer to the partition of Ireland in 1921), been just six ministries—Finance (clearly the premier department), Home Affairs (the next most senior in the order of precedence that was then solemnly observed), Labour, Education, Agriculture and Commerce. This last department had at first come under the same minister as Agriculture but had become a fully independent department by 1937. Home Affairs dealt not only with police and the courts but also with local government, health, housing and the poor law. Finance gave me the impression of a certain élitism, if not actually of snobbism, and was rather aloof though not quite so much so as the Cabinet Secretariat, which one was not allowed to approach or even to telephone, or so I was told.

The magnificent Parliament Buildings at Stormont, where I was to work, had by then been built and occupied. The founders had been far-seeing and had placed the centre of the provincial government and the symbol of devolved authority well outside the city of Belfast. They endowed it with a distinguished setting in a handsome, formal public park. The building itself, a neo-Georgian edifice of four storeys in Portland stone with neo-Greek columns and pediment, was carefully sited on a hill-side, facing south and looking across to the Castlereagh hills and beyond to the soft contours of the Lagan valley. The views from the two ends of the building were even more striking—to the west a view over the city and the huge shipyard gantries rising up from the waters of Belfast Lough and standing stark against the green hills of Antrim; to the east an idyllic vista of county Down and Strangford Lough. Even though the city has expanded, even though motor traffic has multiplied many times over, even though the city boundary has been extended to take in the Stormont estate, the setting still holds its attraction, its dignity and its quite exceptional functional value.

To resume: Parliament Buildings were occupied then, when I was joining in 1937, by House of Commons and Senate, and the administrative accommodation on the higher floors was occupied by Finance, Home Affairs, Labour, Agriculture and the Exchequer and Audit Department. Commerce were very sensibly located in the city. Education were somewhere else. That struck me as being odd, at the time; but they have always been 'somewhere else' and have been less intimately bound up with the rest of the service than any other department. They are now at Bangor, County Down and are the one example of a department wholly 'dispersed' from the main seat of government administration.

One of the most striking incongruities was to me the personality of the permanent secretary to the Ministry of Finance and head of the service, Wilfrid Spender. I could scarcely absorb the fact that this retired army officer (he was known as Colonel Spender at the time), a survivor from earlier conflicts and, more apparent even than that, a survivor from a bygone era of English colonial life, should be heading the civil service in Northern Ireland. Remote, kindly, lisping, out of touch, hospitable, croquet-playing, correct, wary of political interference in civil service affairs, Spender little knew what an extraordinary conundrum he presented to someone like me, a raw recruit from the Queen's University. I suppose he embodied much of what made up the service in those days; and on the principle of the responsibility borne by those at the top he must be accorded credit for what was good in the service then as well as blame for its shortcomings, given the spirit of the times.

Not only did the permanent secretary of Finance seem something of a surprise to me as an Ulsterman entering the Ulster civil service but indeed so did all the permanent secretaries of the day. Blackmore at the Cabinet Offices, Conacher at Labour, Magill at Home Affairs, Scott at Commerce, Scott Robertson at Agriculture, Bonaparte Wyse at Education, Duggan and Petherick the top men in Finance—not a single one of them was a local man! This had a powerful effect on a new local recruit, creating the image of a public service that, far from being parochial, was international in its flavour.

As it was to the Ministry of Labour that I was assigned on entering the service, that was the department I got to know best and which influenced me most. I was posted to the factories department

and was from the very first day plunged into real work in a real
live setting. My job was to read the reports of the factory inspectors,
which they made and submitted each week on the inspections of
factories and workshops. There were four of them, as I recall, all
graduates, each covering an area of the province and each carrying
also a special reference for engineering, chemical or textile trades
and so on. They pursued a rigorous programme of inspections over
five days a week, coming in to the office only on Saturday mornings
in order to hand over their reports and to prepare their programme
for the following week. I was struck by many aspects. There was
the care with which those reports were written, and written by
hand. There was the great amount of detail covered: safety of
workers, guarding of machinery, hours of work for women and
young persons and so on. There was the impartiality and detachment with which the inspectors reported on faults and shortcomings. And there was the stern follow-up action in the shape of
stiff letters going out to the managers and in some cases prosecu-
tions being started in the courts. There was the fact that these industrial specialists reported to us as lay administrators.

I describe all this to indicate the salutary lesson which even a
glimpse of such work provided for a raw young man fresh from
delightful but quite irresponsible debates in the university only a
few miles away across the city.

After being allowed to attend some negotiating sessions at trade
boards—statutory bodies representing employers and workers in
the less well organised trades such as women's garment-making and
retail bespoke-tailoring—I gathered courage and began to look
around the ministry. Everywhere I found the same story—real
work being done, under legal authority, by extremely knowledge-
able men and women totally unknown to the public but serving
them to the best of their ability. The ministry was dominated then
by its work on cash benefits—unemployment, sickness, widows
and old age pensions. This was a formidable machine, both at headquarters and in the labour exchanges. Elderly men would pore
over documents, insurance cards, stamps and cancellations, calcula-
ting benefits and entitlement to benefits. The brain centre resided
in H Branch where specialists grappled with questions of insur-
ability. Till then I had fondly thought that employees had to be
insured, employers not; and that was that. Little did I know.
H Branch wrestled daily with the legal position of clergymen of
various kinds, of part-time farmers, of share-fishermen, of drivers of
cross-border railway trains, and developed some highly esoteric
rules. We, in our branch, had the task of preparing a new factories

bill as we were operating under an old code that fell short of requirements. We studied the English legislation, took a sideways look at how they were managing in the Irish Republic but above all we had to distil the lessons of those factory inspection reports and frame proposals that fitted the needs of our shipyards, our ropeworks, our flax scutch mills and the other industrial operations peculiar to our area.

Unemployment overshadowed all our departmental thinking, for it was the major economic and social problem of the day. State intervention had not made such headway and our contribution was —apart from cash benefits—largely in the form of relief schemes. The Green Card which we issued, entitling a man to a job on an aided scheme, was much sought after. And we fostered a few puny efforts by voluntary bodies such as YMCA. This side of our work struck me as being feeble and amateurish in contrast with the professionalism of factories act and insurance act administration; but nevertheless fresh efforts were constantly made. One took place in the summer of 1938 when the ministry arranged for a voluntary body, the Northern Ireland Council of Social Service, to be set up, appointed the first members and seconded me as secretary. I had only a few months there when I was recalled to act as private secretary to a new parliamentary secretary, Billy Grant.

A new world opened for me, and for many others as well.

The Ministry of Labour had been managed—I use the word advisedly—for many years by its minister, J M Andrews of Comber, an austere man, a thrifty man, a mill-owner who had been brought up in a hard competitive world and knew the value of every penny. He had been followed by D G Shillington, a Portadown iron-founder cast in much the same mould. John F Gordon followed, a very different type and, of all things, an elocutionist who carefully rehearsed every phrase and every gesture. But Billy Grant was unique. He was a huge, rugged man; a shipwright from the Queen's Island; a plain man; a man's man, a football fan; a strong teetotaller ('The moderate drinker is the curse of the country' he would vouchsafe to me); an Orangeman; a Labour-Unionist; a man of immense courage. He used to tell the story against himself of a trade union comrade bursting out 'Billy, it's a blessing that you're a teetotaller for you're coarse enough when you're sober.' He was one of those ministers who attract business. (Austin Currie was another, thirty-six years later.) He had a huge letter-bag. Members of Parliament of all parties and all religions flooded him with cases of poverty, unemployment, sickness and every social ailment. How often did we send letters for example to Paddy Agnew MP, 12 Railway Street, Armagh, for Paddy stood at the chapel gate every Sunday morning and collected handfuls of bits of paper from the poor of his constituency. Billy Grant himself would come into my room in the mornings searching his pockets for a scrap of paper on which he had written the outlines of a case. 'A fellow came up to me at the tram stop this morning' or 'I was having my hair cut yesterday and would you believe it the barber was getting at me about a pension for the wife's mother.'

One of the features which impressed me as a new entrant from the radical and highly critical world of the Queen's University Students Union was the pleasant leisurely atmosphere, beguiling and deceptively easy-going. We came in at 9.30 or so. Most of us went out for lunch. And we finished at 4.45. I observed that when an officer, within even that gentlemanly time-table, acquired some piece of dreary information about a case he would laboriously write it all down on a piece of paper and place it in a tray labelled 'Out' where it would rest undisturbed until an ancient *mutilé de guerre* would see fit to lift it, take it to some central repository along the corridor, whence it would eventually be transported to another gentleman across the room who surprisingly appeared to have desire, or need, to receive it. Why my friend did not, in the first place, simply walk across the room and tell him, I could not understand. Later on I did. And the place abounded in characters.

There were ex-servicemen from the trenches who regularly disappeared on each monthly pay-day, went on the drink and did not return for several days. There was the officer who kept a bottle in his desk and could never start to dictate his letters till he had fortified himself; and, the story went on, no one in the whole department could dictate such a brilliant stream of epistles. And so on. Saturday morning meant plus-fours for the senior men. One elegant fellow brought his dog to the office on Saturday mornings and spent his energies getting the enormous hound to lie quietly in the well of his desk.

In spite of all this the work went on. The insurance laws were enforced. No citizen entitled to a cash benefit went without his cash on the appropriate day of the week. No pension was over-paid for a single day after the recipient died, for diligent clerks combed the death columns of every provincial newspaper, lest the relatives should somehow forget to notify the office. Factories were inspected, working conditions improved, labour relations fostered. The needs of parliament were met.

Chapter 3

THE EARLY YEARS

Such then were the personal impressions of a young man entering the civil service. It is now necessary to look at the service of those days more objectively and to examine its problems and its achievements.

June 7th, 1921 saw the start with the opening of the newly created Parliament of Northern Ireland by His Majesty King George the Fifth in the Belfast City Hall; and with the creation of the Departments of Executive Government. All this has to be seen in perspective. Belfast had never been a capital city and had never been the seat of a parliament or government. Although a busy industrial and commercial city it was essentially a provincial city and had nothing in the shape of national institutions. It was Dublin that had been our centre for public administration over centuries and for legislative and parliamentary activities at certain times as well. In Dublin were situated the principal law courts, museums, libraries, art galleries, the record office, the registry of deeds and so on. And consequently Dublin had its established corps of government and other public officials.

The Northern Ireland service had therefore to be started from scratch, apart from the labour exchanges and a few other local branches of Dublin departments. Times were hard. The wartime boom of 1914–18 had collapsed for industry and agriculture. Unemployment was extremely high, amounting to twenty, twenty-five and even twenty-seven per cent of the insured population at various times in the early twenties.

But it was also a time of civil war in Ireland. The bitter outburst in the south that greeted the 1921 settlement spread north and aggravated the unrest that had prevailed since 1918. Hundreds were killed, thousands injured and a huge amount of property destroyed. Both politicians and officials felt obliged to carry guns. The very task of getting hold of the existing documents and records needed to enable consistent and orderly administration to be started was exceptionally difficult. These lay in Dublin. Some were destroyed by fire. Officials there were cooperative towards the North but were being intimidated from openly helping to sort out and despatch the documents needed in the North. In the end these had to be removed by stealth and brought through a hostile countryside up to Belfast in the guise of a load of old waste paper! And of course there were no suitable offices ready and waiting to receive them. Stormont did not exist. Departments had to be housed wherever accommodation could be found in rented suites in commercial office blocks—Finance in Donegall Square West, Home Affairs in Ocean Buildings, Education in Assembly's College, Agriculture in Wellington Place, Commerce in Chichester Street and Labour scattered over the YMCA, Upper Queen Street, Arnott's Buildings and 124 Donegall Street. Parliament itself had no home for many years. After the opening in the City Hall, parliament moved to the handsome Theological College of the Presbyterian Assembly near the Queen's University where it had to sit for ten years. The elegant book-plate still used by the parliamentary library today features that building as its centre-piece.

If the practical difficulties were great, the political and psychological difficulties were even greater.

The creation of a separate state in Ulster and the setting up of its own government were no joyous occasion, no happy culmination of national aspirations as is the case so often with the launching of a new separatist country. No one had been campaigning for a separate state. To the protestants and unionists the new settlement represented a second best, a barely acceptable substitute for continued integration with Britain. To the Roman Catholics and nationalists it represented such a bitter disappointment, such a set-back to their aspirations for a united Ireland, that they could not find it in their hearts to give their loyalty to it. Both these attitudes persisted and deprived the system of much of the moral support it needed. The honourable members of the first House of Commons included such famous people as Eamon De Valera, Michael Collins and Arthur Griffith, Southern leaders elected for Northern constituencies! These members of course did not take their seats nor did any of the Roman Catholic nationalist members for the first few years. This resulted not only in the absence of any formal opposition but also in the real criticism of government measures coming from its own backbenchers, a phenomenon that was to persist throughout the life of the parliament till the 1970s.

Some local councils refused to recognise the new government and insisted on still posting their departmental correspondence to an address in Dublin!

There were equally serious shortcomings on the constitutional front. The basic act of the Westminster parliament—the Government of Ireland Act 1920—had been designed for a very different situation. It provided for two parliaments in Ireland, one in the North and one in the South, and both operating within the United Kingdom. It provided also for a Council of Ireland with certain statutory functions and designed to lead eventually to an all-Ireland parliament. The South, for good reasons of their own, departed from the idealistic concept of the 1920 Act and set up (in agreement with the British government) the Irish Free State. The Council of Ireland never came into being.

The North, accepting the 1920 settlement, found itself therefore operating under some sections of an act designed for a radically different situation; and found itself, in fact, in the extraordinary position of trying to function under a fragment of a constitution—and of a written constitution at that. Even that fragment—given that it was politically tolerable in the quite unusual circumstances—imposed countless limitations on the practical workings of a parliament and government. Many important matters were 'excepted' from our sphere of operation; these included, quite understandably, the crown and the succession, foreign affairs, war and peace, treaties and so on. But there were also 'reserved' to Westminster many matters which as the years went on proved to have the most serious consequences for government administration: trade outside Northern Ireland, shipping, posts, radio, the savings bank, the supreme court. Furthermore, the constitution contained restrictions on the acquisition of property for public purposes, on the regulation of trade and on taxation which, until they were later removed in amending acts, were to prove positively harmful to the country's social and economic development.

The functions 'transferred' to Northern Ireland could be summed up under the general heading: peace, order and good government, to use the actual words of Section 4 of the 1920 act.

It was not so much the principle of the constitutional restrictions or the exception and reservation of certain matters to Westminster that caused the trouble; it was the inability of Northern Ireland to legislate (or to administer) in any field which touched upon those matters that created the practical difficulties, because of course excepted, reserved and transferred functions interacted at many points and the dividing lines were not always clear. In those days the courts and in particular the local courts tended to construe constitutional limitations much more strictly. Section 5, for example, as it was passing through parliament, had had six words inserted: 'or take any property without compensation'. Clearly framed with the laudable intention of making sure that the two new parliaments in Ireland did not savage their people and confiscate their homes and hearths, the phrase proved to have the most inhibiting effect on town and country planning and slum-clearance legislation. It dogged all efforts in the North for forty years and was responsible for many of the eyesores to be seen in our physical environment today.

The picture I have painted here—of three categories of functions: excepted, reserved and transferred—is a fair picture of the situation as it eventually emerged. But the actual situation at the start was much more complex and much more difficult for administrators to handle. The difficulty lay with the middle category of reserved functions. Some were reserved outright to Westminster, for example the main field of taxation. Some were held in suspense pending the setting up of an all-Ireland parliament, for example the post office, the supeme court, the land registry, the registry of deeds and the public record office. Some, such as the land purchase acts, were being reserved pending the completion of the buying out of the tenanted farms. Some, like the Royal Irish Constabulary, were being reserved in 1921 for a stated number of years (even though the RIC came to be disbanded in 1922). And finally some functions were being reserved not to Westminster but to the Council of Ireland. Examples of these were railways, fisheries and diseases of animals. What uncertainty for the administrator! One can well imagine his problem in advising his minister on any matter touching on those functions, for there are few aspects of public life so inimical to good administration as sheer uncertainty about basic responsibilities.

Just consider the very first parliamentary question put in the new parliament. It was asked by private notice on Tuesday 20 September 1921 and sought information 'as to which authority the duty of the maintenance of the peace in the City of Belfast and the Northern area generally is at present entrusted…eighteen lives lost…unnecessary delay in our intervention of the police and military...what are the powers of the Northern Parliament for the enforcement of law and order?'

The first numbered question printed on the order paper was answered on 26 September 1921 and was concerned with 'large quantities of arms and ammunition having been brought in by Sinn Féiners...Sinn Féiners constantly engaged in drilling...and if the Government will approach the Imperial Government...'

And the second numbered question was equally concerned with instability: 'several Public Boards in Northern Ireland declaring their determination to resist the decrees of the Northern Parliament'.

To complete this picture of legislative and administrative uncertainty as our predecessors saw it at their desks in 1921 I quote some phrases which recur in the 1920 Act:

section 2	'with a view to the eventual establishment of a Parliament for the whole of Ireland'
section 3(2)	'on the date of Irish Union'
section 35(1)	'as from the end of the financial year in which the date of Irish Union falls'
section 36	'if at any time after the date of Irish Union'.

And of course the 1920 Act left the new parliament with extremely limited financial powers overall.

The very boundaries of the state were uncertain and remained in serious doubt from 1920 right until the 1925 agreement with the South was signed. This may seem hard to believe today but is a matter of proven historical fact with a profound influence on administration at the time.

A thoroughly disheartening start, one might say. But the civil service administrator is above all a realist. He wastes no time in regretting the past, or in finding excuses. He deals with the situation as he finds it—with the 'as is', to use present-day office jargon.

What then was the 'as is' in June 1921, the practical situation as the senior officials found it?

Sir Ernest Clark, Permanent Secretary to the Minister of Finance and Head of the Civil Service of Northern Ireland, had probably the most daunting task. He had no civil service to speak of. He had no exchequer. He had no Comptroller and Auditor-General. He had no financial system going. He had no arrangements for government borrowing. He was an Englishman, trained in the Inland Revenue, and thoroughly competent; he was meticulous, hard-working and hard-driving; and he needed to be.

Lewis McQuibban at Education had probably the least of all to build upon. Education was in a parlous state. Administratively the schools had come under no fewer than four separate departments in Dublin: The Commissioners for National Education, The Intermediate Education Board, The Commissioners of Education (commonly called The Endowed Schools Commissioners) and the Department of Agriculture and Technical Instruction. All four, with their differing traditions and methods and with their respective staffs and records, had to be quickly blended into one. There were enormous shortages of school accommodation, the parliamentary secretary confessing in the House of Commons on 21 September 1921 that he understood there were twenty-four thousand schoolchildren without accommodation in Belfast alone! On the same day he roundly declared 'that secondary education was handed over to the Northern Parliament in a condition which is undoubtedly and absolutely deplorable'. One always has to be careful in accepting the judgment of people taking over from others the administration of a public service; they are heavily inclined to denigrate it and those who were earlier responsible, in order to show their own achievements in the best possible light. One has seen this—and still sees it today. But there is much evidence to support the view that school accommodation and school administration were in a poor way in 1921. In a useful and closely documented chronicle of the work of the Belfast Education Authority, *Exactly Fifty Years* (Belfast, 1974) the author Norman McNeilly gives a most careful and precise account of the state of affairs at the start; and it is pretty grim. I can further bear this out, for at St Jude's Public Elementary School on the Ormeau Road, Belfast the physical accommodation was appalling. Two classrooms, at least, had no desks. Miss Orr's class of nine-year-olds had no fewer than eighty pupils in it. And one class in turn always had to occupy 'the floor' and do its work standing throughout the period, with neither desks nor seats.

J S Gordon at Agriculture had equally few advantages. Agriculture was in a poor way and was operated without much scientific backing or educational support.

Cecil Litchfield at Commerce had little to build on. Commercial intelligence was rudimentary in the extreme, traditional industry was declining and the legal powers he possessed were trifling. But he enjoyed one remarkable inheritance: an extensive railway system.

The province was served by rail to an astonishing degree. I

reckoned at the time that, looked at from Belfast, there were at least a dozen main lines and I remember travelling on all of them: to Bangor and Donaghadee on the north-east coast of county Down; two separate lines, no less, to the watering-place of Newcastle at the foot of the Mourne mountains in mid-Down; to Newry on the way south to Dublin and to Warrenpoint on Carlingford Lough in south Down; to south Armagh; to Enniskillen and Belcoo in county Fermanagh; to the Atlantic via Omagh, Pettigo and Belleek; two distinct systems to Londonderry, one south and west of Lough Neagh, the other east and north of that lake by Coleraine; a line to the Stranraer ferry boat at Larne; and a lengthy line right across the middle of the province from south-west to north-east via Dungannon and Cookstown to Coleraine. Then, on top of that, there were a dozen or so branch lines running to such places as Ardglass, Newtownbutler, Castlederg, Limavady and Dungiven, Portrush, Ballycastle, Parkmore, Tobermore and Draperstown, as well as the unique electric tram to the Giant's Causeway. A prodigious legacy from commercial enterprise.

J A Dale at Labour must have viewed a more encouraging if patchy scene. The cash benefit services—as we came to call them—had all been established and were a going concern. So also were the factory acts and the workmen's compensation legislation. The most dismaying feature on his landscape was undoubtedly the high rate of unemployment and the limited tools at his disposal for dealing with it.

Sam Watt at Home Affairs was in a totally different position. Law and order was his big worry. The Royal Irish Constabulary was breaking up and the new regular police force for the North had still to be created. There was a special constabulary—already created by Westminster on 22 October 1920 under Westminster legislation going back as far as the Special Constables (Ireland) Act of 1832—and his mind must have turned gladly to thoughts of expanding and using it in the terrible conditions of the early years of the new state.

It is hard to do justice in a few lines to the burdens of administration and legislation caused by the threats to the state from within and without its borders. The second-reading speech by R D Megaw KC when introducing the Civil Authorities (Special Powers) Bill on 21 March 1922 has to be read in order to gain even a glimpse of the practical problems facing the Northern administration. It was destined never to escape wholly from them.

On the housing side of his work Watt inherited a miserable patrimony—a huge legacy of wretched nineteenth century dwellings in Belfast and Derry as well as even older cottages in the rural areas; a rising population in the towns; little or no new building since the outbreak of war in 1914; and many houses being damaged or destroyed under his very eyes during the troubles of those days.

Watt found he had one useful standby, namely the poor law system administered by the Board of Guardians. Although it has for long been customary to despise and reject that system for the simple reason that it survived into an age for which it was unsuited and in which it became increasingly unpopular in the light of evolving social policy, it nevertheless was—in its Irish form—a highly successful aspect of government. Sam Watt found that he had inherited 27 out of the 144 Poor Law Unions in Ireland. Each union was a most convenient area of local government, namely a union of parishes based on each market town and an area of some ten miles radius around. In the language of today the elected Boards of Guardians can be said to have gradually developed, since their foundation in 1838, a comprehensive health, welfare and cash benefit service—hospital, dispensary, doctor, midwife, workhouse, boarded-out children and outdoor relief in cash— all under their own hand. The terms were harsh, the residential accommodation spartan and the social atmosphere discouraging; but in the conditions of Ireland in the nineteenth century and up till the time when the Northern government took over, the system brought great benefits. As I say, the permanent secretary of 1921 must have been mighty grateful to see it functioning. On the general public health and epidemiological side of his work the permanent secretary could have been excused if he had muttered a word of despair across his broad desk: tuberculosis was rampant (or consumption as it was commonly called then); maternal mortality was disgracefully high and so also was infant mortality.

Those then were a few of the facts which stared the administrators straight in the face when they sat down at their desks in 1921. Before going on to appraise the achievements and failures of fifty years of local administration (1921–1972) it is well to remember that the situation which they took over in 1921 was inevitably an inheritance from the past, for better or for worse. London had, in one way or another, been governing us for eight hundred years, sixteen times as long. Politicians, according to their standpoint, will refer to that period as eight centuries of English misrule or as our precious heritage. To the civil servant all that is immaterial; he deals with the present and, as far as he is allowed, with the future.

It was the duty of the permanent secretaries to bring to the notice of ministers the facts as they found them, to suggest alternative courses of action, with their advantages, disadvantages and attendant dangers. It was for the new ministers to decide in cabinet what they wanted to do. And it then became the duty of the permanent secretaries to see that those decisions were carried out and legislation prepared or such other action undertaken as the situation required. The record of activity is impressive.

In preparation for a debate in the student union of the Queen's University during my first term there in 1932, I calculated that in its first ten years the new parliament had passed into law about three hundred public and general acts promoted by government, to say nothing of the private and local acts promoted by others. The very first was the Exchequer and Audit Act (Northern Ireland) 1921, laying down the basis of our system of control of public expenditure. Incidentally the usage was quickly established of inserting the words 'Northern Ireland' in round brackets after the word 'Act' and before the year, in order to indicate a measure passed by this parliament. A measure passed by the parliament of the United Kingdom but dealing specifically with Northern Ireland would have the words Northern Ireland inserted before the word 'Act'. Many other acts followed, dealing with financial provisions, government borrowing and government lending and so on. The well-known local savings scheme that takes the form of Ulster Savings was enacted as early as 1922. The Census Act of 1925 was another early measure providing for basic requirements of good government. Debates and legislation on intoxicating liquor featured prominently in the twenties for the sale of liquor was one of the great controversial issues of those times. Local Option was one of the platforms on which candidates fought the 1929 election. Valuation, rating and that ugly word de-rating all appeared on the statute book.

A small but unusual scheme for house-building was developed under the auspices of the British Government, namely the Irish Sailors and Soldiers Land Trust composed of officials nominated by the governments of the United Kingdom, Northern Ireland and the Irish Free State. By the outbreak of the second world war 1251 houses for ex-servicemen had been built in the North, mostly in Belfast and Londonderry (of which ironically a dozen were destroyed by enemy action in 1941). The houses still carry touchingly evocative name-plates on the doors: Mons, Somme, Thiepval, Jutland, Messines, Courtrai. Fifty years on, the Irish Sailors and Soldiers Land Trust was replaced by a new voluntary housing association, providing flats for elderly people and going

under the name of the 'Milibern Trust', so that the Irish soldiers
at least are remembered.

And the interests represented by each department featured in
turn on the parliamentary order paper: a Roads Act in 1923
laying the foundations of what was to become in time the best
road system in the British Isles; a Housing Act in 1923, the first
of a great many; a Livestock Breeding Act, also in 1923, wisely
providing for the control and quality of bulls as a basis for the
whole cattle industry of Ulster in later years; the Marketing of
Eggs Act 1924, the forerunner of many schemes for the better
marketing of agricultural produce to the manifest benefit of our
farmers and of us all; a National Health Insurance Act in 1922;
no fewer than eight acts, I reckoned, dealing with unemployment
insurance between 1922 and 1925—a sure sign of social and therefore administrative turmoil; a Workmen's Compensation Act in
1923, adding to a most complex code of law that eventually became too complex even for the courts to handle; a Rent Restriction Act in 1925, taking another step along a seemingly
endless road of involved legislation of questionable value; a Trade
Boards Act in 1923; a Contributory Pensions Act in 1925; and
so it goes on, bread and butter business, certainly. But they did
not confine themselves entirely to bread and butter issues. They
found time to promote legislation on less material matters as
well. As early as 1923—that is to say in only the second year of
legislative activity—the departments promoted a public records
scheme which laid down the ground rules for the acquisition and
maintenance of records, one of the more civilized activities of any
state. Today we have, I assert, the most attractive and well-staffed
Public Record Office in these islands. And to anyone who thinks
that in making such a claim I may be exaggerating, my answer in
this and every other case is to invite him to go and see for himself.
Parliament passed the Game Preservation Act in 1928, the Wild
Birds Protection Act in 1931 (the only piece of legislation successfully promoted by the opposition) and the Grey Seals Protection
Act in 1933. And meantime they had found an opportunity to
deal with Deceased Brother's Widow's Marriages in 1924.

Many of the parliamentary bills were highly political in content and correspondingly controversial in the country. The
government were scarcely in power when they decided to abolish
the proportional representation system of elections which the
British government had introduced for local government in the
last months of their regime in Ireland. The bill had passed
through all its stages in Commons and Senate (including the

Commons' consideration of many Senate amendments) by 5 July 1922. Royal assent, which would normally be expected within a few days, did not arrive; and still did not arrive. The Lord Lieutenant was being advised from London not to give assent to this contentious bill; and the administrators, being the ham in the sandwich, waited anxiously from week to week, not knowing what to do for the best. In the end London agreed, authorised assent on 10 October and put the officials out of their misery. Likewise the bill which abolished proportional representation as the form of election to the Northern Ireland House of Commons created bitter controversy in the country when it came forward in 1929.

Meantime there were even more bitter battles to be fought with the protestant population over religious education in schools —a subject on which the ordinary protestant people felt strongly and which called for several hard-fought parliamentary bills before the issue came to rest in 1947.

Relations between the Northern administration and the high courts were far from cordial in the early years. The courts and their staffs were no doubt wary of the new departments growing up under a surbordinate parliament, and there is equally little doubt that the Ministry of Finance had its problems in settling the many administrative and financial points of common concern. No judge can be beholden to any political executive; civil servants do not find it easy to do business with judges.

Successive parliamentary draftsmen, whose business it is to work closely with both the courts and the executive, have spoken of the problems they had in repairing the damage of the early years. By the time of the 1939–45 war relationships were on a proper footing and since then have worked happily and well.

The Northern Ireland service was extremely fortunate in its first parliamentary draftsman, Arthur S Quekett, the officer whose duty it was to convert the instructions of the departments into legislative form and to guide both departments and parliament generally in legislative and constitutional matters. Quekett served from 1921 till 1945, when he died within a few hours of his retirement. I recall being sent as a junior officer to consult him and being overawed by this precise little man sitting in a huge office surrounded with shelves of law books from floor to ceiling on all four sides. He was hard to satisfy and quick to point out flaws in departmental arguments. It may have been prudence that caused my older and wiser colleagues to send me along instead of going themselves. But these youthful impressions of mine are worthless compared with an assessment of A S Quekett which we are fortunate to have in published form. It is by Sir Cecil Carr KC LLD, counsel to Mr Speaker at Westminster, and takes the form of a foreword to volume III of Quekett's definitive work, *The Constitution of Northern Ireland* (HMSO, 1946).

After tracing Quekett's origins in Somerset and his legal training in Dublin, Carr goes on:

'Arthur Scott Quekett was selected to go to Belfast. It was a happy choice. He was blessed with an unruffled temper, a great capacity for hard work and an unerring instinct for patiently tackling first things first. He had an orderly mind, a lucid style and a scholar's learning. He was master of his trade and of his materials. Amid the exigencies of those formative years the statute-book of Northern Ireland built up its high standards of technical competence.

'Though neither the present volume nor its predecessors hint at any such claim, he has written of events in which he himself played no insignificant part. He saw the Government of Northern Ireland come into being as part of a symmetrical pattern including both the North and the South, though the other half of the design was fated to be rejected and replaced. He knew the difficulties of transition and adaptation: he shared in their solution. He watched over the stages whereby, as confidence in the Belfast administration grew, fresh powers and responsibilities were added. The framing of these extensions, though they were to be enacted at Westminster, was largely his work. The statutory pitfalls on the border-line between reserved and transferred matters were warily evaded though the day's work might bring problems which the makers of constitutions could hardly have foreseen. Not least important, the contacts between Stormont and Whitehall were preserved from friction, thanks in no small degree to his vigilance and discretion and to the personal contribution he could make to official relationships—a manifest singleness of purpose and an engaging charm of manner. Men relied upon his disinterested judgment. It was by no means unknown for visitors to Belfast, seeking guidance on enigmas far removed from the drafting of Bills, to be advised to their great advantage to "see Quekett first". A Parliamentary draftsman indeed seems nowadays to be drawn ever more frequently into consultation over the general and particular tasks encountered in the widening field of departmental decision. Even were that not true, his own indispensable duties are in themselves exacting and formidable. His handiwork affects the lives and interests of thousands. A mistake is unlikely to escape notice; its consequences may be grave. He works under heavy pressure. Loyalty to the proven principles of his art may bring the draftsman into conflict with the wishes of his masters whose main concern, naturally enough, is to be shown the shortest cut to some immediate political goal. The ignorant may scold him for results really due to the dictation of policy and to the uneasy conditions in which "government by discussion" evolves a people's laws. By a good fortune not always adequately recognised, men have been found who devote exceptional qualifications to the anonymous service of the State instead of seeking the more glittering rewards which forensic ambition is entitled to pursue.'

Legislation is of course the business of parliament, the responsibility of ministers, of whips and of politicians whether they support government of opposition. The role of the administrative civil servant in the legislative process is harder to summarise: he assembles facts; he acts as secretary to investigating bodies; he advises ministers; he takes their mind; he instructs parliamentary draftsmen, he briefs ministers on technical points; he attends in the officials gallery of parliament; he notes the trend of debate; ministers consult with him on tactics, timing, concessions and so on; and once the bill is passed into law, it becomes his job to enforce the act and carry out its administrative provisions. How he does all this; how it feels; how it affects his life—all this I shall try to describe in later chapters.

Chapter 4

THE NINETEEN THIRTIES

The year 1931 in some ways marked a turning point.
It was the year in which parliament and the main departments moved out to the splendid new building at Stormont. Not only were all concerned being released from temporary and unsuitable accommodation but they were also being physically brought together for the first time. There were two dimensions to this concentration. First, a number of departments—Finance, Labour, Home Affairs, Education and Agriculture—were housed under the same roof so that the opportunities for personal contact, for acquaintance, for collaboration were immeasurably improved. Second, departments were brought into closer touch with parliament. Senior officials whose work involved them in parliamentary business were housed only a few paces, or a flight of stairs, away from the lobbies or the galleries. Attendance of officials during debates became much more frequent and their understanding of politics improved correspondingly. And one cannot work in the same building as other people, enter by the same doors, use the same lifts or meet in the corridors without making personal contacts and friendships.

The year 1932 saw the great depression hit the Ulster economy. Unemployment rose to high levels. The first act allowing direct aid to new industry was placed on the statute book (as distinct from guaranteed loans) and the first step taken on the long road of state intervention in industrial promotion.

It was unfortunately also a time of deteriorating relationships with the South. The Cosgrave Cumann na nGaedheal regime was giving way to the De Valera Fianna Fáil, to more extreme nationalism, to a break with Britain and eventually in 1937 to the new Éire constitution.

Public funds were becoming even scarcer as the world slid into the great depression, for the British economy was in poor shape and ours was in a still worse condition. What money we had we were forced to husband most stringently. As always happens in the making of cuts in public expenditure, it turns out to be impossible to make uniform reductions in all services. Two services simply demanded funds—cash benefits for the needy, and the law and order function. The others consequently had to suffer quite disproportionate reductions. Those two were not by any means dissociated from one another. Unemployment brought idleness and unrest; unrest brought civil disturbance and, in the circumstances of Ulster, sectarian riots on the streets of Belfast in the summer of 1935. I can myself remember seeing the mourners in a funeral cortege in Royal Avenue scatter like chaff in the wind at the harsh sound of rifle fire from Smithfield Market.

Departments were all the time pressing ahead with such development of their services as the difficult conditions allowed.

The Ministry of Agriculture was probably the department that knew its own mind best. It had recruited a team of leading agricultural scientists and, what is important, had given them positions of influence in the administration. The result was seen in a record of quite striking progress. They gave pride of place to agricultural education. Early on they had opened a further agricultural college at Greenmount in Muckamore, County Antrim, in addition to those at Cookstown, west of Lough Neagh, and Strabane on the Donegal border, so as to give young men and women from the farms throughout the province the benefit of some formal training. Next they developed their advisory service to farmers: I can recall the sensational gossip at firesides in remotest Magilligan over the arrival of the Hen Woman in the 1920s.

But in some ways perhaps the most notable achievement of the Ministry of Agriculture was the link with the new faculty of agriculture at The Queen's University of Belfast. This was nothing less than a stroke of genius resulting in an admirable arrangement under which the university teachers became ministry advisers and ministry advisers became university teachers! If any similar arrangement were to be mooted today for giving departments of government the right to propose the appointment of academic staff, one can imagine the cries of protest about infringement of academic liberty and so on. The whole emerging pattern gradually became clear; research in agricultural science; teaching of university students; advice to ministry; flow of background advice of the highest quality to the teachers in the agricultural colleges; recruitment to the ministry's staff of a continuous flow of university graduates in agricultural sciences; stiffening of the inspectorate and of the general advisory service to farmers—all forming part of one continuum. Little wonder that the Ministry of Agriculture never wished to see agricultural education become part of the work of local education authorities as in England. No wonder at all that they were unhappy at the suggestion, many years later, that the faculty of agriculture should break its link with the ministry and be transferred to the New University of Ulster at Coleraine. The suggestion foundered, to the surprise of no one who knew the ministry.

The achievements of the Ministry of Agriculture in the field of marketing are well known and recorded; less well known are their outstanding contributions in the field of animal health and veterinary research. It is to their unremitting efforts and their firmness that Ulster owes an animal health status that is one of the highest in the world. Foot and mouth disease and swine fever are rare, so also is Johne's disease, and sheep scab is unknown. The foundations of these successes were laid by the ministry's veterinary research division in the Stormont estate in the 1930s that we are now reviewing. On those foundations the ministry was able to develop a multivalent vaccine to control neonatal enteritis in piglets (now in world-wide use), as well as testing methods for brucellosis in cattle that are now employed throughout Europe. This was top-level pioneering work by a ministry that had the knowledge, the foresight and above all the self-confidence to survey its field of work, assess the needs and then decide upon the solutions.

Much else was happening in the departments. It is hard for people today to imagine the strong passions aroused by the liquor licensing laws and in particular by proposals to abolish that most convenient of arrangements, the spirit grocer. How often was I dispatched as a child by a friendly neighbour, Mrs Rafferty, to McQuillan's shop to buy a quarter pound of tea; and while I was in the shop would I just buy her a glass of whiskey as well? Looked at in the spirit of the times, these shops embodied a number of social evils: too easy access to drink for shoppers, too big a temptation for housewives to spend the housekeeping money on whiskey and stout, and above all, an undesirable atmosphere for children running messages, to use the vernacular. The puritan protestants were determined to use their new local legislature to put an end to all three evils, and this they did within the first couple of years of the new parliament by abolishing the licenses and compensating the licensees. Thus emboldened, Home Affairs turned their attention in the thirties to those other pirates, the private bus operators who used to compete with one another in the most buccaneer fashion for the lucrative end of the road passenger trade, while leaving the less profitable ends somehow to look after themselves. I have the picture still in my mind of the rival firms of Nutt and Hutchison racing one another through Bellarena and Magilligan to capture the few pence that were to be collected. Even as a child I was struck by the noise, the rattle and the makeshift arrangements of these so-called services. Home Affairs set to, bought them out and cleared the way for the Northern Ireland Road Transport Board which in 1935 was a pioneer in the field of nationalised transport.

There was more being done by departments in those days in the sphere of public works than is generally appreciated. Drainage was one of the great needs, and I can recall as a child in Magilligan much stormy talk amongst farmers over the improvement of the only sizeable watercourse in that flat and sandy raised beach, the Big Drain. It was a momentous day when my grandfather took me by horse and cart to the Courthouse in Coleraine to listen to a public discussion on that subject. I assume now that it must have been a local inquiry into proposals by the Londonderry County Council.

Enormous discussion attended the efforts of the Ministry of Finance to lower the level of Lough Neagh and to improve the drainage of the whole river Bann basin. The drainage of Lough Erne followed and, later, that of the river Quoile. These were the first essays in what eventually became a widespread and most energetic programme of land drainage under the auspices of the Ministry of Agriculture.

The modernisation of the educational system had meanwhile been pushed ahead by our colleagues in that department. One of their very first steps, away back in 1921, had been to set up the R J Lynn Committee of Inquiry, with the hope of doing two things at once: introducing an up-to-date system of state schools and encouraging Roman Catholic parents to send their children to those schools. From the very start, however, their hopes on the latter point were dashed, for the Roman Catholic community found themselves unable to take part either on the Lynn Committee or in submitting evidence to it; and the inevitable followed in the sense of Roman Catholic unwillingness to share in the new Public Elementary Schools set up all over the country under the Londonderry Act of 1923 which flowed from the Lynn Report. My object in recounting this particular piece of history is to demonstrate one of the many tasks of exceptional difficulty which confronted my predecessors and still confronts my colleagues fifty years later. It fell to the officials in Education to devise workable ways and means of ensuring that Roman Catholic children, even though not attending state schools, nevertheless received the amount, quality and standard of education to which they were entitled, in schools adequately subsidised by the ministry and under teachers recognised by the ministry as competent. That they succeeded in doing so over all the years, and that they built up friendly relations and mutual trust with the clerical managers of Roman Catholic church schools has been frequently and amply attested by the bishops on public occasions.

Electricity Acts in 1930 and 1931; an Adoption Act in 1929; numerous acts dealing with the marketing of agricultural produce throughout the thirties; the monumental Factories Act of 1938 —these and many other acts and schemes testify to the positive activities of departments.

But the overwhelming administrative problem remained the continuing high level of long-term unemployment. The Ministry of Labour struggled to devise schemes for sending men and youths to where the work was available; and increasingly this was 'across the water' to Great Britain. Under the stress and strain there was, I fear, little clear thinking on policy. One tiny episode stands out in my memory and may have marked something of a new departure in thinking about the bases of the problem. The Ministry of Labour was being blamed for not finding more work. I was sitting in the officials' pew in the House of Commons one night when the minister was being attacked on that score. As he showed increasing signs of distress we sensed that some supplementary briefing from us would not be amiss. A senior colleague, F C Moore (author of that amusing book on office life in Dublin, *My Countrymen by an Irishman*, Blackwood 1930) scribbled a few words for the minister on a scrap of paper: 'Our task is to find men for the jobs, not jobs for the men'. That represented something of a clarification in the respective roles of Ministry of Labour and Ministry of Commerce; but to me it represented, much more vividly, the value of crisp, succinct briefing, of terseness, of monosyllabic impact. Had F C Moore not been there, I should have done the briefing. In my anxiety and my enthusiasm I should have written all I knew about the subject, and I should have been of much less help to a harassed minister on his feet.

The central task of the Ministry of Finance, all this time, was of course to finance all these beneficent activities. Starting from scratch, as I have shown, they set up an exchequer and a consolidated fund; a system of annual estimates and supplementary estitmates with a consequent appropriation bill system, departmental book-keeping and appropriation accounts; an exchequer and audit department to guard the exchequer, headed by the Comptroller and Auditor-General to audit our departmental accounts and report on them to a Public Accounts Committee of the House of Commons; a system for raising loans for government purposes; a government loans fund from which local bodies could borrow capital; a system of trading accounts for those activities of departments which brought in trading revenues and could therefore show a profit or a loss; and much else besides. These of course were but the outward forms. The more telling arrangements were those which actually controlled the flow of day-to-day expenditure as well as the accuracy, care and integrity with which payments, contracts, grants, purchases, disposals and so on were handled within departments. Here the key to the lock was held by one man in each department, namely the accounting officer and he was almost always the most senior official, namely the permanent secretary. A vast amount of the working of government flowed from this clear and simple arrangement.

The other important side to the work of the Finance officials lay in their handling of confidential relations with HM Treasury, an esoteric cult which would deserve a book to itself. Suffice it now to say that those relations worked and worked well. Through good times and bad, in peace and in war, under Conservative, Labour or Coalition governments in London, no matter what the vicissitudes of fortune produced in Northern Ireland, the Ministry of Finance managed to make the system work to the great benefit of this province. No one can say otherwise. The joint exchequer board; the residuary share of reserved taxation; the imperial contribution; step-by-step; parity; leeway; the re-insurance agreement; the social services agreement; the remoteness grant; the guaranteed price system for agriculture; the Development Programme 1970–75; paragraph 86 in the 1973 white paper on constitutional proposals—all strike a chord in the memory of everyone who follows the course of our public affairs and all reflect the practical arrangements worked on by Ministry of Finance officials right since 1921.

Let us consider the arrangements. The basic point is that the main provisions were actually embodied in the 1920 act, which (considering the unsettled conditions of the time) seems today to have been a hazardous thing to do. The act provided for separate public accounts (the word 'separate' was in the act); for certain extremely limited powers of taxation for the Northern Ireland Parliament (indeed for the two parliaments because one must always remind oneself that that act pre-supposed a parliament in the North and a parliament in the South, with a Council of Ireland working towards an all-Ireland parliament eventually). The act provided for a joint exchequer board to make certain determinations and apportionments in the financial relations between the three governments. Tightest of all perhaps was the arrangement laid down for the payment by Northern Ireland to the United Kingdom of an 'imperial contribution' in respect of its share of the benefits accruing from certain imperial services listed in detail in a schedule—the national debt, the armed forces, the civil list, the diplomatic service and so on. The point to be specially noted is that this was to be a first fixed charge on local revenues.

Separate accounts; extremely limited powers of taxation; an imperial contribution; the pre-supposition of a Southern parliament also 'working the act'—in those four elements lay the makings of constant difficulty and misunderstanding.

Separate accounts were bound to throw into relief any aid received from the United Kingdom and made the regional government appear as a poor relation always having to be subsidised. Separate accounts for Cornwall or Cumberland would have revealed a similar situation there, or in any part of the United Kingdom that happened to be less well off in financial terms than the average of all parts, and moreover would fail to show the contribution which that part made to the national well-being in other ways such as agricultural produce, or water supply or tourist facilities or recruits to the armed services and so on.

Limited powers of taxation also weighted the scales against the new administration. The act envisaged at worst a static economic situation and failed to foresee continuing unemployment and deepening economic troubles. With rising expenditure on social benefits and other public services, and no power to increase taxation, how could any regional administration balance its budget? The imperial contribution as a fixed first charge offered a standing target for criticism. If it dropped to a low point, critics of the administration could easily point to the failure of the North to pay its way; if it rose to a noticeably high level, critics could claim that money was being handed over to Britain that could with greater advantage be spent on the improvement of local services.

With the South opting out of the Government of Ireland Act of 1920, a customs control had to be quickly imposed on the border by an act of 1922, creating a new and unforeseen situation that hindered trade, and resulting in a customs revenue smaller than it might have been under the full terms of the 1920 act.

So far as government administration is concerned, the 1920s and 1930s were dominated by those inherent financial difficulties and the day-to-day problems that flowed from them. Ministers were determined to keep the level of social benefits equal to that in the rest of the United Kingdom. The room for manoeuvre which they left themselves on other services was therefore correspondingly restricted. Then yet another dilemma emerged. If in any year the British government decided to reduce national taxation, for ordinary fiscal reasons, Northern Ireland suddenly found itself with a reduced 'residuary share' of that taxation, and a reduced revenue, even though the circumstances of the region demanded more money that year, not less! Equally of course if Britain raised its tax rates, Northern Ireland enjoyed an unexpected windfall when perhaps no expansion of services had been planned.

The outcome for the departments was two-fold: uncertainty and extremely limited funds. It was a struggle to secure approval to an extra pair of hands in the office; indeed, the engagement of one additional clerk called for a major battle. And allocations of funds to particular services were counted out in single pound notes. The wonder is not only over the system but also over the fact that it managed to work at all.

The system came close to breakdown on two big issues. One was the need to carry out a general revaluation of all property in the region as a basis for local rating and also for the Schedule A aspect of British income tax. Valuations had become notoriously out of date. Public opinion shied away from the dreadful prospect of re-valuation and its all too clear consequences, and it was only under the threat of the Westminster parliament legislating over Stormont's head that the Northern parliament was eventually persuaded in 1932 (at the depth of the depression) to pass the necessary legislation authorising the general revaluation that came into force amidst public outcry in 1936.

The second issue arose out of the contribution which local rates were making, or not making, to the cost of the local education services. This again stirred popular feeling and eventually parliament had to impose 'the Pollock shilling', that is to say an additional shilling on the local authority rates for the purposes of education. The Belfast corporation challenged the validity of this measure on the grounds that it imposed a tax outside the powers of the Parliament of Northern Ireland and took the issue to the judicial committee of the Privy Council. They lost their case, and the Lords upheld the legislation; but it was a close-run thing and again illustrated the debilitating uncertainty which beset departmental administration under a fragmentary written constitution.

The history of these events has been carefully and sympathetically traced by Professor R J Lawrence in his scholarly work, *The Government of Northern Ireland—Finance and Public Services, 1921–1964*. He relied on published material, on public accounts and on statements and debates at Stormont and at Westminster. How these unworkable arrangements were actually made to work he just could not fathom; he wrote plaintively but quite understandably of secrecy in public finance, of calculations made each year that were never published, of crucial calculations that could not be worked out by an outsider, and so on. That the system was made to work is in retrospect the great achievement.

This achievement deserves a closer look. For long the financial relations between Stormont and Whitehall were shrouded in secrecy and protected by a veil of nothing less than make-believe. The principles had been laid down in the 1920 act. The Northern Ireland accounts were regularly drawn up, audited and published. A budget was presented each spring. The outcome in practice was not at all bad. Whether the internal arrangements were consistent with clear principles of inter-exchequer finance is of less importance. The Royal Commission on the British Constitution sitting from 1969 to 1973 was in a position to examine the Treasury as well as the Ministry of Finance, and reported with refreshing candour. Its report speaks openly of 'the collapse of the financial arrangements laid down in the 1920 Act' and of 'total breakdown soon after the Act came into effect of the financial arrangements which it provided and the substitution, though ostensibly within the framework of the Act, of some very different arrangements'. Going still further, the Royal Commission speaks of 'the maintenance of a façade' and of the Northern Ireland Budget being regarded by some as 'a farce'.

The Royal Commission significantly concludes that the whole financial story is a monument to British pragmatism. In that context the officials of the Ministry of Finance played their part by making themselves well known to the Treasury, by working closely with them, by building up confidence and by joining actively with the Treasury officials in adapting the arrangements to the changing needs of the province while scrupulously preserving the outward

forms of the 1920 act—maintaining a stiff upper lip to the public.
The pity is that they took so long to get the money flowing. I remember that it was popular at the time to blame the British
Treasury. But that is always easy to do—from a distance. Some of
the blame may well have lain on the Ulster side. Both of the top
officials in the Ministry of Finance (Ernest Clark and G C Duggan)
had come from the London civil service and it is possible that they
may have been over-zealous in showing their new independence of
London. This often happens when a subordinate officer goes out
from a parent office to head a lesser one. So anxious is he to show
that he is no mere tool or yes-man that he bends over backwards to
be independent, even to the point of becoming awkward. I have
found it hard to ascertain the facts in this instance, but the essence
of the matter was that the Northern Ireland departments did not
become flush with money until the war came.

Throughout the twenties and thirties the Northern Ireland civil
service remained distinctly unpopular with the public. No bureaucracy sets out to court popularity and all bureaucracies are inured
to misunderstanding and to criticism. But if the service started off
in conditions of such obvious difficulty as I have described, built
itself up gradually by sound recruitment and performed in practice
in the way I have tried to summarise here, why then was it unpopular amongst its own people?

There were, I believe, many reasons contributing and here again
I draw as much on my own experience of living in the community
as a child and youth as I do on my official knowledge. First, it must
be remembered that a civil service operating in their midst was
something new for local people. Most people in active life of any
sort had of course been accustomed up to a point to the presence of
government officials; they knew of the inspector of schools, the
postmaster, the labour exchange officials and so on. The new
factors were the sudden springing-up of headquarters offices, of
enlarged staffs, of private secretaries to ministers, of expanded recruitment of clerks and typists, as well as the gossip that all this
activity generated in a small and predominantly farming community. Next, times were hard and the spectacle of a mandarin
class in secure, well-paid and pensionable jobs must to a great many
people have seemed objectionable. Officials appeared to work short
hours and to enjoy long holidays, an obscenity to a puritan society.
Some appeared positively lazy and indulged in conspicuous display
of their comparative affluence. There was much popular gossip
about civil servants not having enough to do, about women clerks
knitting at their desks and about young girls treating as extra

holidays their entitlement to seven days sick leave without a medical certificate. Many of the duties they performed did not endear them to the populace—collecting taxes, enforcing the factory and workshop acts, inspecting insurance cards and detecting fraud and so on. This applied, I remember, with particular force to officials of the Ministry of Agriculture, for their work bore heavily on the small farmers in the shape of inspection of potatoes, insistence on the cleanliness of eggs (what is wrong anyway with a bit of hen dirt sticking to an egg? and sure I can wash it with soap and water, can't I?) and many other such activities designed to raise the standards of the very produce on which the farmers' livelihood depended. How often did I as a boy hear Magilligan farmers justify to one another their hatred of that estimable parliamentary measure, the Noxious Weeds Act? All this, and much more, was laid at the door of those under-worked, over-paid, useless college boys up at Stormont.

There was yet another reason why the service attracted criticism and it sprang from an unusual quirk in our constitutional history. In our arrangements it was the ministry (not the minister) which was the legal entity and the corporate body. (The title was changed to department in 1973, but that is irrelevant.) In Great Britain it is almost always the minister. With us of course the minister is the political head—he commands his ministry—he answers for it in parliament and elsewhere but the fact remains that, because of our legal succession from the Lord Lieutenant of Ireland in 1921, the ministry was, from that date onward, the statutory body. Formal letters to the members of the public used to open with the formula 'I am directed by the Ministry of Labour'. This was hardly calculated to endear the officials to their public. Sir Wilfrid Spender used to warn us, 'Be careful of the weak minister; in time of trouble he will use the ministry as his lightning conductor'.

The atmosphere has greatly changed for the better. The public has long since accepted its civil service. Fewer people nowadays have reason to envy us our rates of pay. Security of tenure in a job for life is not as priceless an asset now as it was in the thirties. We seldom can manage to take our quota of holidays. Our work is much better known and, let us hope, appreciated. But the greatest change of all has come about through the huge increase in publicity of all kinds surrounding ministers. The limelight has long since shifted from the ministry officials to the political heads and the public have come to attach to them the responsibility, the credit or the blame.

For ministers are responsible and always have been in our

government service: let there be absolutely no doubt. This book is basically about officials, not about ministers or politicians. I am trying to tell the story of what the officials have done over the years and what they are doing today. Let this not in any way or in any degree take away from the responsibility of the political heads. We are still in this chapter speaking of the 1930s. The ministers then were important public figures. James Craig dominated the scene without a doubt. Others have written of his achievements; let me simply record the impression I had of him coming in to a sitting of the Commons. It was an impression of authority, of dignity and above all of ability to quell an argument and to still the factions. H M Pollock, Minister of Finance, I knew slightly for our family attended the same church as he did, May Street Presbyterian, where he was regarded as shrewd and businesslike. Dawson Bates at Home Affairs naturally attracted the greatest weight of political criticism, especially to us as undergraduates at Queen's. Milne Barbour at Commerce seemed to us then the caricature of an Edwardian figure in the heyday of the linen industry. Edward Archdale was less in the forefront but conveyed a sense of competence and knowledge of his subject. Lord Charlemont who succeeded Lord Londonderry at Education and also as leader in the Senate was a witty speaker and a man of considerable taste and culture.

Reverting to the work of the service, what were the achievements of those two early decades? In a word, I think, the setting of standards. All the rest was bread-and-butter business and only to be expected of them—the administrative schemes, the preparation of legislation and so on. But it was the setting of standards that was to count in the long run—integrity, checks and balances, accuracy, fairness, impartiality, and perhaps above all the spirit of continuity and the determination to carry public administration on, no matter what the circumstances. Our predecessors may have been complacent, they ought perhaps to have striven harder for social change, they could perhaps have done more to help bring the Roman Catholic community into collaboration with the administration. I believe all that to be true. But I do recognise that they created for us the nucleus of a first-class civil service that was in fact to make good those shortcomings when conditions developed a generation later.

In looking back and trying to assess the achievements and failures of a period long past, it is easy to fall into the error of using hindsight. Sensible writers know this and discount their assessment on that score. Those of us looking back from the extraordinary circumstances of Northern Ireland in the 1970s have to cope with a great deal more than hindsight; we have been through a period of anxious soul-searching about the history of the province, soul-searching that for many of us involved regret and even anguish.

Discounting heavily, therefore, for all that we now know, how do we assess the achievements and failures of our colleagues in those first two decades?

They succeeded in helping to create the machinery of parliament and government and to get it to operate. They helped ministers and political leaders to legislate over a wide field. Above all perhaps they managed to establish British standards of public administration—administrative skills, accuracy, integrity, accountability, the checks and balances necessary to the healthy operation of government, systems of purchasing, contracting, acquisition of land and many other features—that were to prove of great value to Ulster in later years. The going may have been rough in the early years but in the years to follow it was to prove rougher still. It is easy to include in such a passage as this a word or two about establishing standards. But what is involved in practice? A permanent secretary does not set standards in the field of placing contracts, purchasing supplies, buying land and so on simply by preaching at people nor even by composing an elegant memorandum. He has to proceed by fighting individual cases; and very often he comes into the picture only in mid-case, so to speak. For example, I was told that in the very earliest days of the Ministry of Home Affairs the minister decided to meet a request from the inspector-general of the Royal Ulster Constabulary for motor-tyres for the police fleet by telephoning the managing director of a business firm in Belfast and placing an order. Why not? The ministers were amongst the leading business and professional men in the city. They knew the trading community and had for long been doing business with them. They knew who were reliable businessmen and who were not. Why not take the sensible, quick course and place the order where they knew the ministry would get good service? Why bother to go through a long rigmarole of tiresome civil service procedure, advertise, receive sealed tenders, open them pick the lowest tender, only to find that the tenderer turns out to be an unreliable, inexperienced supplier who lets you down? Local ministers understood the practicalities of business in Belfast a great deal better than a lot of strange officials newly arrived from London, or, worse still, from Dublin. To the government's political opponents of course the matter seemed an open-and-shut case of unionist and protestant ministers favouring unionist and protestant businessmen, a clear example of discrimination. To the permanent secretary it was a matter of getting hold of the problem, taking it by the scruff of the neck and imposing some sort of order on administrative chaos.

But it was a complacent service. There was little urge to press on and break new ground. Above all there was little urge to bring about social change. Social attitudes and structures changed much less in those decades than in the decades that were to come. Some stirrings were noticeable in the later years just before the war; a deeper concern about unemployment, especially unemployment amongst young men, was being felt. One small token of this was the formation by some of us in the summer of 1938 of the Social Service Society of civil servants, a voluntary group dedicated to various forms of spare-time work with unemployed youth. We took a disused linen factory in the back streets of west Belfast, rigged it up as a set of clubrooms and started to make what contribution we could. It may have been significant that the chairman was the comptroller and auditor-general of the day, W R Maconkey, a stern Methodist from a small farm in county Fermanagh.

Digging deeply into the recesses of my memory, I cannot recall the subject of religion being even mentioned in the Social Service Society. Our efforts were to be available to all; we had no thought of religious differentiation or segregation. Our attitude—if we thought about it at all—would have been to welcome Roman Catholic boys and men in so far as they took part in our activities; in so far as they did not, then we would have regretted the fact but not been put out or surprised in the least. We all knew that Roman Catholics had their own point of view on such matters and we respected it. It would not have occurred to us to attempt to press or cajole them into the clubrooms, much less to construct any system of bridge-building or integration. In a very small way I suppose our philosophy reflected that of the service as a whole at the time.

Still wary of hindsight and subjectivity in forming a definitive judgment of the civil service of those days, I quote with greater confidence from an independent authority. In his exhaustive and fully documented history, *Northern Ireland in the Second World War*, published in 1956, Professor J W Blake (then at the University College of North Staffordshire) starts by reviewing the genesis of Northern Ireland and assesses the administrative position in 1939 in these terms: 'The architects of Government in Northern Ireland, by a combination of skill, determination, hard work and imagination, had by 1939 produced a working system of administration capable of adaptation without undue loss of efficiency in

the event of an emergency. The machinery of government, central
and local, was in fact at once made available on the outbreak of
war. If not perfect it had stood the test of nearly twenty years of
hard experience. The circumstances of the genesis of Northern
Ireland, being unusual, had called for much improvisation on the
part of the civil service and the staff of the local authorities. The
lessons learned in such a school were likely to prove useful in time
of war when flexibility and improvisation often become imperative.
Among the assets which Northern Ireland could boast, the men and
women employed in the service of government should justly be
given a prominent place' (Chapter 1).

Chapter 5

IN HUMAN TERMS

Who were those men and women? Who made up the civil service of those early days? Where did they come from? How were they recruited? To try to answer those questions we need to take a few broad sweeps through the social and administrative history of the last century, because the recruits to the service came from many different sources. It was to a quite surprising degree a multi-national service and has remained so to this day.

The basic arrangement was embedded firmly in the Government of Ireland Act 1920. There were to be allocated to the new government of Northern Ireland those existing Irish officers who had been employed up till then in the Dublin administration and who had been concerned solely with the administration of public services in Northern Ireland. So ran section 59(1) of the act but to understand its full import we need to look back a lot further.

The northern part of Ireland, like the rest of Ireland, had since the coming into force of the Act of Union in 1801 been subject to the British parliament and its laws. Nevertheless, under one of the characteristic anomalies of the British constitution, administration in Ireland was delegated to a Lord Lieutenant, a public figure of very considerable dignity and authority. He was assisted by a Chief Secretary, who as time went on assumed great power and influence until at various periods in the late nineteenth century it was hard to say which was the senior personage. At times one was a member of the British cabinet and at times the other. Arthur Balfour described the arrangement as a 'practical paradox'. Relationships were not always easy. Between them they were responsible for the civil administration of Ireland and over the generations till 1921 they built up a full-blown administrative system for the whole of the country from Fair Head in Antrim to Mizen Head in Cork.

It is probably fair to say that the system was competent but bureaucratic. It was highly centralised in Dublin, with little power delegated to subordinate local bodies. Even the impact of the major Local Government Act of 1898 which set up the elected county councils and district councils was more apparent than real, for Dublin ruled with a strong hand and controlled financial matters tightly. But within the Dublin administration there was little coordination.

As each new set of problems arose, the temptation had been to set up a new board to deal with it. There were something like twenty-eight of these by 1921. As early as 1889 a new under-secretary, Ridgeway, an Englishman trained in India and arriving into the Chief Secretary's Office in Dublin, castigated the system: 'Nothing could be more chaotic and effete than the present system of government by boards. For at present Ireland is ruled by a congeries of boards who are by statute semi-independent and by Treasury in London.' (The intention here is to emphasise that the boards were largely independent of Treasury control.) 'These boards have the power and licence to commit blunders but on the Chief Secretary rests the responsibility.' Not only was there a Local Government Board for Ireland but also a Congested Districts Board. Not only a Royal Irish Constabulary but also a Dublin Metropolitan Police. As we saw earlier there were no fewer than four departments dealing with education. And so on.

It is not that they were poorly staffed. Even before 1855 two of the main offices—that of the Chief Secretary and the Poor Law Board—had been applying tests of competency to candidates for clerkships. Shortly after that the Irish offices generally adopted the system of competitive examination for recruitment and were amongst the first anywhere in the British Isles to do so. Larcom, the top official, wrote to London in 1854: 'Everything here was in former days so soiled with politics and religious differences that people thought it the most natural state of things'. By 1871 competitive examination had become the normal mode of recruitment. The next great need was to divide up the work inside the offices so that educated and able minds were not wasted on routine tasks. Between 1870 and 1890 the broad classification of administrative (or first division), executive (or second division) and clerical grades was established, with recruitment appropriate to each. Another distinguishing feature of the Irish service was the fact that recruits were drawn from all over the British Isles as a matter of deliberate policy. As the vice-president of the Local Government Board told a royal commission in 1914: [An office in which English, Scots and Irish are mixed is] 'perfectly equipped. The Englishmen have been stolid, sensible, highly competent persons. The Scotchman is a rock of commonsense, accurate and cautious. The Irishman is brilliant, resourceful and quick, but he is rather impulsive and wants the steadiness of the English and Scotch.'

The many Dublin offices were notorious for their spirit of independence and their *grá* for departmental autonomy. It was supposedly the duty of the Chief Secretary's Office to bring them together but it had an uphill task. The measure of that task is well illustrated by Sir Henry Robinson when he described in his *Memories: Wise and Otherwise* how he stubbornly and successfully resisted the efforts of the Chief Secretary's Office to intervene in the affairs of the Local Government Board, of which the Chief Secretary was the president! The board would answer only to the political chief and not to his minions because Robinson firmly believed that there was no point in two sets of officials combing over the same work and still less in the English political head being advised at second-hand by English officials when he could have, for the asking, advice from his Irish officials at first-hand. A much more effective form of co-ordination between departments was to be found in the personal contacts that existed between senior officials whether in their offices, thir homes or more significantly in the Kildare Street Club. Chief Secretary Wyndham coming from London found to his puzzlement that the government of Ireland seemed to be 'conducted only by continuous conversation'. It is not that the senior Irish officials were opposing the political heads or in any sense ganging up on them. None of the evidence available, written or oral, points in that direction so far as I can see. It is simply that the Irish officials were so familiar with the scene and so concerned about the practical problems that they found it a waste of time to keep on explaining matters to a succession of less well-informed English officials.

At the risk of wearying the reader but in the hope nevertheless of throwing as much light as possible on Irish administration past and present, let us devote another moment to that formidable machine, the Local Government Board for Ireland. Formed out of the earlier Poor Law Commissioners in 1872 it had a wide range of highly important functions—local government generally, the poor law in all its many aspects, lunacy, child care, hospitals, roads, housing, sanitation and a multitude of miscellaneous functions. The Chief Secretary, that is to say a political figure, was its president and titular head. Its effective head was the vice-president, that is to say the top permanent official and a very considerable power in the land. And there were three other commissioners, one

being always a medical doctor. The first vice-president was Henry
Robinson. His son, also Henry Robinson, became vice-president
later and dominated the scene from the 1890s till the end in 1922.
His son, in turn, Adrian Robinson, served also in the board and
eventually became permanent secretary of Home Affairs in
Northern Ireland, the virtual successor to his father and grandfather. Small wonder that Adrian Robinson talked of himself as a
'congenital civil servant'.

The Local Government Board occupied part of that most handsome of public buildings, the Dublin Custom House on the Liffey
(where, again significantly, the board's successors are housed today
under Gerry Meagher). The Chief Secretary's office was housed in
Dublin Castle, across the river and in one of the oldest parts of the
city. No love was lost between these two offices for reasons which
are not hard to find. The Local Government Board knew Ireland
extremely well. They employed a team of inspectors, not headquarters inspecting officers in the ordinary sense, but out-posted
officers of very considerable standing and education who acted both
to hold the hand of the local authorities and to do the job of eyes
and ears for the board in the Custom House. It was a remarkably
good arrangement and above all it was effective in doing exactly
whatever the board from time to time wished to see done. (A
modern equivalent is the development officer service in Northern
Ireland today.) The board also carried out a close system of local
government audit, with a team of well-qualified auditors (lawyers
as well as accountants) who covered every elected local body leaving them no discretion to opt out of government audit. Inspectors
in time moved to headquarters bringing with them their first-hand
knowledge of the country. All three Robinsons for example started
life as inspectors. That amusing Irish writer, George A Birmingham, found at the beginning of the twentieth century that it was
impossible to walk the length of any railway platform in Ireland
without meeting two or three inspectors. A cheerful but pardonable exaggeration, it was certainly indicative of Irish administration.

These arrangements gave the board at the Custom House enormous advantages over the Chief Secretary's office at the Castle.
The Chief Secretary came and went with the fortunes of the
political parties in London, Conservative and Liberal Chief Secretaries succeeding one another at intervals of a few years or a few
months. They tended to be heavily preoccupied with problems of
politics, law and order, violence and insurrection. Their senior
advisers, coming (generally at an advanced point in their careers)

from London, or even from the Indian civil service, could not possibly have the knowledge of places, people and events possessed by the Local Government Board. And on top of all that the Chief Secretary and his office had to keep a wary eye on the Lord Lieutenant and his people across the city in Phoenix Park. It is little wonder that George Trevelyan, when Chief Secretary, complained to W E Gladstone that 'the life I lead is not a human life at all', describing his post as 'this terrible office'. Robert Ball, a clerk in the Chief Secretary's office (and a man of letters and scholarly attainment) grumbled about 'the soul-subduing slavery of Castle work'. (A comparison with Stormont Castle under direct rule suggests itself forcibly.)

Summing up all these aspects of the Irish administration and viewing them through civil service eyes in the 1970s, it is fair to say that it was essentially a bureaucracy, a bureaucracy in many senses of the word. For one thing, it was well-staffed; it had a fine blend of recruits from many fields and countries; it was not accustomed to working closely under parliamentary control, for access to parliament was through an English political head and an English cabinet to a parliament three hundred miles away across the sea and none too anxious to become any more involved in Irish local administration than it was forced to be. Bureaucratic also in the sense of not having a competent and virile local government or other elected local system to which to respond from day to day; indeed the character of the local bodies—for the most part—and the disturbed state of the country justified the Dublin bureaucracy in governing with a pretty firm hand. And in the absence of local political ministers answerable to local electorates the departments came to play a noticeably large part in the government of the country.

For the most part, be it noted. The exceptions were the local bodies in the north of Ireland who seem to have caused the Dublin administration surprisingly little trouble. Sir Henry Robinson, realising how difficult some people would find it to believe that statement, devoted a paragraph to the point in his *Memories* written in 1922:

It may perhaps be remarked that in my story of the problems and difficulties which beset the Local Government Board as the central authority for supervising the administration of local bodies, no word has been written of Ulster. The truth is that there never were any difficulties in Ulster arising from the hostility of local bodies to the central authority. Ulster prided itself upon its loyal support of the British Government, and recognized the status and powers of the public departments responsible to Parliament, and submitted to their rulings as a matter of course. The Local Government Board's administration in Ulster in these circumstances was straightforward and uneventful.

Finding it hard to credit this extraordinary encomium I checked it closely in 1975 with Adrian Robinson who had had the advantage of serving as Local Government Board Inspector for both the Cork area and the Belfast area simultaneously. He supported the tribute without reservation, saying that the Ulster local authorities were renowned in Dublin for their competence and business efficiency 'even if they had their own ways of doing things'. By contrast (if we may allow ourselves one mischievous quotation) one board of guardians in the south indignantly rejecting Chief Secretary Balfour's offer of a seventy-five per cent grant on relief works, instructed their clerk: 'Write and refuse and tell them to go to hell. The people of this district are unanimously in favour of a large and liberal grant of pecuniary assistance from the Government which is the curse of the country.'

I have concentrated largely on the Local Government Board here partly because of the wide span of its activities, partly because these activities were all to be carried forward into the new Northern Ireland administration and partly because they have been particularly well written up and documented. The many other public offices in Dublin before 1922—dealing with education, health insurance, police, agriculture, the courts, the records and so on—would, if studied in a similar way, have a comparable story to tell of relatively self-contained offices, of remoteness, of strong administration by competent staffs.

Now — to return at long last to the main thread of our story— the relevant point is that it was from those staffs, employed in those offices in the British administration of all-Ireland, that the main stream of our civil servants came in 1922. The law laid it down, as we have seen, that officers concerned solely with work in the north of Ireland in 1922 were to be allocated to the new government of Northern Ireland, while those concerned solely with work in the south were to go to the southern government. So far so good. Sydney Eraut, for example, was HM inspector of factories in the Belfast area and became chief inspector of factories under the new Ministry of Labour in Northern Ireland—the classic case. Likewise R R Bowman, manager of the Belfast labour exchange moved automatically to the employment branch of the ministry, along with his staff. And there were other similar straight transfers.

Those engaged on general duties over the whole of Ireland (and by definition stationed at the central offices in Dublin) were to be allocated to the northern government or the southern government by a statutory civil service committee consisting partly of persons nominated by the British, the Southern and the Northern governments and partly of persons elected by the existing Irish officers themselves. And the law further provided that the civil service committee would (subject to the exigencies of the public service) endeavour to give effect to the wishes of each officer. There lay the personal dilemma. What were the wishes of the Dublin staff? How were they to make up their minds whether to opt for the North or for the South? Those I have spoken to confess that it was indeed a hard choice. They were living in Dublin. They had houses there and families with friends, schools and a host of personal and social connections. The Dublin offices would obviously carry on, whereas new offices had to be set up in the North. The South was patently the bigger place and there would presumably be better career opportunities in its service. And life in Dublin had always seemed to them a pleasanter prospect than life in the Black North. Argument thus reinforced natural inertia and predisposed them to stay where they were. But times were extremely unsettled in the South. The British were clearly relaxing their hold in the country and preparing to withdraw. Sinn Féin had been getting bolder since the 1918 British general election and were openly challenging the legitimate authorities. Local councils had been ordered in 1921 to swear allegiance to Sinn Féin. Adrian Robinson once confirmed to me that he personally warned the Local Government Board in 1921 that neither the Board nor the Chief Secretary ruled west Cork; the effective governor was the Sinn Féin storekeeper of the local workhouse. Civil war was imminent. There was no knowing what the future held for the loyal and conscientious civil servant in the South. Perhaps it would be wiser to throw in one's lot with the North and move one's house to the Antrim Road or to suburbs with names such as Balmoral or Belmont or Sydenham. But how secure would one's job be? How stable would the new, untried, provincial government prove? How fair would they be in their treatment of staff coming up from Dublin? The fact is that they made their choice and a great many came North. Most were Protestants but by no means all. Many had Ulster connections but many were true Dubliners with rich Dublin accents that rang through the corridors and canteens of Stormont undiluted for many a year.

Starting with the more senior people there was G C Duggan, a distinguished southerner, a double gold medallist at Trinity College, Dublin, and (having started his career in the British Admiralty in 1908) employed in the Chief Secretary's office from 1910. A P Magill had been private secretary to the Chief Secretary. His brother Walter Magill had been secretary and accountant to the Dublin Metropolitan Police. W R Maconkey had been on the finance side of national health insurance. J A Cole had been an inspector of schools, while W A Houston had been assistant commissioner for intermediate education. Bonaparte Wyse, a prominent Roman Catholic, had been secretary to the Board of National Education. Dr Bryan had been a local government auditor. Pimlott and Getty had been inspectors of agriculture; Turner an inspector of horticulture; Gordon had been chief inspector of agriculture for all Ireland; Elliott with the Estate Duty Office; Abbott with the Stamp office; Dr Chart with the Public Record Office. All these strange new men moved straight into senior posts in the new Northern service and helped to provide its leadership for up to thirty years. Hard on their heels came a cohort from that excellent Dublin legion, the second division clerks. They came from all the Dublin offices and formed the backbone of our executive and managerial teams. Each name as I mention it will strike a chord with those who know something of the Northern administration of the 1920s, 1930s and 1940s: William Allen, Hugh Anderson, J E Gorman, Barney Ahern, L J Mason, G T Fidler, J S Godden, Thomas Elwood, A Dann, H C Montgomery, G W Brownell, C W Grant, William Henderson, W C Glover, Harry Diamond, H J Campbell, R V Laurenson, Alfie Russell—a truly formidable file of non-commissioned officers who proved their worth so fully that they all in time took over substantial commands in the various ministries.

But, in the chaotic conditions of 1921 and 1922, it took quite a while to allocate and transfer these men. Meantime the new parliament and government had started work on 7 June 1921 and needed staff. A number of key positions had to be filled at once and so the first appointments were announced on 27 September 1921. These were of officers either lent to Northern Ireland by the British government or transferred outright by them: Ernest Clark (who had been preparing the transfer of services from a temporary office in Belfast) went to the key post of permanent secretary at Finance and head of the civil service; James Huggett, also from London, became comptroller and auditor-general; Cecil Litchfield from London became permanent secretary at Commerce; and A I Dasent from the clerks table at Westminster became clerk to the Houses of Parliament. Others followed from London such as Robert Gransden from the Treasury, Charles Blackmore from the Admiralty, J A Dale from the War Office. Lewis McQuibban of the Scottish Education Department became first permanent secretary at Education. A strong team from a quite different set of stables.

The demands of parliament, of ministers, of policy-making and of legislation called for a quick strengthening of the junior administrative cadre and for an inflow of younger men. The service set to and recruited a number of bright young men, on a temporary basis, to act as private secretaries to ministers, secretaries to investigating committees and so on. This was the first real opening for local young men of talent and the list is again a recognisably distinguished one. William Greer (who was later to leave, enter the Church of England and become Bishop of Manchester), L G P Freer, W A B Iliff, Claude Blake Whelan, J A McKeown and W N McWilliam.

Specialists had also to be recruited: D A E Harkness, an agricultural economist from Scotland, later became permanent secretary at Agriculture and eventually head of the service. A A Farrell from the West of Ireland was engaged as an accountant to deal with the compensation of spirit grocers when they were put out of business and he eventually became a senior administrator. H Conacher came to the Ministry of Labour from England, a barrister with special experience of labour management in the railway companies there. And so on.

Up till now we have been reviewing the recruitment, from various sources and various countries, of officers entering the middle and higher grades. Where did the junior clerks, the messengers and the manual workers come from?

They formed the main stream of local recruitment from the local labour market. The background is well-known: heavy unemployment; many ex-servicemen who had (in the absence of conscription in Ireland) volunteered for service with the British army in the 1914-18 war and were still finding it hard to get a job in the world that was to be fit for heroes to live in; many had been wounded and some had been gassed. The 36th (Ulster) Division had suffered enormous casualties in the battle of the Somme on 1 July 1916 and the feelings amongst the people were still emotional. The labour exchanges were constantly submitting from their

registers the names of people suitable for government employment. Against that background the new government decided on
a firm policy of local recruitment of junior staffs, giving preference
to ex-servicemen and, through the operation of the King's National
Roll, giving special preferences to private firms employing dis-
abled men. The new government felt obliged to reward some of
its more ardent supporters with jobs and made a few pretty blatant
minor appointments. When I entered I was amazed to find Colonel
Fred Crawford, for example, of gun-running fame in 1914, still
harmlessly occupying a chair, unnoticed and undisturbed. On the
negative side they adopted a stern policy of total prohibition on
the employment of married women in the civil service, a policy
to which they adhered right until the 1960s and which clearly
reflected widespread public opinion.

The ministers of the day were of course interested in all forms
of recruitment—to the senior ranks because these were the men to
whom they would be looking for advice and help in framing their
policies, and to the junior ranks because of the social factors
sketched above and to which enormous public and political
interest attached in those years. So great was their interest that the
Minister of Finance took charge of recruitment and was appointed
by His Excellency the Governor to be chairman of the Civil Service
Commission, the body charged with responsibility for standards
and methods of recruitment. By present-day ideas this must seem
an odd arrangement, for civil service recruitment is held to be
strictly impartial matter to be conducted by the whole-time
salaried service itself. It has long been so in Great Britain. But
would it have been such an acceptable idea in Ulster in the twenties? A new parliament had been set up. Members were intensely
interested in the make-up of the emerging service. The early debates in parliament bear testimony to this interest, with criticism
of 'the hordes of officials' matched by criticism of the influx of
English and Scottish recruits. The members understandably looked
to the Minister of Finance to answer to them for what was being
done. Giving a minister power in such a matter has the effect also
of making him responsible. The day when recruitment could be
left to officials came later. It came gradually, first with the Minister
of Finance fading out of the picture in practice, ceasing to take
an interest in recruitment and becoming more and more a figure-
head like the Archbishop of Canterbury on the old Board of Trade.
Eventually he disappeared even from the formal list of members
of the commission.

It was part of the duty of the senior officials in the early years to persuade ministers in this as in other respects to lessen their involvement in day-to-day management and to rely on officials to conduct it on their behalf according to recognised procedures. A big step forward took place in 1926 when a competitive examination was introduced for admission to clerkships in the service; and competitive it certainly was with far more candidates than places available. This competition quickly became attractive and drew good-type recruits from the Ulster and Irish grammar schools. The intake year by year was a valuable one in building up the ranks who were to help run the service twenty or thirty years later —J E Greeves, J E Aiken, L B Jagoe, Paddy Shea, Dick Rogers, Ewart Taylor and many more. Amongst these there was a steady stream of entrants from one particular school, namely Mountjoy in Dublin: R F R Dunbar, G W Nixon, R R Butler, L C Dennis, W J Arthurs, A H Henderson, J S H Gaw—about three or four each year out of a total of ten to twenty entrants a year, a truly remarkable state of affairs and a tribute to the enterprise of the Mountjoy staff.

An even more surprisingly courageous step in many ways was the decision in 1929 to start recruiting direct to the first division or administrative grade by means of the London Civil Service Commission competition. This was the top competition in Britain, by which cadets were recruited to the home civil service, the Indian civil service, the colonial service and the diplomatic service. It represented the pinnacle of written examination procedures with a complex series of three-hour sessions, first on general topics and then on specialised subjects selected by the candidate, stretching over several weeks with an interview on top of everything else—a marathon not only of knowledge but of skill and stamina. By a particularly cruel dispensation the marks obtained by every candidate in every subject were published in a printed book—along with the Question Papers!—for all to read: HMSO, price four shillings. It is hard to believe that provincial ministers in a beleaguered Ulster should entrust the manning of their top administrative cadre to that system. But this is exactly what they did in 1929. Each year from then on there arrived at the doors of Stormont one or two young men from Oxford or Cambridge: Alderson, Plumb, Wolferston, Holmes, Fisher, Jones, Lowry, Holden, Arnold and so on. Some, notably Jones, Lowry and Holden, rose to the highest positions in the service; some drifted away; one or two died; the war claimed others in one way or another. But the point of interest, invariably overlooked by critics of the service, was that here was a recognised method of entry, controlled by impartial forces in London, through which anyone with the required determination could enter. It is significant that, with the exception of myself, every one of the twenty assistant principals who entered between 1929 and 1940 were from across the water, educated at English and Scottish schools and universities. The great tragedy of course was that no Ulster Roman Catholics saw fit to enter by this competition. Not until the late 1960s indeed did the first Ulster catholic enter as an assistant principal through the British competition. But that was only a part of the tragic disregard which catholic families and catholic schools showed for the Northern Ireland civil service as a career, for during the twenties and thirties they could see no merit in sending their boys and girls to the service—with a small number of notable exceptions. The outcome was inevitably an unhappy imbalance of religions in the service and a shortage of catholics coming up through the ranks in the thirties and forties to occupy senior posts of responsibility and influence. Attitudes changed after 1945 and the outcome is clear today in the greater numbers of catholics holding senior positions on merit.

After these wanderings in time and space we must return to the main stream of our narrative. We have looked at the work of the service in the twenties and thirties; and we have now perhaps a better idea of who the men were who established the standards that were to enable us to face the new problems presented by the second world war.

Chapter 6

THE WAR YEARS

For Northern Ireland as for the rest of Britain the war began in earnest in June 1940.

We had of course been preparing for a long time. We had passed our Air Raid Precautions Act in 1938 and a further Civil Defence Act in 1939. British war-time laws including the defence regulations came into force in September 1939. Many of our office colleagues left to join HM forces in the autumn of that year. Dunkirk was the signal for action, and the fall of France (with the capture by the Germans of valuable French ports giving access for enemy warships and submarines to the Atlantic shipping routes) converted Ulster into a strategic bridgehead on the now vital Atlantic front.

The conduct of the war and the disposal of the troops, the ships and the aircraft, together with their manning and their equipping, were matters for the United Kingdom government, it goes without saying. But it was the policy of our government to cooperate to the fullest extent and this they certainly did. Facilities of every kind were placed at the disposal of the forces; airfields sprang up at Nutts Corner, Ballykelly, Aughanloo, Long Kesh, Aghadowey, Bishopscourt, St Angelo and many other places. A flying boat base was set up at Castle Archdale on Lough Erne. The Londonderry port and naval station assumed an enormous significance in the battle of the Atlantic. Troops were stationed over the province— at times as many as 100 000 men. At the front gate of the Belfast City Hall there is a memorial to the first landing of the American troops in Europe; and the GIs dominated our street scene from 1942 till 1944.

The shipyard, the aircraft factory and countless other factories were rapidly converted to wartime production. The farms of Ulster performed prodigies of production. Acreage under crops rose by over 30 per cent. Acreage devoted to oats rose by 50 per cent and to potatoes by 65 per cent. For the first time milk was exported to Great Britain. Poultry rose by 70 per cent and provided about one-fifth of Britain's egg supply. In civil service terms all this involved a huge increase in work and in the intensity of work. De partments came to act more and more as agents of wartime London Departments. There was much contact with London and a great deal of travelling back and forward—by sea and rail—often in conditions of some danger. It was a stimulating experience and officials rose to the occasion.

My own participation started on a note of high excitement. Just before the war and on into the early months I had been serving as private secretary to the Minister of Labour and to the parliamentary secretary. Suddenly in June 1940 a new war-time department was created: the Ministry of Public Security. Major John Clarke MacDermott QC MC, member of parliament for the Queen's University constituency, was recalled from service in the Royal Artillery to become the political head of the new ministry. Major William Angus Boyd Iliff was likewise recalled to become its permanent secretary. These were two very big men. MacDermott was a lawyer of great distinction, a man of dignity and bearing, a son of the manse and a man of stern morality. He was altogether a formidable personality. So too was Bill Iliff, but how different. He was just about the most brilliant, the most forceful, the most racy and the most irascible of men. I was made private secretary to the minister and thus found myself wedged firmly between these two balls of fire. Everything was at a high pitch of importance and urgency. We were given offices in Stormont Castle, that dignified, comfortable Scottish-baronial edifice in the trees within Stormont Estate, hitherto the exclusive preserve of the cabinet and its secretariat (and later to be occupied by Willie Whitelaw, Francis Pym, Merlyn Rees and Roy Mason under a very different regime in the seventies). We were given priority and precedence by the Ministry of Finance in everything we wanted to do.

We worked night and day. For me this was no hardship, as I was young, fit and a bachelor. I lived within easy walking or cycling distance of the office (and many of us were in the habit of cycling to work). We built up an excellent staff around us. The permanent secretary selected two outstanding assistant secretaries, equally able but totally contrasting in style. Eric Scales was a Dubliner with a light and happy touch. J A McKeown was from county Armagh, also a Trinity Graduate, but a dour and taciturn man; he had a most formidable brain which he used to the utmost. His minutes and letters were masterpieces of thorough analysis and presentation. It was said of him that when he had finished picking an administrative bone there was nothing left on it for the dogs.

Our work was relevant, pressing and fascinating. It was the first time any of us had been engaged on work which immediately and directly affected the lives of the entire population in a literal sense and which that entire population followed with active concern. Staff morale was extremely high. We had under our supervision the police and the special constabulary; the civil defence; the local defence volunteers, later known as Home Guard; the women's voluntary service; anti-invasion measures; and, at a slightly later stage, evacuation of women and children from Belfast. As I recall, we first set about the reorganisation of civil defence in the city of Belfast. The task was proving too heavy for the Belfast Corporation and so the minister decided to transfer the functions to a new statutory body which he created, namely the Belfast Civil Defence Authority.

This worked well. The various services responded; they had a remarkably good set of leaders whose personalities I clearly remember today: the wardens under a meticulously correct quantity surveyor H W Gooding; the casualty service under Professor Flynn, professor of zoology at the university and father of that acrobatic hero of the cinema screen, Errol Flynn; the rather neglected rescue service whose flagging spirits were lifted by their brave, cheerful leader Billy Martin the builder; the welfare service under two men who were later to play a big part in Ulster life, Lucius O'Brien and Herbert Bryson. The fire service were in a much more difficult position. They had a fine set of enthusiastic officers and men but the organisation was ill-fitted to local authority units and areas. We found ourselves obliged to create a new national fire service, which turned out to be an excellent force. The fire service commander throughout the entire period of its existence—and in a sense on into the peacetime organisation—was David Andrews, the grain miller, who gave all his time to this labour of love.

The provision of shelter protection against air-raids occupied a lot of our time and absorbed a lot of our money. We provided a few Anderson shelters (inverted u-shaped affairs which one half-buried in the garden or open ground); we provided rather more Morrison shelters (steel structures which one put together on a do-it-yourself basis); we helped factories to do the best they could to build protection for their workers, but our biggest contribution to the landscape was, alas, the building, at high speed, of thousands of hideous brick shelters on the streets of Belfast, half blocking the footpath and half blocking the carriage-way. For years until they were finally demolished by a destructive ball-and-chain contrivance I winced as I passed through the little streets of Belfast and thought of men, women and children huddled together on a winter's night in those ghastly black holes. Underground shelters of any kind were out of the question in Belfast because of the phenomenon of sleech, a wet, moving subsoil which underlies the older parts of the city.

The distribution of gas masks to the population provided some light relief. Quite a mammoth task, it provoked reaction ranging from the indifferent to the resentful to the baffled to the outraged. Our people are eloquent on such matters.

Finding the personnel to man the services is seldom a problem in time of national emergency. Volunteers will always come forward and offer help. Between June and August 1940 for example we recruited 26 000 men into the Local Defence Volunteers, and our experience was similar with the other services. Buildings, equipment and telephones are a different story. My recollection of office work in those war years is overshadowed by our unremitting efforts at securing quotas of stirrup-pumps, tin hats, mobile pumps, 50 foot extension ladders, turn-table ladders and goodness knows what else. Our most frequent contact seemed to be with the post office telephone manager, begging him to drop every other assignment and lay extra telephone lines to keep us in touch with Londonderry. Our operational centre was the war room, a fortified establishment in the woods near Stormont Castle, comprising operations room and intelligence room. It was a most simple form of central control; if a war room were being designed today it would be a lot more complicated, I feel sure, though possibly no more efficient.

But work at the office represented only a part of our endeavours. We spent a lot of time in the evenings and at weekends visiting civil defence posts and fire stations, attending training courses and taking part in exercises. Oh, those exercises! Endless affairs in forlorn places waiting for pointless messages to come through when one could see the true position for oneself perfectly well, while wet coils of fire hose were sadly accumulating around one's tired feet. The recompense was found of course in the friendships and the hospitality which generally followed exercises in the country towns. Roast suckling pig and Irish whiskey in Derrygonnelly.

Our work in Public Security fell into three clearly defined parts. First, from June 1940 till April 1941, we were devising schemes, making preparations and generally helping to harness the energies of the people for civil defence. Then in April and May 1941 came the air raids themselves. We had one curtain-raiser on 8 April when thirteen people were killed and eighty-one injured. The most serious occurred on 15 April, Easter Tuesday, when large parts of Belfast were devastated and at least seven hundred people killed and fifteen hundred injured. There were some slight incidents also in Bangor and Derry. The third raid took place on 5 May; this time about one hundred and fifty people lost their lives and seven hundred were injured. This was largely a fire-bomb raid and enormous damage was done to working-class houses as well as to shops and factories. The shipyard was of course the obvious target and lying as it does at the head of Belfast Lough and the estuary of the river it was not hard for the navigators to locate. It was around the shipyard and in various flight paths of approach to it, and of escape from it, that the greatest damage was done. Frankly all this destruction, killing, maiming, burning and upset far exceeded anything for which we had prepared; it made our schemes look woefully inadequate. The civil defence services worked well and much heroism was shown. Dublin generously sent fire engines and much equipment as well, but the scale of the event outstripped our capacity. The third phase of our work—from the air raids of April-May 1941 until the end of the war—was really a period of starting all over again and of making much more far-reaching civil defence preparations for further air raids that never came.

Nowhere was the sequence more clearly seen than in evacuation, that is to say the organisation for the planned evacuation of mothers, children and other priority categories from Belfast to the countryside. Elaborate, well-thought-out arrangements had been made in good time in 1939 and 1940 for planned evacuation, with persons registered, transport organised, leaders appointed, receptions planned and hosts lined up at the receiving end. I remember vividly the occasion on which ministers, having decided not to introduce evacuation on the outbreak of war, eventually decided at a meeting in Stormont Castle to pull the switch that would send the whole of the dependent population of Belfast out into the green countryside. It was the biggest administrative decision the cabinet had taken up till then.

Sunday 7 July 1940 was to be the day. Everyone was notified, organisers were at their posts at the break of day and trains got up steam—and hardly any evacuees came! There were a number of reasons. There was the fear of the unknown, the worry about schooling in the country areas, the natural reluctance to leave fathers and brothers; there was the confusing fact that, although they were being exhorted to leave Belfast as a danger zone, people were coming over from the known dangers of London to live in the peace of Belfast! There were even official discussions about the possible arrival here of sixty thousand refugees from Belgium and Holland! So, for whatever reason, the mothers and children decided on Sunday 7 July 1940 to stay in Belfast, and we the administrators were forced to think again. The air raids when they eventually came the following spring caused many thousands, literally countless thousands, to flee from the horror of death and fire in their little streets and to become the nightmare of the administrator: the unplanned, unrecorded but terrified refugee. I quoted in the previous chapter Professor Blake's reference to 'improvisation' and this was indeed the time and the scene in which improvisation was truly needed in terms of hostels, schoolrooms, field kitchens, bedding, food, sanitation, medical and nursing care and a hundred other services. The arrangements which we then went on to make for proper evacuation to billets in the country were admirable—but after the event and of course superfluous as it turned out.

Of all the periods since the 1920s which I am trying to record this wartime administrative process is, I find now, one of the most difficult to summarise and to present.

For one thing my memory of the process is patchy and, while I can clearly and accurately recall episodes that happened earlier, I am forced to consult the written records of wartime work in which I personally took part, in order to be sure of the facts and the dates. Some happenings had escaped my memory completely while others have remained vivid in my mind. (I should admit here that I married in the middle of all this so that my mental aberration is in truth a tribute to my young bride, Stella Ritson, from the hills of Cumbria and the Quaker School at Sidcot in Somerset.) Again, we were acutely ashamed of our failure to foresee and prepare for the phenomenon known as 'the homeless'—the great exodus of Belfast people to the suburbs, the countryside, 'funk-holes' (as many themselves put it) in the shape of huts and shacks on the main roads running out from the city. On the other hand I can remember Herbert Morrison, English Minister of Home Security, telling us on a visit that we had done better than any other city he had visited in Britain in the business of clearing up and making good the physical damage of heavy air raids.

As administrative officers we were well aware of our limitations in dealing with the immense human problems created by the raids, indeed of the relative futility of paper arrangements in face of fire, death and fear. In those days of air-raid sirens, of black-out and of long nights of fire-watching in the office we used to cheer ourselves up by composing doggerel verses. The game was to parody our own administrative activities, using layer upon layer of irony. One of us for example had to interview a distressed housewife who arrived on the dignified forecourt of Stormont Castle with six children entreating us to evacuate the lot immediately even though we had never heard of her before and had no knowledge of her true circumstances; in a word, she had not filled in the proper form! The interview ran:

The logic is uniquely clear
As you will now perceive, my dear:
This scene would never have occurred
If you had been pre-registered.

Or the minute that recorded in one stanza the administrative efforts of two of our colleagues—William Duff and Jack Donaldson —their human concern, the problems of hygiene with overtones of sectarian differences treated with commendable impartiality:

The Duff man and the Donaldson
Scanned the evacuees
They wept like anything to see
Such quantities of fleas
Such lousy little Protestants
Such nitty young RCs

(Incidentally the whole human side of evacuation has been best caught and most charmingly recorded by Robert Harbinson in his delightful book, *Song of Erne,* the middle volume in a trilogy of childhood in the hard, impoverished world of evangelical, loyalist Belfast).

Religion in fact played little part in the wartime administrative story. All were at risk and all played their part in the processes of survival, aid, neighbourliness and defence in general. Understandably the aspects of organisation and of uniformed service had a greater appeal for Ulster protestants for they are, by nature and tradition, organisers and devotees of order and efficiency. Anything in the shape of a call to duty or an appeal for national service evoked a readier response from them than from catholics since they identified themselves more fully with the British state than many catholics did. As in the first great war so again in this war

HM government thought it wiser not to apply conscription to Ulster, as they knew that many catholic extremists would resist. Some catholics nevertheless volunteered for service in the British forces, as of course did many from the South as well. On the home front the catholic contribution lay rather more in neighbourliness and spontaneous help. Catholics took part in all the civil defence services but less prominently and with some inhibitions. Royal visits for example were an embarrassment to them. And there was the recurring problem of the oath of allegiance which, as always, uncovered a divided loyalty in the hearts of many catholics. It fell to me personally to administer the oath of allegiance to one thousand full-time firemen on the conversion of the local authority auxiliary fire service into one national fire service on 1 April 1942. While only six refused outright and had therefore to leave the service, many others made it clear to me that they were taking the oath with varying degrees of 'mental reservation'. Throughout the whole of the war I cannot recall any manifestations of sectarian strife seriously affecting the administration of services: for a contentious people we were remarkably unified in face of the dangers of war.

The underlying problem lay, as always, in our position in relation to the South. Here we were, part of the United Kingdom, actively helping to fight her battle (and ours) against the German threat, with a neutral country immediately across a land border. Here we were, enforcing strict blackout regulations even in remote country areas while, one hundred miles to the South, Dublin was ablaze with lights, a navigational beacon for bombers skirting England to the west on their way up to Liverpool, Belfast or Glasgow. Here we were waging conscientious war against 'careless talk' and rumours that could lead to 'alarm and despondency' while the envoys of Germany, Italy and Japan had free run of Dublin and their outrunners were doubtless taking the train from Amiens Street to Great Victoria Street any day they chose. This all contributed to make our job very hard indeed.

Even deeper risks appeared when we came to compile our anti-invasion plans. Part of the British strategy was of course to prepare against a possible landing of foreign agents. One thought of Kent, one thought of Norfolk, but where better than Donegal or Sligo? And what handier fifth column inside the United Kingdom than the IRA in Derry or Fermanagh? We were keenly aware at the time that this was adding an Irish dimension to our already difficult problem, though we did not come to use that term for another thirty years or so.

Chapter 7

A POSITIVE ERA

Well before the war was over, our government decided to carry out a reorganisation designed to cater for the work of postwar reconstruction that surely had to come.

On 1 June 1944 the Ministry of Public Security was wound up and a new Ministry of Health and Local Government created. The staff of the wartime department formed the nucleus of the new department but an important element was added in the shape of the local government side of the Ministry of Home Affairs. This was not an easy blend. It was a matter of amalgamating a go-ahead group of miscellaneous staff who had carried out the wartime emergency services and who, in doing so, had developed unorthodox methods as well as a sense of camaraderie, with on the other hand a cadre of severely orthodox officials from one of the oldest traditional offices that derived from Dublin Castle and the Local Government Board for Ireland. We were concerned with health, hospitals, poor law, workhouses, planning, housing and local government. It was obvious that many changes would have to be made in the structure of society and that we would have to take the lead in a lot of that work. Much of the rest would fall to our neighbouring department—the Ministry of Labour—who would have to carry out the vast changes that were foreshadowed for the cash benefit services (unemployment, sickness, old age, injury, family allowances, widows and death benefits). The basic social philosophy had been worked out for us all by then in the form of the Beveridge Report of 1943. It is hard to realise today what an impact that monumental piece of work had on social thought and how comprehensively and effectively it shaped the plans of governments.

In the last year of the war, therefore, from June 1944 till August 1945, from D Day till VJ Day, we were getting ready administratively to tackle the task of social reconstruction which we clearly saw ahead. We were well equipped. We had an admirable minister in Billy Grant, a man who could make up his mind and then defend himself before all comers—the ideal leader for a department about to enter battle. In Eric Scales we had an open-minded, flexible permanent secretary; in Ronald Green an assistant secretary of brilliance, wit and energy; and in George Hamilton a lawyer of clear, cool analytical capacity. And, what proved to be of immense help to us, we had cordial working relations with the parliamentary draftsmen to whom we were going to have to turn so often, Jack Caldwell and Bill Leitch.

But before we could put our hand to the exciting work of reform we had to get to grips with the humdrum affair of running the existing services—public health, poor law, housing and so on.

At first glance this seemed a dull chore. What could be less exciting, one might think, than supervising and answering for the administration by local authorities of nineteenth-century enactments relating to sewers, drains, privies, burial grounds, canal banks, cesspools and so on? In fact it proved to be a worthwhile exercise, enriched by a most remarkable textbook. I refer to the *Green Vanston,* a huge volume of some thirteen hundred pages of close type, and bound in green cloth, written by George Vanston, legal adviser to the former Local Government Board in Dublin. The first edition had come out in 1892 and we were using (in 1944 and for twenty years after that) the second edition of 1913. This valuable book enlivened the whole task of administering those far-seeing public health statutes of 1878 and later years. As every local authority office had its copy of the *Green Vanston,* it was possible to conduct a continuous and extremely well-informed dialogue about definitions, bye-laws, decided court cases and so on. In the same way, when we turned our hands to the job of administering the poor law acts, we were supported by another stupendous text-book, Mooney's *Compendium of the Irish Poor Law 1887,* another thirteen hundred pages of statute, regulation, case law and advice. These acts went back to 1838 but, though out of date in every sense of social policy, were still effective instruments for local administration.

In the other basic field of administration, the general local government structure of county councils, county borough councils, borough, urban and rural district councils, we found we had ready to hand three further textbooks of the highest quality. First there was the *Red Vanston,* George Vanston's three-volume work on local government law in general, brought out within a matter of months of the fundamental Local Government (Ireland) Act

1898. Second, there was Vanston's *Law of Municipal Towns*. And third, there was Vanston's *Municipal Corporations*. I am most happy to record the tribute of many of us working at Stormont to these invaluable works by a Dublin lawyer who must have been a man not only of ability but of prodigious energy. The deafness which prevented him from hearing the Sinn Féin rifle fire during the attack on the Custom House may well have aided his concentration, for his books were masterpieces of care, accuracy and faultless detail.

Having got to grips with the day-to-day work we had to decide which of the reforming jobs we ought to tackle first. I am genuinely sorry now that we did not put in hand at once the job of reforming the local government structure. It would have paid handsome dividends in later years, and a strong, modernised local authority system might possibly have saved the country some of its troubles twenty-five years later. At the time, that need stood very low on our list of priorities. In retrospect, this seems to have been a serious error of judgment on our part.

We argued in the office about the problems of greatest urgency and we picked out three: housing, tuberculosis and the poor law.

In housing we decided that we needed some extra impetus over and above the efforts of the local authorities whom we were just then launching on their postwar programmes with additional powers and subsidies. We needed new thinking, new men, new methods, new courage. And by one of those happy turns of fortune in public affairs, we got all four.

In welfare work arising from the air-raid bombings of Belfast, and the problems of refugees and evacuees, two men of stature emerged—Lucius O'Brien and Herbert Bryson. These were well-known businessmen with Quaker associations who saw a clamant need to project into peacetime something of the united effort of wartime and who wanted to help with the task of house-building across the province. They offered their services for nothing. Ronald Green in the ministry converted their ideas into workable form and threw himself into the task of preparing the legislation. The permanent secretary was receptive. The minister put his great weight behind the idea and by 1946 we had created the Northern Ireland Housing Trust with O'Brien as chairman and Bryson as vice-chairman. This was a statutory board with power to build, to clear slums and to re-build. To some extent there was a parallel with the Scottish Special Housing Association but the trust had more identity of its own and it managed and looked after the houses it built or acquired. The standards it adopted were high. Its estates were well laid out. It was generous with green spaces and with trees. And it pursued a housing management policy on Octavia Hill lines. In no time the trust estates became recognisable. The ordinary member of the public would comment, in passing by, 'that must be a Trust estate'. The good siting, the superb landscaping and the distinctive house-types of the housing trust represent a high watermark in British housing and a lasting tribute to members and their staff. The members of the five-member board took a close personal interest, visiting sites, approving layouts and supervising management methods. Having built the annual output up to two thousand dwellings they were hard to persuade to go much beyond that figure, so intent were they on keeping the organisation to a size that they could personally manage. And they were stern moralists in financial matters— Gladstonian liberals, we used to say, in their repugnance to anything savouring of deficit financing. They had indeed a remarkable financial record. To some people they may have seemed paternalistic—to some they may have seemed self-satisfied; they certainly had their detractors amongst the local authorities—but all in all their achievements stand up to most criticisms and it was tragic to see the trust subsumed into the bigger Housing Executive in 1971.

If housing struck us in 1945 as one great social problem, tuberculosis was undoubtedly another: the Captain of the Men of Death, the greatest killing disease amongst young adults. Ireland was still suffering then from the ravages of phthisis or consumption and we made up our minds in the ministry to create the machinery by which all the best available remedies could be brought to bear; surgery, rest therapy, chemo-therapy, home visiting, education, early diagnosis, cash benefits, rehabilitation and so on. Once again we were lucky and managed to focus our resources on the problem. It called for intense effort but by 1946 we had created another unique body, the Northern Ireland Tuberculosis Authority. The best testimony to the success of this body was the fact that within ten years it had worked itself out of a job and could be wound up as redundant.

Those were two legislative and administrative achievements that grew out of our administration, were wholly indigenous and owed nothing to precedent or pressure from elsewhere.

The third of these early postwar reforms concerned the poor law. Here we were clearly some dozen or more years behind Great Britain; and it was no surprise to anyone when we decided to abolish the boards of guardians and all their works. The greater problem lay in arranging a proper succession, for as I mentioned in an earlier chapter the Irish poor law was a truly comprehensive health and welfare system embracing (in the terminology of later years) a hospital service, a general medical service, a domiciliary midwifery service, a home nursing service, residential accommodation for the elderly and for children in need of care and attention, a boarding-out service and finally a cash benefit service.

We knew of course that we would be establishing a national health service shortly and that Ministry of Labour would be creating a new national insurance and national assistance scheme.

Meantime as a first step we made up our minds to make the administrative break and create a fresh system based on the counties and county boroughs. We went out of our way to make this a distinctive service in its own right. We therefore legislated to oblige each of the councils to set up a statutory committee for health and a statutory committee for welfare; and to oblige each such committee to appoint not only a medical officer of health but also a health secretary, not only a county or county borough welfare officer but also a welfare secretary. We were determined to mark the break with the old poor law and create a new machine clearly designed to perform a new set of tasks in the idiom of the times. At the same time we plunged into the business of sanitary inspection and sanitary officers. Within a few years we saw the bad old system of part-time unqualified sanitary sub-officers-cum-relieving-officers transformed right across the country into a modern corps of qualified and highly respected sanitary officers (or public health inspectors as they rather regrettably chose to call themselves in later years). These were a particularly dedicated lot of men, constantly striving to equip themselves for their tasks in the fields of sanitation, smoke abatement, food hygiene, food composition and labelling, meat inspection and house inspection. In the many difficulties which have beset us since then the unobtrusive work and quiet success of these excellent men are generally overlooked or taken for granted. This is a pity, for the country today would be a much poorer place without their contribution. I was especially proud to be connected with them and their professional association.

There was quite a ferment in our offices in those heady days and many of our officials were reaching out for new ideas. Some of us in the office had taken a part-time study course at the Queen's University in 1941-42 and obtained a certificate in social studies. Not satisfied with that, we had kept together as a study group in the years 1943 and 1944 and taken a special interest in social problems as we actually found them in Ulster, not just as they were told in textbooks. It was therefore an exceptional experience to be able to play a part within government in helping to set up the administrative systems needed to alleviate the ills we had discerned.

The other source of satisfaction was the extraordinary amount of cooperation we received from local authority members and officers in making all these radical changes. Ulster is a contentious country and its people are skilled in the arts of rhetoric and invective. Undoubtedly we ran into criticism and opposition; much of it we created ourselves by what now seems bad timing; but there was a surprising amount of unity of purpose and a notable absence of religious controversy in administrative affairs.

The reforms I have been mentioning here were isolated measures, not to be compared with the huge undertaking of devising and setting up the national health service in 1948, covering the whole range of hospital, specialist, nursing and technical services, ambulances, blood transfusion, facilities for medical teaching and research, the general practitioner medical service, the dental service, the pharmaceutical service, the supplementary eye service and much else besides. Here there was little original work for us to do; the lead had been given by Nye Bevan and Clement Attlee's government in Great Britain. Our task was the more mechanical one of carrying out the multifarious negotiations, mounting the legislation and setting up the new bodies. We managed to do all that in time for 5 July 1948, the D Day for all the new social services in the United Kingdom. But we managed, I think it fair to say, to do something more; we managed, with the help of many people throughout Ulster, to create a better and above all a happier health service than was done in any other part of the kingdom and one that has patently stood the test of time—and the fire of unparalleled civic disturbances, violent deaths and injuries.

Those were a few of the legislative and administrative developments with which I was associated as a junior officer from 1944 onwards. I look on it as one of the most constructive periods in my time in the office.

Other departments were making similar advances in their fields. The Ministry of Education had been making giant strides with their education act of 1947, setting up the tripartite system of grammar school, intermediate school and technical school and bringing the historic voluntary grammar schools into the state system on sensible and acceptable terms; establishing a three-year training regime for teachers, well ahead of England, and generally keeping education in Ulster abreast of the times. Commerce had the task of promoting industrial growth in Ulster, as well as tourism, harbours, electricity, gas and much else. Agriculture pursued in single-minded fashion the objectives they had set themselves—maximum production from the land, a fair living for the farmers, extensive forestry, pasteurisation of milk, the eradication of, first, tuberculosis and, then, brucellosis from cattle and the development of a huge trade in pigs and poultry. And Finance were steadily broadening out from negative control to positive backing for the activities of other departments, earning respect from those departments and avoiding the obloquy which generally attends the Treasury function.

I have touched on the work of the Ministry of Labour in setting up the comprehensive insurance and assistance services that came to be stigmatised, unreasonably in my view, as the welfare state. It was this development, fully as much as my own ministry's work in health, welfare and housing, that stimulated me to undertake an academic study of the thinking behind all these affairs, the movement of thought over the centuries and the philosophical basis for these extraordinary activities of the state. I had the good luck to be encouraged by Alexander Macbeath and John Faris at the Department of Philosophy in the Queen's University who patiently steered me through a doctoral course in a philosophical analysis of the presuppositions and implications of the welfare state. Ironically I was at my busiest when I plunged into this difficult undertaking. Work in the office was at a peak in the sense that the administrative problems arising from the national health service and the new social welfare service were far more troublesome to us than the initial problems of policy and legislation had been. Stella and I had three children at the time and in addition were building ourselves a new house five miles from home with all the running back and forward (on bicycles) that that involved. Still I was keen to explore the unknown territory of philosophical thought and set off on a lengthy journey that took me through epistemology, moral philosophy and political philosophy. Starting with Plato and Aristotle and working through many of the great thinkers of the past, the plan was to try to trace some philosophical thread of concern for the weaker members of society and of the obligation of others for them. From this there emerged, first, the basic idea of 'the good life' and then the role of society and of the state in fostering the good life. Ought it to be the job of the state to make people happy? Can the state make people happy? Or is it a matter of the state helping to create the conditions within which the individual can achieve his own fulfilment? The outcome was enough to get me a PhD but not good enough to publish, I thought.

At that time I was engaged not only in helping to administer the statutory social service but in other approaches of a personal nature as well and was completely immersed in voluntary social work. This is easy to manage in Ulster because of the regional system that prevails and because of the way in which so many bodies operate coterminously within the region. Ulster is the one region in the United Kingdom that defines itself and is instantly recognisable. Our work in the office was concerned with the public and statutory social services through the region and linked up naturally with the main voluntary body in social work, the Northern Ireland Council of Social Service. There was also the Federation of Boys Clubs in Northern Ireland, the Northern Ireland Council for Orthopaedic Development, the Northern Ireland Committee of the Institute of Almoners and several other regional bodies of the same kind. Not only was there voluntary social work but part-time teaching and lecturing on the social services at the Queen's University and at Trinity College, Dublin. When the British Association for the Advancement of Science held its meeting in Belfast in 1952 it fell to me, as the most conveniently placed local person, to read a paper on our fundamental approach to the care of old people:

> Age is opportunity no less
> Than Youth itself
> Though in another dress.

I seem to remember that I was vainly struggling to establish there a new concept which I called social humanism, an attempt at placing the emphasis on the individual and on his capacity to lead the good life with the support of a comprehensive system of statutory and voluntary social care. I thought I saw at that time a danger that the social services could become ends in themselves and that the essential elements of individual initiative and individual fulfilment could be lost sight of in the very effort to provide state services which were incapable in themselves of making people either healthy or happy. But my notion of social humanism did not win many disciples.

Chapter 8

ON THE DEFENSIVE

The IRA kept attacking the Ulster community spasmodically for six long years between 1956 and 1962. The campaign was largely a rural one and was concentrated on the border areas. It was naked terrorism and was not based on the support of the local population. The targets were the familiar ones: railway lines, roads, bridges, customs posts, police stations, water and electricity installations and farmers in lonely places. With 605 recorded incidents there was much distress and destruction as well as a great deal of intimidation. Six policemen were murdered. By comparison with the troubles that were to come seven years later, in 1969, these were small affairs and people in Belfast, Antrim and Down saw little of them. But they had a depressing effect and struck a ominous note.

In administrative terms the campaign called for the spending of extra effort and extra money. Police had to be reinforced, the Ulster Special Constabulary mobilised, stations fortified and patrols mounted to check the movement of vehicles and persons. Ministers spent much of their time inspecting the border area, encouraging the police, attending funerals, visiting victims in hospital and reassuring the population.

The harm caused by the campaign was contained and reprisals prevented. But the greatest cost may be measured by the effect which the IRA campaign had on the administration. For one thing it was a serious distraction of attention and effort. For another it drove the government and the general public into a defensive and negative posture at a time when they might have been striking out on positive lines of political action. And it helped to make the political climate totally unfavourable to change. Let us recall the position as seen by the administration.

The main work of postwar reconstruction had been completed, the damage made good and the new social systems set in motion.

Hospitals and schools were flourishing. Housing though still patchy was moving rapidly forward. We completed our one hundred thousandth new postwar dwelling in 1962. We had just seen enacted the housing act of 1956 dealing with slum clearance and with improvement grants; it also took a second bite at the rent restriction cherry which had been first broached in the act of 1951. Handsome new roads and bridges were appearing all over the province. And as for new industry, let me list a few of the firms which had been attracted to Northern Ireland and had set up factories in the outlying part of the province: Reed Corrugated Cases in Warrenpoint, Bairnswear in Armagh, Adria in Strabane, Du Pont and British Oxygen in Londonderry, Daintifyt in Limavady, Chemstrand in Coleraine, UK Optical in Lurgan, Slack and Parr in Enniskillen. Nestlé in Omagh—to say nothing of the many in and around Belfast. Some of these factories had been purpose-built; in other cases the companies took over advance factories which the Ministry of Commerce had put up and held ready at some considerable financial risk.

From such a sound base we might well have been moving forward to political reform, the removal of causes of discontent and the attraction of Roman Catholics into full participation in public life in greater numbers and with greater enthusiasm. But the atmosphere in the country was being soured by the long-drawn-out campaign of terrorism. The attitude of many people in positions of authority or influence across the country was becoming negative and defensive. Appointments to senior positions in the civil service were timid, mediocre men were being encouraged, grey figures were beginning to predominate. I recall the head of the civil service advising me: 'Your main job is to keep your minister out of trouble'. When it became clear that Ronald Green, at once the most imaginative and the most energetic man in our senior ranks, was never going to be given the really influential post of head of the civil service, I began to feel worried. Local authorities—of both political complexions —were losing their wartime and postwar sense of purpose and willingness to collaborate; and a few were playing unworthy games in the location of new housing estates in relation to electoral wards and in the allocation of tenancies. As administrators we drew attention to these practices and warned of the dangers. We may have been at fault in not being more forceful in our advice. These tensions were well illustrated by our personal relations with the minister who dominated our office lives throughout most of the 1950s, Dame Dehra Parker. Here was the leading woman in public life in Ulster, a woman of education and distinction, a patron of the arts, with American connections which she cultivated, capricious, an adroit politician and a most formidable operator. When receiving visitors from abroad she could be charm itself, drawing on a lifetime of travel and conversing easily in French and German. When receiving a deputation from Belfast or Fermanagh, she could be a lot less charming and relied rather less on elegant phrases. She could grasp, every bit as well as we officials could and perhaps a lot better, the arguments in favour of changes in electoral affairs or in housing allocations or (more aptly) in the relationship between the two; but she could grasp even more clearly the political case for leaving such sensitive matters as they were. She would not be moved; and that was her right. Each of us had his own method in briefing sessions with her: Leslie Freer's was magisterial coolness, Ronald Green's biting wit and mine brisk argument. Perhaps we ought to have been more obstructive; but was that our job? Perhaps one of us ought even to have resigned; but what good would that have done? It might have created a small sensation for a few days but would have been quickly forgotten. We believed at the time that our duty lay in carrying on, in continuing to offer to Dame Dehra our impartial advice whether palatable or not, and in providing all the while the best administrative service we could. Having experienced the ups and downs since then and having seen many turns of political fortune I believe even more firmly today that that was indeed where our duty lay all along. We knew well in those days that 'liberal' observers, old college friends and so on thought otherwise and vaguely imagined that we ought somehow to have sabotaged the machine or else reformed the political system; but they were observers not executants. Time has, I believe, amply demonstrated, in the eyes of the world, the supreme difficulty which any political party (for a whole number of reasons) must have in running a full and faultless democratic system of government within Northern Ireland; and has confirmed also that officials will be doing their job if they fulfil their threefold duty of offering the best advice they can, of getting decisions from ministers and of providing the most efficient service to the people.

It was in this negative period that we suffered some of our most unhappy relations with the Belfast Corporation. Here we had the inherently difficult situation of a large city and a small government; we had the juxtaposition of a city of some considerable standing that dated from the seventeenth century and enjoyed a

royal charter, with a parvenu parliament and government dating
only from 1921. Relations had never been easy. The city clearly
resented interference by government. They resented even more
any attempt to equate them with other local authorities. They felt
superior to the others and disparagingly referred to all other local
councils as 'the local authorities'. They were convinced that the
country members of parliament conspired to depress the city's
position. Their deputations were testy with ministers, when not
actively hostile.

The big issue with the Belfast Corporation was their yearning
for an extension of the city boundary so as to take in large tracts
of surrounding territory. Their argument was that the city was
too densely developed (which was true) and that they therefore
needed virgin land on which to build houses and schools and to
create parks and playing fields (which was true on the surface but
not valid in the wider context of the development of the country
as a whole). But the problem was greatly exacerbated by the
simple fact that their claim had really come too late. To have
granted Belfast a moderate extension in order to take in virgin
land for building might well have been reasonable in the 1920s
but by the time they presented their local bill to parliament in
1947 the city had already been ringed around with surburban
growth. In order to take in green fields one would have had to
take in first of all a belt of modern suburbs, with the result that
the full extension required would have been enormous. Parliament—not government—rejected the claim; and the rejection
rankled with the City Hall for many a long year.

I am convinced that the instinct of parliament was sound. A
city of some 440 000 people was big enough in relation to a
province of approximately 1 600 000. An Irish city of 440 000 is
probably big enough in itself, leave alone all comparisons with
province or government. In terms of rateable valuation the city
embraced over forty per cent of the wealth, the limited wealth,
of the province. The other local authorities surrounding Belfast
did not relish the thought of being absorbed into the city or even
of being forced to surrender some of their valuable rating resources.
This resistance, though soundly based, antagonised the Belfast
councillors and made them still more unresponsive. They themselves contributed further to the confusion by staging acrimonious
and destructive debates in the council chamber. They took an
unconscionable time to get a policy proposal through their
Byzantine committee and party channels. They were weak on
the social but somewhat stronger on the trading services; they ran

a competent enough electricity generating and distribution service; one of the better gas services in the kingdom; and an excellent tramway system and later trolley bus and omnibus system until outside difficulties overtook them in the 1970s. The diplomatic trouble the ministry had at the end of the war in bringing them to the point of agreeing to set up a mass radiography scheme was in sharp contrast with the excellence of the unit which they eventually built, equipped, staffed and managed. Their executive skills far outran their political capabilities.

All this meant endless trouble for their officials and ours. The constant disputes between City Hall and Stormont were but the tip of the iceberg; beneath the surface was a continuous struggle to keep relationships going and to carry on effective administrative and financial business. Within their staffs there were many able men but they needed leadership and would have responded if they had got it, I am quite sure. We, for our part, in the ministry were not free from blame and a more mature and generous spirit might well have softened attitudes and eased the tension. It was one of those situations in which we were in the right but could have handled relations much better.

Building outside the city boundary was the crucial issue in the defensive years of which I write here. The ministry wanted them to do much more in the way of new housing, to plan their estates more generously and to refrain from using up every square yard of available land in the city. They argued that this was impossible without a boundary extension. The ministry argued that neither the surrounding local authorities nor parliament would grant them one. They argued that there was therefore nothing they could do. The ministry argued that the latest housing act of 1959 gave them fresh powers to undertake slum clearance and then to redevelop the land. They argued that this would create untold problems in the religious and party political arenas. The ministry argued . . . And so it went on, endlessly, bitterly and unprofitably, until one day in an unguarded moment a Belfast city deputation went so far as to say that they might be agreeable to build a few houses outside the boundary provided the ministry appointed an independent assessor to select the sites and advise upon them.

We seized on their suggestion immediately. We approached Robert Matthew of Edinburgh, a leading national and indeed international figure in architecture and planning. Our chief architect and town planner, James Aitken, and I travelled at once to Edinburgh in March 1960 in order to settle the arrangement. Matthew, naturally unwilling to step into a situation of controversy and act simply as referee, preferred to make a proper study of the whole situation, analyse all the relevant factors and give us the benefit of a development plan. For a mere twenty-five thousand pounds, I recall, he undertook to set up an office in Belfast under the care of that most talented, versatile and meticulous planner, Cecil Newman, and within a couple of years to produce for us all a Belfast regional plan. This he did. It was in the form of a most handsome pair of volumes, graced with Newman's incomparable photography and mapping. In many ways it broke new ground in regional physical planning in the British Isles. And it placed our feet on a path from which we were never to turn back, the path of a positive, activist approach to the physical and economic problems of the province.

Chapter 9

A NEW START: FROM MATTHEW TO MACRORY

The publication of Matthew's *Belfast Regional Plan* and the announcement of a number of government decisions implementing his advice took place simultaneously on 26 February 1963.

This was of course by no means the first time that the administration had taken an activist role in tackling problems. Far from it. Nor was Matthew necessarily the cause of all the activist policies that were later adopted in various fields. But it is true to say that his *Belfast Regional Plan* represented the undisputed origin of a huge programme of government involvement and of the assumption by government of responsibility for the physical development of the country; and secondly that the popular impact of his *Plan* in 1963—which was much more striking than that of most government reports up till then—at least coincided with (if it did not actually fire the starting pistol for) a whole series of other important departures in public policy.

The essence of Matthew was that the community should take a firm grip on land and on physical development and begin to shape the country in the long-term interests of prosperity and quality of life. He recommended what was then the revolutionary idea of drawing a stop-line around the total urban area of Belfast and its suburbs, in order to stop all further suburban sprawl; the preservation of a strictly controlled greenscape around the city; the creation of a counter-magnet to Belfast in the form of a new regional city that would embrace the boroughs of Lurgan and Portadown as well as the land between them and surrounding them on the southern shore of Lough Neagh; the wider concept of growth towns for planned industrial growth; the preservation of the countryside and the coast; the creation of a single planning authority in place of the forty which then existed; the payment of compensation for outright refusal of planning permission; and a great deal else.

Act of parliament followed hard on the heels of act of parliament; scheme followed scheme; new town commission followed new town commission; nature reserve committee followed countryside committee; and so on in a series of rapid moves that sought, as Matthew advised, to give the community a bigger say in the physical shaping of the country. One flaw existing in the edifice dogged the government for years. The hard realistic constraints of the Ministry's battle with the Belfast Corporation in 1960, when Matthew was appointed, necessarily confined his work to Belfast and its surrounding area. That was the object agreed with the City Hall; to have insisted on widening the scope would, in the context of the argument of the day about city boundary and local council rivalry, have jeopardised the success of the arrangement. We foresaw that there would be trouble over this, and that, once the benefits of this type of planning came to be generally appreciated, the parts of the province that had been left out would inevitably complain. We managed to have included in Matthew's terms of reference a phrase setting the study in the context of Northern Ireland as a whole, but that was not enough. The plan appeared under the title of *Belfast Regional Plan.* Londonderry, Tyrone and Fermanagh gradually began to complain. They alleged that they had been deliberately omitted. Matthew had, for objective planning reasons, sited the new city in county Armagh and east of the Bann. Fuel had been unwittingly added to the fire of the 'west of the Bann' grievance that was then beginning to burn.

Physical planning had been broached. Next it was to be economic planning, and Professor Tom Wilson, Adam Smith Professor of Political Economy at the University of Glasgow and a distinguished Ulsterman, gave Ulster the Wilson Economic Plan of 1965 that urged us to set about guiding the economy in a purposeful way. But regional planning is not a static, once-for-all exercise. It must move with events. The government therefore brought back both Matthew and Wilson in 1967, along with Jack Parkinson of Nottingham, to prepare for us the Development Programme 1970-75. This programme, the government white paper that accompanied it and the machinery set up for monitoring the progress of the programme, proved remarkably effective and placed us in the forefront of regional work in the British Isles and earned us a respectable place even in the calculations of the European Community institutions.

I said that Matthew in 1963 at least coincided with a number of other departures if he did not actually fire the starting pistol.

Positive action was in the air and barely a year passed before the government decided to reorganise the ministries so as to provide a more effective machine. For years the physical or environmental functions of government had been distributed over several ministries for various reasons that seemed good in each particular case. Roads and transport had been moved from Home Affairs to Commerce after the war, as the ministry concerned with industry, commerce and tourism. They were later transferred back to Home Affairs in an effort at broadening the scope of a ministry too heavily identified with law and order. Home Affairs also looked after nature conservation. We in Health and Local Government, founded at the time of D Day in 1944, were responsible for planning, housing, water and sewerage but of course we could not concentrate wholly on those matters as we had also to look after health and welfare. The sorting out which took place in July 1964 resulted in the health and welfare work being moved alongside the cash benefit services and the employment services into a new Ministry of Health and Social Services. The Ministry of Development was created to bring together a wide range of physical services: planning, roads, transport, airports, housing in all its forms, water, sewerage, nature conservation, amenity lands, new towns and local government. There was great excitement in the office over the prospect of closer coordination and interlocking, of greater drive and of better service to the public and to incoming industry.

The interlocking arrangements worked in a number of ways. First the permanent secretary finding himself responsible for all those services realised that he had an equal responsibility for promoting all of them, for ensuring that all got fair treatment in the allocation of staff and resources and above all for welding the various separate staffs into one team. Engineers, as well as working on road projects, became available to advise on housing; quantity surveyors previously concentrating on housing could be called on to help with problems of contracts or materials or costs over a much wider field; the highly specialised skills of the geologist or the landscape architect could be used in helping small services such as amenity lands that could not justify the employment of such men on their own. The central issue was of course town and country planning and especially the regional plans and the area plans which we were developing from the time when Robert Matthew started work with us in 1960. With us planning became essentially a bringing together of a number of disciplines such as architecture, road engineering, transport, economics, sociology and geography (itself a synthesis of many different approaches to the environment). It was a matter of looking forward to the needs of the people and of industry and commerce for some twenty years ahead, trying to foresee their demands for land and then of budgeting in terms of space and time. In regional and area planning we found ourselves engaged in work that was at once the most all-embracing in public affairs and the most stimulating.

Apart from the problems of bringing other ministries, with their own ideas and their own timetables, to see the benefits for them in long-term land budgeting, we had problems inside our own ministry as well. The hardest part of the new grouping of services to digest was the roads branch, illustrating one of the fundamental human dilemmas in office organisation. How far should one recognise energy and drive and give a branch its head, regardless of the finer points of coordination with others; or how far should one merge it with other cognate services for reasons of greater precision in public policy, at the cost of dulling its edge and slowing it down? In the roads branch of the 1960s Northern Ireland had a Rolls-Royce machine, staffed by high quality people who were fully on top of their jobs, were clear about their own priorities and extremely capable at getting on with the business of designing and building modern roads and bridges, either directly themselves, or through the splendid team of county surveyors, who in turn (for reasons running back a long time in Ireland) were something of a law unto themselves within their counties. The excellent roads of Ulster today are a tribute to the single-minded energy and self-assurance of the roads branch and county surveyors in an era before 'public participation' loomed as large as it does today. All very well, but were their efforts always in the best direction? Was there a risk of building roads for their own sake? Should road planning not be an integral part of general planning strategy? Naturally there was tension. Those virile men in roads, I had the impression at first, took a poor view of the old women on the planning side, concerned as it seemed with pretty scenery and scandalised at the sight of honest-to-goodness concrete post fencing.

Nor was the wide range of physical services under the Ministry of Development as complete as it might have been. Forestry and forest parks remained with Agriculture as did also land drainage and water recreation. Road safety stayed with Home Affairs, associated with police supervision and with their responsibility for the safety of the individual, despite the fact that our road engineers had to advise the road safety branch. These and other anomalies caused slight wrinkles and delays but in this matter of the distribution of government business amongst departments there is no finality and there can be no finality. Times change, priorities change, politics change; organisation must change with them. Between us all we worked out a number of techniques for making the parts of this splendid machine fit smoothly, over and above the normal procedures of minuting, submission of files, office meetings and informal man-to-man talks. I was particularly keen on bringing groups of officers together regularly for a free-for-all discussion. The cost in time was repaid in improved communications and understanding. We operated a system of concentric circles. Every Monday morning at 10, no matter what was happening, I would meet my three deputies in my room for a blowing-off of steam. At 10.30 we would be joined by all the assistant secretaries; there were nine of them at one stage. Our press officer was privy to these deliberations. We had no agenda and kept no minutes. It was simply a matter of running round the table asking each in turn to tell his tale. It was generally a tale of woe, an account of all that had gone wrong in the previous week and of all that could conceivably go wrong in the following week. They seemed to take the successes for granted and seldom remembered to report them. Then on stated days we would be joined by the professional heads of roads, water and sewerage and planning. On yet other days we had with us all the heads of professional services—the lawyer, the architect, the auditor, the quantity surveyor, the Alkali etc. Inspector (*sic!*), the public health inspector and so on. To put it at its very lowest we arranged in that way that not more than a week or a month or whatever, as the case might be, could pass without all the various senior people at least meeting all their opposite numbers and exchanging worries. At one level the process was hard on me for it brought me face-to-face prematurely with horrible problems and clashes of discipline that I could well have done without. At a deeper level there was the knowledge that the process was contributing to a better-knit public service.

I recall one meeting, of an even less structured kind, that I held in my room late one Friday evening soon after the Ministry of Development was created. We had a lot of people present from all sides, including some junior men away down the ladder, but with interesting remits. The group was greatly stimulated by hearing Bailie Russell speak on his long-term road strategy. He stood at my wall-map and with his finger traced some of the old historic routes in Ireland. With brilliantly imaginative strokes he described to us the line he had in mind for a motorway to Derry; and picked out the Gap o' the North in south Armagh which he was keen to follow when it came to building a really monumental motorway from Belfast to Dublin, by-passing Dundalk and Drogheda on their landward sides. Those two motorways have still to come.

Much of our work was aimed at meeting ordinary social needs: more and better houses, more and better roads and transport and so on. But much of it was devoted to the support of industrial development. Our working links with our colleagues in the Ministry of Commerce became closer and closer. Houses were built to suit the shift-working requirements of a new factory; houses were specially designed for business executives; road access was planned as new industries took shape and their transport needs became known; huge schemes were worked out to meet the heavy demands of industry for water; industrial effluent had to be disposed of. This approach of providing the infrastructure (as it was called) became increasingly important in the sixties and played its part in attracting top-class industry to the province. Cooperation with our colleagues in the Ministry of Commerce was not always easy. Relying on the importance and urgency of industrial development and on the backing which that gave them, without fail, in political circles, they were exacting in their demands on us. We did not mind this nearly so much as their habit of implying that if we could not guarantee to provide some facility by an impossibly early date the company they were dealing with would simply transfer their project to Scotland or Wales or West Germany; and the blame for losing the valuable factory would fall on us. This put great pressure on us in providing roads, water, sewerage, disposal of effluent, housing and so on. But we felt the pressure even more keenly in relation to the apparently simple matter of granting planning permission for the use of a particular piece of land. The site often seemed to us to have been selected by the foreign businessman without a great deal of thought (as we used to say, probably through the window of the Ministry of Commerce Austin Princess as it sped through the beautiful countryside). The land would turn out to require a quite unreasonable outlay of public money on services and to make harder the task of preserving the countryside and its amenities in the long-term interest of all of us, businessman included. And yet all we needed to do was to say yes. We in the Ministry of Development were probably over-sensitive on our side. We may have taken too conscientious a stand on defending the regional strategy. We were haunted by the fear of opening the floodgates where the Matthew regional plan had spoken of the need to treat as sacrosanct the Belfast stop-line in order to safeguard the orderly growth of the region. I know that I was prickly on that subject. As a result there were many hard exchanges, one or two quite nasty, but the outcome was a combined service to incoming industrialists which has been widely acknowledged. Altogether it was a satisfying experience for us and for the staff of the local authorities who were then the responsible executive bodies.

The local authority system was being severely tested by all this. Created in the nineteenth century to meet nineteenth century conditions, the system had outlived its usefulness by the time we are speaking of. The fault lay with the antiquated system rather than with the councillors and officers struggling to operate it. There were too many authorities; many were too small; most were too poor. The two-tier system of county and district was wasteful and confusing. The sharp distinction between town and county, between urban and rural, so important in the nineteenth century, had become not only meaningless but a positive hindrance.

For those reasons we launched in March 1966 a campaign to reshape our local government system. Following widespread consultations, a white paper embodying some preliminary suggestions was briskly prepared and issued in December 1967; further and more detailed proposals were published in a second white paper, but unfortunately not until July 1969. All were designed to create a simplified, single-tier, strong local government system with a full range of powers including housing. Since later events in this local government saga received a lot more publicity than these early steps, the memory of those important proposals tends to become blurred. It is therefore fortunate that the Command Papers 517 and 530 are on permanent record demonstrating clearly the direction in which the Ministry of Development was moving. Although those steps served to get opinion moving, there was diminishing agreement as to what ought to be done. There was diminishing agreement on everything, for we were by then well into the civil rights campaign and the troubles which were to tear the community apart.

To complete the story of local government reshaping even at the price of jumping ahead a little, a crucial decision was taken by ministers in October 1969 in consultation with James Callaghan, then British Home Secretary. This was to lift the whole subject of housing in all its forms out of the hands of local councils and the housing trust and give it to a new statutory board (the Northern Ireland Housing Executive). Everyone saw that whatever the merits of this decision it would tear the heart out of local government as we knew it and render it impossible to create a new system with anything approaching a full range of functions in the British or Irish tradition. The consequence was understood and accepted. Clearly then a fresh start had to be made with reshaping. A review body was set up under the chairmanship of Patrick A Macrory, which noted the two earlier white papers and the housing decision, made a realistic survey of the chances of gaining local agreement to any new pattern and in the remarkably short time of five months—January to May 1970—produced a clear, firm and workable set of proposals. These were accepted by government and acted upon. A huge programme of consultation, preparation, legislation, interviewing of staff, allocation of premises and equipment followed, culminating in the total reorganisation of our local administration on 1 October 1973. The reorganisation was on a more radical scale than in England or Scotland and preceded them in time. Macrory stamped his imprint as indelibly on the administrative scene as, ten years earlier, Matthew had done on the physical.

Other departments had been moving forward rapidly during all this time. Education had in 1964 published their white paper setting guide lines for the future shaping of schools in consonance with the times. Labour were making enormous strides in industrial training, far ahead of what was being achieved in Great Britain or for that matter anywhere else. And Commerce stood high in the big league of industrial development. Companies of international standing had been attracted to Ulster and were running manufacturing plants here: Courtaulds, ICI, UK Optical, Michelin from France, Grundig and Hoechst from Germany, Enkalon from Holland, Oneida, Bridgport Brass and Hughes's Tools from USA, to mention only a few of the better known names from amongst several hundred companies, large and small, foreign, British and local, that entered into settlements with the Ministry of Commerce.

As well as their constant activities in the work of farm production, our colleagues in Agriculture were concerning themselves more and more with land drainage and with forestry, creating incidentally some forest parks of distinction and beauty.

Only Home Affairs were unable to join as fully as other Departments in this positive movement forward. Caught in an unhappy position between disturbed protestant feeling in the Terence O'Neill era of political experiment and on the other hand the rumblings of civil rights (all taking place in a crescendo of heated publicity on television) they could make little impact on their major fields of concern: electoral law, prison reform, policing, public order, the prosecution system.

But the problems ran deeper. The Ministry of Home Affairs had never been adequately staffed in the senior ranks. Regardless of the threat of ill-informed accusations of bureaucracy, it is the positive duty of every ministry to make sure that it has senior officers who are not only capable of studying and advising upon all the functions of the ministry, but also in practice free to do so. There is often a reluctance to arrange this in a small department that has little or no executive, clerical or manual work to do and therefore no broad base to its pyramid (unlike, for example, the Ministry of Agriculture or the department handling social security benefits). A small department does not want to appear top-heavy, nor to consist of 'all generals and no privates'. And this is the very mistake that Home Affairs fell into. They remained under-staffed in the higher ranks. The result was that year after year the rest of us could see from their staff chart that some unfortunate assistant secretary was responsible for vivisection, greyhound racing, liquor licensing, law and order, road safety, the marriage laws etc etc. Or perhaps accounts, personnel, prisons, dangerous drugs, electoral law, betting shops, administration of the lower courts etc etc. No man in that situation could possibly devote the time, the reading, the travel and the thought needed to promote constructive reforms in the key issues of electoral law, penal reform or law and order.

The problem, again seen purely in administrative terms, ran even deeper still. It is doubtful whether Home Affairs ever really 'administered' the police and police activity in the manner that other ministries administered, say, industrial promotion, educational policy or agricultural marketing, and that I shall be trying to describe in part II. From the earliest days police policy was regarded primarily as a matter for ministers, and successive inspectors-general of the Royal Ulster Constabulary had a tendency to report straight to them with their troubles. The outcome was first of all that the main activity of the ministry in relation to the RUC was largely reduced to 'police maintenance', in other words the supply of barracks, uniforms, equipment and so on. Many a thick ministry file solemnly concerned itself with such weighty matters as the provision of a knee-rug for the inspector-general's car! Second, the early administrators seldom had a chance of studying police policy and methods, or police relationships with the community. No doubt a hard-pressed police in the early years would have felt 'frustrated' if they had been subjected to 'bureaucratic interference' by bright up-and-coming young graduate administrators in Home Affairs and would have complained sadly of 'delays'; but the result might have been better. This is a most difficult and sensitive field of administration, especially in Ulster, and one comments only with the greatest care. But to put the matter another way, and still in civil service rather than political terms, it would be hard to see law and order, the police, the prisons and electoral law all developing as they did, if say, a vigorous department like the Ministry of Agriculture or the Ministry of Labour had been in charge. Although, as I shall analyse in some detail in part II, ministers willingly carry the political responsibility, there is no sense in evading the undisputed fact that the quality of the departmental administration and of the service given to ministers does have a bearing on results and on the wellbeing of the country. Parallels could be produced in most countries. It seems to me to be one of the great unrealities of present-day politics and political science that this big factor in public affairs is so seldom studied. Nevertheless a great deal was accomplished by Home Affairs after the war and, given the poor reputation that that department had, it may be worth recording some of it. First of all they managed to contain the IRA activity of 1956–62 to a remarkable degree, to keep it from spreading to Belfast, and to prevent anything in the nature of protestant retaliation. Those three facts are generally overlooked. So far as the Royal Ulster Constabulary itself was concerned the ministry made unobtrusive progress in the way of disarming the constables on the beat, for the first time ever, and of building village constable stations designed to bring the police into closer and easier contact with the civilian population. Recruitment from grammar schools and universities was encouraged and serving officers released on full pay to attend courses at the Queen's University. Arrangements were made for police chiefs from England and Wales to visit the police college at Enniskillen so as to keep young policemen in touch with the best practices of the civilian English forces.

For a department that is generally thought to have neglected its responsibilities in the field of social affairs and legislation, the facts speak differently. Here is a summary of the acts of parliament promoted by the Ministry of Home Affairs between 1946 and 1971, under the nine broad headings of the ministry's responsibilities:

Law reform and family law	43
Administration of justice	37
Protection of the individual	29
Criminal justice	12
Wild birds and animals	9
Liquor, betting, clubs	12
Elections and franchise	9
Police, offenders and probation	10
Children and adoption	5
Total	166

More than half of those acts were enacted between 1946 and 1960, fewer than half between 1961 and 1971. What matters of course is the content of those 166 Home Affairs acts, not simply their number. A numerical count is a crude measuring-rod, if perhaps no cruder than the sweeping generalisations made by distant critics. But the statute book is there for any impartial person to study. One of the gaps in the Home Affairs record was any attempt at converting the B Specials into a modern police reserve. The end of the 1956–62 IRA campaign might have been a good time to do it. But Home Affairs, like any department, could work only within the limits of what was politically possible.

On 5 October 1968 a civil rights march in the city of London-derry came into open physical conflict with the Royal Ulster Constabulary. The troubles can be said to have started on a recognisable scale, with unforseeable results for the civil service as for everyone else, on that day.

Chapter 10

THE TROUBLES—1968 to 1974

It is no part of my plan to analyse the causes of the civil disturbances which wracked the province for several years nor to trace the course of those events. I confine myself to the effect which they had on our work and on our lives.

Like the rest of the population we had been accustomed to a certain amount of instability and violence in Ulster. It had been thus over the centuries. But like the rest of the population, again, we had found ourselves under increasing strain as year succeeded year from 1968 onward. I believe that we took about four or five years of disturbance without noticeable effect; when it became clear in about 1972 and 1973 that, despite all that had happened and despite the endeavours of William Whitelaw, violence was going to continue, the strain began to tell. As in the population at large, war-weariness was setting in with us in the service. It was not only the bombs, the shootings, the destruction and intimidation; it was the counter-measures and the ever-encroaching limitation on day-to-day life, on freedom, on shopping and on social activities that began to tell. More poignant still was the sight of a whole generation of children and young people growing up never knowing any other life than a life dominated by violence and lawlessness. And when we began to notice the drifting away from Ulster of many of its young men and women we began to feel the first intimations of despair—as Keats wrote:

Where youth grows pale, and spectre-thin, and dies;
Where but to think is to be full of sorrow
and leaden-eyed despairs.

But we had a job to do; and one of the simple rules of the service is that we do our job, and carry on, no matter what our feelings are.

Doing the job was far from easy. I did not have, personally, the most difficult passage; my colleagues in Health and Social Services probably had a rougher time. Taking the whole of our sphere of action in the Ministry of Development (including the transport bodies, the housing bodies and the local authorities) we had our quota of violence; bombs, shootings, destruction of water installations, destruction of offices, loss of records and much else of the same kind. Transport suffered particularly, with the hijacking and burning of buses, bombs on the railway lines and destruction of signalling equipment. At one time we counted that in Belfast alone some thirteen hundred buses had been destroyed or damaged out of a total of three hundred and fifty! In other words, some had been damaged, repaired and damaged again and again. Serious though the damage was, there were other aspects that made continued operation extremely difficult. The bomb hoax was disruptive of office work; staff had to be got out to safety; but what about money, documents and other valuables important to the public, left unattended? Imagine the problems of running a parcel delivery service from a depot subject to bombs and bomb hoaxes to areas where no vehicle may enter, or may enter but not stop, or stop only if someone remains in the driver's cab as a surety while the parcel is delivered, and where the recipient may in the end prudently hesitate to accept the parcel lest it prove, itself, to be a bomb. Businessmen, manufacturers and shopkeepers had of course similar problems, with fewer resources behind them than we enjoyed. Power stations and transmission lines were repeatedly damaged or threatened so that electricity supply to industry hung many times upon a thread.

A few of the problems particular to our kind of work need to be put on record.

The demand for housing and for slum clearance was clamant in some areas; those were however the very areas where building contractors found it hardest to carry on. On some sites there was sporadic shooting; on some there was cold-blooded murder; on many the labour supply was controlled by intimidation. How does one enforce the time limit or the final cost of a building contract in such conditions? And what does one do if the builder decides he must leave the site and abandon the job? Twenty-six thousand tenants of publicly-owned houses went on strike and stopped paying rent. Painted notices appeared on the streets of modern housing estates: RENT SPENT. Squatting was a widespread, sporadic and recurring feature. However much one sympathised with the plight of individual families—and one often did—one could not take the same view of squatting deliberately stimulated by political bodies or organised for gain. The measures to counter widespread rent strikes and organised squatting are not altogether easy to devise or enforce. The strains on the whole system were acute. Little wonder that four urban district councils ceased altogether to function. For a number of highly practical reasons I was personally appointed sole commissioner to discharge all the functions of all four councils—as far as we know a wholly unprecedented and unheard-of burden. I hasten to add that as soon as I assumed these dignified municipal functions I delegated them to little teams of anonymous officers in the ministry who did all the work and ran all the risks.

Administrative life was going on all the time; we were not just concentrating on emergencies, not by a long chalk.

In 1971 we were setting up the Housing Executive, a body without precedent or parallel in the British isles; and transferring to it the function, properties, assets and liabilities as well as the contracts, tenancies and problems of sixty-one local authorities and the Housing Trust. And in readiness for 1973 we were preparing the immense Macrory reorganisation of local administration, leading to elections for the new councils and appointments to a host of new boards. Indeed in 1973 there were three polls: the border referendum in March, the local council elections in May and the elections to the new Parliamentary Assembly in June. All the while departments were striving to fulfil the ambitious objectives which they had set themselves in the Development Programme 1970–75.

More than that, as we passed the midway point and began to foresee the ending of that programme and the time when we would run out of targets and objectives, we put our hand to the shaping of another programme to follow. The Development Programme 1970–75 had been strong on the physical and economic sides but weak on the social side. If the troubles had taught us anything, it was that a great deal more attention had to be paid to the deeply rooted social problems of the province. Thus, the new programme was entitled 'Social and Economic Programme', and under the leadership of the Ministry of Finance all departments set about preparing objectives, studying the constraints and planning to allocate resources. Many of the social objectives such as the reduction of poverty, the better training and occupation of young people or the improvement of the quality of life in residential areas cut across departmental boundaries, and this work therefore had much to do with accelerating fruitful co-operation between departments, not the easiest of tasks. Shortage of money

Grandfather Henry Sherrard of Magilligan, born 1845.

The author's parents in 1930.

A primary school class of the 1920s. The author was one of eighty pupils in his class in 1922.
E. E. Sandford.

The author's student card, issued by the University of Bonn in Nazi Germany, 1936.

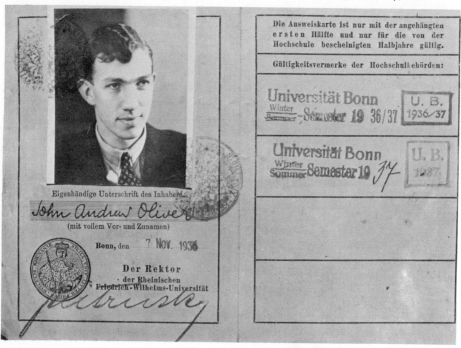

forced ministers eventually to abandon this programme in 1975. Another large volume of imaginative and positive work thus disappeared without trace.

The Ministry of Finance were meantime giving a lead in another positive development during these years of violence and turmoil. This was the British PESC or public expenditure survey committee system for drawing up five-year budgets of all public expenditure by all public agencies in addition to the traditional system of annual estimates of voted cash. The PES arrangement is a most sophisticated one, making great demands on departments and promising to provide them with a useful tool of management. I cannot honestly say that I ever saw that promise fulfilled and I seriously questioned its value for Northern Ireland. But the innovation illustrates the type of new work being undertaken in spite of the uncertainties of the times. The Ministry of Finance have further ideas for reforming the traditional estimates so as to show more clearly to parliament how much money is being sought in support of each of the main functions—industry, schooling, housing and so on—all forms, direct and indirect, and regardless of the department concerned. The traditional form of estimates throws the emphasis on departmental responsibility rather than on functional objective, so that I am sure the new system will give a better service to parliament in future.

One of the really constructive efforts which we undertook and saw through to a conclusion at the height of the troubles was the creation of three executives under the Ministry of Development. We had been charged under Macrory with direct responsibility for managing—not just supervising or administering—three important blocks of practical work: roads (including streets, road and street maintenance, bridges, car parking and street lighting), water and sewerage, and town and country planning. We had a host of formative decisions to take that would shape public work for a long time to come. As usual it was a matter of balancing advantages and disadvantages, and of keeping our eye on the long-term interest. In the end we decided to lean heavily in the direction of decentralisation; while retaining in headquarters at Stormont the power of making policy, of settling priorities and allocating men and money, we set up a decentralised system under which named professional officers, known to the public in their areas, would carry on the day-to-day work in offices across the province and take the practical decisions. There were obvious risks for us in the system, but we were prepared to take those risks rather than congest the system and annoy everyone by having all problems come to the centre to be settled in the corridors of Stormont. We also found time, in the midst of all our difficulties, to devise and set going an entirely novel arrangement under which development officers were appointed and allocated to the district of each elected district council. These were experienced all-round men whose job it was to help make the various new government services operate smoothly and in harmony as far as possible with the attitudes and responses of the elected councillors, whom we had pledged ourselves to consult. We took quiet amusement from the knowledge that we were reviving, in a modern form, the system of inspectors started by the Poor Law Commissioners for Ireland in 1847. And in the Ministry of Development we had the added task of trying to arrange for a measure of urban renewal and town centre development; negotiations with London property companies for leases to build hotels and offices (while the bombs were blasting on the very sites) presented some unusual features.

A word is needed to record the special steps which we took to carry on the administration of the city of Londonderry. When it became clear during the autumn of 1968 (and that is one of many reasons why unlike most commentators I date the troubles from 1968 rather than from 1969) that the county borough council was unable to carry on, we had to devise some form of substitute. We struck upon the idea of using our new town legislation which fortunately had been cast by parliament in a generous mould when first worked out in 1965. We had power to designate a wide area of country as well as town, to take over planning powers as well as development powers and, what is particularly relevant, to give the commission whom we appointed for each new town the powers of a municipality as well as those of a development corporation. We had tested all these powers in the new city of Craigavon; and we had used some of them in Antrim and Ballymena which were really town expansion operations. We were able to use all these valuable powers (and also draw on recent experience in the province) when the Londonderry Corporation and the Londonderry Rural District Council were eventually abolished and the Londonderry Development Commission set up in early 1969. This worked well.

If I have already succeeded in conveying some impression of the effect of the troubles on our administration, I have still covered only a fraction of the ground.

As well as meeting the direct effect of the troubles, it fell to the administration to help carry out the constitutional changes that

took place. The last six months or so of the former parliament
and government of Northern Ireland before their winding up in
March 1972 were a time of great difficulty, with parliament not
functioning fully and with various proposals for constitutional
change being examined. It was at this time that we were having
our most unhappy relations with the Home Office in London.
Suddenly they began for some unknown reason to be difficult
with us. Anything we put to them was regarded with suspicion
and handled with tongs. The tragedy was that this attitude on
their part was quite needless and that they could have better
served the interests of their political masters by being frank with
us and seeking our cooperation on a straightforward professional
basis. We discovered subsequently that their unreasonable and
unhelpful attitude to us was known and regretted by other Whitehall departments concerned with other aspects of our affairs. The
whole difficult subject of the Ulster question was later to be taken
from them.

When in August 1969 the army was called in to aid the civil
power, the British government took on heavy new responsibilities
and it was only natural, in civil service terms, that they should
send over to Belfast one or two of their officials to keep an eye
on matters for them. Oliver Wright of the Foreign Office was
attached to the Cabinet Office and given a room at Stormont
Castle; A S Baker of the Home Office took up his place inside
the Ministry of Home Affairs on the third floor at Parliament
Buildings. Both arrangements worked well and were looked on
by our staffs as sensible and helpful. Baker did not stay for long.
Wright was replaced by Ron Burrough, then by Howard Smith
and later by James Allen. The pity was that these officers withdrew from direct contact with our departments, set up elaborate
establishments elsewhere and gradually built up a system of contacts and operations outside but largely in parallel with the
ordinary stream of government business. This was as unnecessary
as it was demoralising to the indigenous Northern Ireland staffs.
One never knew what was going on nor where one stood. These
estimable (and very likeable) men had world-wide diplomatic
experience and political expertise that the rest of us lacked. We
could have learned from them and could have benefited greatly
from having them work with us and amongst us instead of being
dimly aware that they were independently dealing with subjects
that fell within our departmental fields. One outcome—to put
the matter no higher or no lower—was that British ministers
were receiving two sets of largely uncoordinated advice.

Then in March 1972 came direct rule, that is to say the
assumption by parliament and government at Westminster of
direct responsibility for all public affairs. I shall describe in my
next chapter what this involved; it is sufficient to emphasise at
this point that it meant for us a change of constitution, of parliament, of political masters and of the whole method of managing
the upper reaches of the administration. After twenty months
direct rule by Westminster gave way to the new Northern Ireland
Assembly and the new power-sharing Executive of Northern Ireland ministers on 1 January 1974. Again it fell to us to help
operate a new constitution with a new and in some ways strange
set of rules; it fell to us to work under a new, unicameral
assembly; and most important of all it fell to us to serve directly
a new group of local political leaders forming the executive
government or cabinet. I shall describe this experience also in a
later chapter; here I am merely trying to record the sequence of
changes during the troubles. When in May 1974 the assembly
was prorogued and the executive came to an end we were faced
yet again with a new arrangement which it was our duty to make
work and make succeed. Although the secretary of state, Merlyn
Rees, took general charge at once, ministers were not allocated
to departments for some time—in the case of my department, not
for five weeks. During that time we had to do the best we could.
The statutory position was far from clear and we looked on ourselves as operating a sort of quasi-direct rule, let us call it mark II.
The position was clarified in July 1974, when direct rule mark
III was instituted. We fell to at once, and without interruption,
to make it work.

Chapter 11

DIRECT RULE

As soon as Her Majesty's Government in London decided to suspend the parliament and government of Northern Ireland, they arranged for William Whitelaw to take office as secretary of state and to come over to Belfast. He arrived on Saturday 25 March 1972, consulted with his security chiefs and then met the permanent secretaries of the departments and the parliamentary draftsman the same morning. The meeting was an immediate success. William Whitelaw was affable and open with us, created an atmosphere of goodwill and trust and won our confidence at once.

The Northern Ireland cabinet agreed to remain in office for the few days needed to take the necessary legislation—the Northern Ireland (Temporary Provisions) Bill—through both houses at Westminster. This was done by Friday 31 March, the full powers obtained, and Mr Whitelaw enabled to act officially. Events moved quickly. His permanent secretary, Bill Nield, made his influence felt within hours and got the secretary of state's office into order; and with a few days junior ministers had been named and allocated to their departments: Lord Windlesham, Paul Channon and David Howell. William van Straubenzee replaced Paul Channon later on, and Peter Mills was added to the team the following autumn.

These were all dedicated men. They needed to be. Their task in practical and human terms (to say nothing of the political aspects) was a hideous one.

Each had to look after two or three departments. As well as that, each had to share the burden of responsibility for security and law and order, for the military and the police, for prisons and the problems of internment and (later on) detention. Each had to take his turn at weekend duty, for violence in its nastiest form had a habit of breaking out on Friday or Saturday nights.

A fair week's work, one might think. But they also had to do duty
in parliament at Westminster—firstly as members of the government of the day in the chamber and in the division lobbies; and
secondly as departmental spokesmen in parliament replying to
parliamentary questions, winding up debates and moving bills
and innumerable orders in council. Moreover they were all—with
the exception of Lord Windlesham—elected members of parliament with a duty to look after the interests of their constituents,
deal with their problems and visit them in the constituencies.
The physical and mental strain on these men was enormous.
Their lives were made up of interminable journeys by plane and
by helicopter, picking up documents in London to be used in
Belfast and picking up documents in Belfast to be used in London.
They were avid readers of departmental briefs. Their timetables
were a paradigm of interlocking appointments, journeys, desks in
London and desks in Belfast, late divisions, all-night sittings and
hectic efforts to keep faith with promises made to people in Ulster.
And they ran the constant risk of assassination. The lives that politicians lead are normally a matter for themselves and one leaves it
gladly to them. But in these quite abnormal conditions I am happy
to record the favourable impact which these men—as men—made
upon our departments.

The secretary of state was of course the king-pin—governor,
prime minister, commander-in-chief, negotiator, arbiter, host, all
rolled into one. With us he was disarmingly frank, engagingly
indiscreet. He was generous in his thanks and over-generous in
his appreciation of anything we did for him. 'Marvellous, John,
simply marvellous! I don't know anyone in Whitehall who could
have done that job nearly as well as you did.' The little spark of
vanity that is in me responded to the flattery and of course the
result—as he well foresaw—was that I redoubled my efforts next
time. And I was not alone in this, for we all responded. Inside the
office all was easy for him. The conflicting demands made upon
him in the wider scene of Ulster politics were severe. The *Belfast
Telegraph* cartoonist pictured Willie Whitelaw as an embattled
and bewildered Macbeth, crying out:

> Who can be wise, amaz'd, temperate and furious,
>   Loyal and neutral, in a moment?

He took a few of us to Chequers once for a thoroughly uninhibited discussion of the whole strategy in Ulster over a complete weekend. I remember that he utterly rejected the views
which I put to him; but that did not matter. My purpose was

served by saying what I thought and by stimulating a rational argument.

Now to the structure of government under direct rule.

The secretary of state was a member of the British cabinet and with them he worked under, and was answerable to, the parliament at Westminster. Our legislation had to be obtained from Westminster: in the form of bills and acts of parliament in matters that were reserved to Westminster such as the constitution and security, or in the form of orders-in-council in matters that would normally have been dealt with in the Stormont parliament. Parliamentary questions were accepted at Westminster on all aspects of ministerial responsibility in Northern Ireland. For us this meant learning new techniques, for the procedures at Westminster are complex and were in some ways new to us. The scale of operation was bigger and the distance from one's base was daunting. We could easily have got lost in the foothills of the Westminster Himalayas. This is where the new Northern Ireland Office—the secretary of state's department—proved to be of immense help to us at the London end, helping to pilot us and our business through the procedural thickets of Whitehall and Westminster. Our officials had a lot of travelling to do and a lot of time to spend in waiting for our business to be taken in the Commons or Lords where they had to be in attendance.

The centre of action for us was the secretary of state's morning meeting which he held practically every day he was in Belfast. Such junior ministers as were free would attend, as also the defence chiefs and those of our senior officials who happened to be concerned with the business of the day. These were cheerful, brisk sessions; everyone was encouraged to speak his mind; and Willie would wind off each discussion by clapping his hands and declaring 'Well that's it. That's what we'll do', beaming a huge smile all round the one big table at which we all sat.

He also had, under statute, an advisory commission of appointed men and women of distinction in the community who could give him at first hand the benefit of local reactions to situations, proposals and so on. This worked better, we thought, in relation to general public and political matters than in relation to legislation (for they were charged also with the duty of examining and advising upon draft orders-in-council before they were presented in parliament). There was, to us and to them, an air of unreality about an appointed body, without powers, expressing views on legislation. It was this feature that most strongly conveyed the odour of colonial government, however little anyone actually thought in colonial terms. One could not get away altogether from equating the advisory commission with the Legco (legislative council of a British colony) and the secretary of state's morning meeting with Exco (executive council).

The direct responsibility to HMG and to parliament in London carried with it some surprising outcomes. One for example concerned our appropriation accounts (i.e. our departmental accounting for all moneys appropriated to our departmental services and for which the permanent secretary is personally and inescapably answerable); and it concerned more particularly the audit of those accounts. The public accounts committee at Westminster decided to review the comptroller and auditor-general's report in 1973 and summoned two permanent secretaries to appear before them. Ewart Bell of Commerce was one and I was the other. I did not enjoy the experience one little bit. The setting was strange, in a lofty committee room in the Palace of Westminster; the acoustics were difficult; I did not know the members and naturally they did not know me; I found it hard to assess how intimately they were acquainted with our administration—for example we were dealing with the development accounts and the municipal accounts of our new towns, words that did not mean the same thing on one side of the water as they did on the other. Altogether I found the occasion quite a strain.

At the level of the officials under direct rule there were the makings of real trouble. The secretary of state's Northern Ireland office in Belfast was understandably staffed for the greater part with officials from London and was quite separate from our Northern Ireland departments. There were two problems. First, should the NI Office stand between us and the ministers, filter our advice, involve London in everything we did? We saw great difficulties along that path. If anything which we proposed in Education or Health or Housing subjects had to be cleared in London, we saw visions at every turn of some homunculus creeping out from under his Whitehall carapace and nibbling away at our proposals. Bill Nield recognised the danger at once and put a stop to it before it arose. We therefore advised ministers and the secretary of state direct; and the NI Office concentrated rather on security, parliamentary matters and preparations for the constitutional settlement that was to come.

The second problem was on a more personal plane. Here were a number of officials suddenly descending on us from London. They did not know the geography of the area and could not pronounce the place names. They spoke with markedly English accents. They lived in a luxury hotel and were ferried to and fro in official cars. They spoke of being posted to Ulster as 'coming out' and constantly gave parties for colleagues 'going home'. And to my mind they seemed rather numerous. But there was no friction. For their part they behaved with great restraint and tact. For our part we recognised that they came in the course of duty, that the demands of security required them to live in a protected place and to travel under guard, and that they could be of great help to us in making the London end of the machine work. We derived a quiet satisfaction from the growing realisation that, bad though conditions in Ulster were, most of them liked this para-doxical country and were glad to serve here.

There was one point on which the arrangements came close to breaking down in the early months of direct rule. This was in the appointment of private secretaries to the secretary of state and his ministers. In a department of government the private secretary (though generally a young and junior officer) plays an extremely important role. He is attached directly to his minister's office and looks after his telephone, his correspondence, his transport, his appointments, his deputations. Simple though these tasks may seem they harbour infinite possibilities for danger. The private secretary is the pivot on which the day-to-day, hour-to-hour, indeed minute-to-minute arrangements for the minister and his senior officials hinge. He must know the department intimately and must be familiar with the interest groups and others outside the office with whom the minister will have to deal. Under direct rule the ministers were allotted English private secretaries. And, after the London fashion, they kept on changing. We never knew where we were. Muddles abounded. Time was wasted. Blunders were perpetrated. To make matters worse, the direct rule minis-ters preferred to work from Stormont Castle (which is a quite separate building away from any of our main departments) so that the private secretaries did not even have the advantage of being inside the department and getting to know it. We got all this sorted out eventually, and local officials appointed who dealt with local business while the English private secretaries travelled back and forward to London with their chiefs and kept the wheels turning in that way—a thoroughly unenviable task, we concluded. Eventually, in 1977, an Ulster civil servant was appointed private secretary to the secretary of state. This marked a significant ad-vance. Needless to say, he is an Instonian.

One benefit flowed from direct rule which I think will be of lasting value to the administration. With new ministers, strange to Northern Ireland, and a small number of them at that, with part of their time necessarily spent in London and with nothing in the nature of a cabinet system operating here, we saw that there was a great need for departmental business to be thoroughly well processed before being put to ministers for decision. We therefore devised a system under which all permanent secretaries met regularly and frequently, considered Departmental projects before they went up to ministers and reconciled inter-departmental aspects of projects that cut across departmental boundaries. We believe that it may have helped ministers to have their business prepared in this way, but I add at once that it helped us even more and gave the service a cohesion which it had never previously enjoyed. The meetings themselves were workmanlike and worthwhile. Discussion was frank and realistic. Statements made by individual permanent secretaries rarely extended beyond three or four sentences. Interventions were crisp and to the point.

All the time gradual progress was being made by the secretary of state with the forthcoming constitutional settlement. From the departmental stand-point the settlement eventually burst on us in November 1973 with the announcement of the names of the participating politicians and, what meant more to us, the departments which they were to take charge of.

Departmental officials were dismayed. Making every allowance for the political exigencies of the time, we thought the arrangement less efficient than it might have been. This was a great pity for we understood the pressing need for a political settlement and would have been pleased to see a more workmanlike solution.

First, for a small government with severely limited powers under the new constitution there were too many posts: eleven in the executive proper and fifteen in the administration as a whole. Half that number of posts would have been enough, in our view. Second, there was a most confusing arrangement under which some of the activity of government was to be in 'departments' whereas other activity was to be in 'offices'—a lesser entity. But to confuse matters still further, non-executive activity such as information was to become a department while manpower services —with an executive job to do, money to spend and statutory duties to discharge—was to occupy the lesser role of an office.

And there was one portfolio which no one could understand or explain: executive planning and coordination. Experts in metaphysical exegesis assured us that it all acquired a blinding charity once one inserted a comma between executive and planning—as had appeared on the original manuscript version. Unfortunately, it was said, some weary typist at nine o'clock in the evening mistook the comma for a blot; or maybe she was a saboteur in heavy disguise. However, as there was also in the list a Minister for Planning, all remained perfectly clear and logical.

To satisfy the exigencies of political arithmetic, the former Ministry of Health and Social Services was split and a new Department of Manpower hived off. This seemed to us unnecessary but not unreasonable from the working point of view.

The splitting of the former Ministry of Development, however, was a horse of a different colour. Here was a superlative instrument which Northern Ireland had created in 1964 and which had set a pattern in the British Isles. Great Britain followed the pattern by creating a somewhat comparable Department of the Environment. It seemed a pity to undo what we had successfully done. Planning was divorced from roads and transport, water and sewerage from housing. A splendid team was torn down the middle.

Even this mistake was further compounded by the titles which were given to the two new departments created out of the former ministry. Department of Housing, Local Government and Planning was such a clumsy title that few could remember all the component parts, let alone the order they came in. Department of the Environment was equally unfortunate. There was already the Department of the Environment in Great Britain, which operated in Ulster as well and placed building and engineering contracts with the very same construction industry with which our new DOE would be expected to place contracts. And in case all those conflicts were not sufficient, our DOE was to act in one or two matters as the local agents for the DOE—an arrangement hardly likely to commend itself to the long-suffering public who wished to know whether they needed to do business with the DOE or on the other hand with the DOE.

To make doubly sure that all the lines were effectively crossed, a subsidiary arrangement was made under which the care of buildings of architectural or historic merit was to be in the hands of the DOE, heavily staffed with engineers but employing neither architects nor planners, while the Department of Housing, Local Government and Planning were to have the responsibility of exercising control over any development or change of use in those buildings.

Aside altogether from politics or religion, such a settlement had the seeds of trouble within it from the start and was going to have difficulty in surviving.

Chapter 12

THE ASSEMBLY AND THE EXECUTIVE, DIRECT RULE AGAIN

Once again it was our job to help make the arrangement work. But this time there was something more in the air. We sensed in the community a feeling of relief; at last some kind of agreement had been reached; some of the political parties had made concessions; the arrangement should be given a chance; if it succeeded there was the hope that at last violence, turmoil and unrest would subside. In that atmosphere we devoted our energies to making an early success of our part in the business of government under the 1973 Constitution Act. There had been some open questioning in Social Democratic and Labour Party circles of the readiness of the civil service to give their full allegiance to a power-sharing cabinet and some agitation for the replacement of protestants by Roman Catholics in the higher ranks. But as all this was extraneous and misdirected, we carried on with our work as usual.

Well before the executive formally took office, the permanent secretaries met the members, both as a group and individually. We found them extremely keen to acquaint themselves not only with the work of their individual departments but also with the functioning of the government machine as a whole. Soon after taking office the chief minister organised an all-day session, a sort of talk-in, at which each permanent secretary in turn outlined the problems facing his department for the information and guidance of the whole administration. In this way every minister (or head of department as he was termed under the act) came to appreciate early on something of the problems and difficulties that would be confronting his colleagues (who of course might be party colleagues or members of one or other of the two political parties in coalition with his). There was the added benefit for ministers of being able to gauge against the hard realities of fact and of finance the objectives which they had already set them-

selves in their inter-party statement of aims. The minister I was
to serve was Austin Currie. I placed myself very much at his disposal, set out our past achievements and failures, our hopes and
fears for the future of the housing, planning and local government services. I helped him to establish good working links with
our twin department, the Department of the Environment, with
whom we wished to work closely since the splitting of the former
Ministry of Development.

Austin Currie was young, fresh, hard-working and likeable. He
was one of the leading thinkers in the Social Democratic and
Labour Party; he had a radical image, having been identified in
the public mind with both squatting and rent strike. And now
he was Minister of Housing. We believed that he was well satisfied
with the way in which his department had helped him to settle
in to the responsibility of office. But I think that the aspect which
surprised him most was the open way in which I ran the department's relationship with its minister. Let me explain.

It did not take much imagination on my part to see that this
young radical would have been encouraged by his supporters to
look on me as a fuddy-duddy, an upholder of 'the system' if not
actually a committed agent of the former Unionist regime.

Now in any department of government with its pyramidal
structure there is a tendency for all business going up to minister
to be strictly channelled through the most senior officers, if not
through the permanent secretary himself. I had always resisted
that tendency for a number of eminently practical reasons. When
Austin Currie took political charge, I continued with my arrangements. There were young men and women in the department of
the same age and generation as Austin. Some of them had been
at university with him, doubtless taking part with him in all
kinds of student politics there. I encouraged these officers—who
were of course responsible officials discharging their professional
duties—to go direct to the minister, to advise him and to brief
him, and I encouraged him to call on them freely. He enjoyed
getting around the department and meeting people of all ranks
and categories. I was determined that his influence should be felt
throughout the department, and I was equally determined that
the advice and accumulated experience of the department should
reach him fresh and at first-hand from all kinds of young officials
and not be diluted by my personality. This worked well. Needless
to say I had various fail-safe devices. When I foresaw a really
troublesome matter looming up in the distance I would always

make a point of seeing him myself and taking his mind. My room had an intercommunicating door with his.

Business flowed well under the executive and assembly. Our departmental proposals went up to the executive, were considered and came down to us decided. The ministers took many debates in the assembly, answered hundreds of questions and absorbed the impact of political reaction to our departmental activities.

I am acutely aware of one aspect in which we did not have time to give Austin Currie the service he wanted. This was in the handling of his voluminous correspondence which came mostly from house tenants concerned about repairs or improvements and which, he felt, deserved a more sensitive political touch than we could give; by the time the executive ceased to operate on 28 May 1974 we had not found a way of securing a party political secretary for him.

There was also too little time in which to develop one other novel feature of the assembly system. This was the consultative committee, a committee of back-benchers of all parties to cover the activities of each department and chaired by the minister in each case. There was some overlapping membership, which could have helped a lot. Most committees had just met a couple of times when the assembly was prorogued.

For senior officials the interval of weeks between the fall of the executive and the arrival of departmental ministers under the new form of direct rule was extremely embarrassing. Everyone knew that there was a hiatus but everyone nevertheless expected to get decisions and an uninterrupted flow of business. There was a further complication. Whereas in March 1972 a Temporary Provisions Act had been passed through parliament at Westminster within a couple of days, the corresponding legislation in 1974 was not enacted until July. In the interim the Northern Ireland Constitution Act of 1973 had to be operated, with direct rule ministers acting in place of Northern Ireland ministers on the executive; and apart from Mr Rees and Mr Orme there were no ministers. Direct rule mark II was perforce only a sort of quasi-direct rule. There are always shades of arcane meaning within these constitutional arrangements which I have no intention of inflicting on my readers. I confine myself to stressing the truth that political uncertainty is quickly reflected in administrative uncertainty. While experienced administrators in such circumstances can put up a brave appearance of normality, the façade soon crumbles and is replaced by indecision, procrastination and shilly-shallying, that are all too often regarded as civil service attributes. One earns one's pay. After the passing of the new act in July 1974 and the arrival of Don Concannon to take charge of Finance and of Housing, Local Government and Planing, Roland Moyle to take charge of Education and the Environment and Lord Donaldson to take charge of Agriculture, Health and Social Services and Community Relations, the team was complete. Stan Orme looked after Commerce and Manpower and of course Merlyn Rees was in overall command of everything. Direct rule mark III was then in force and operating firmly. There was no advisory commission this time. Assembly members were still active both in general politics and in constituency affairs, even though the assembly had been prorogued. Our Westminster members of parliament were also active in the interests of their people and were making independent representations to the direct rule ministers. It was extremely hard to find a path through all this activity.

At this point I consider it right to draw the veil and bring the departmental story to a close.

There is still one piece of official work to be recorded outside the general run of departmental business, namely work for the constitutional Convention from 1975 till 1976. As this was a distinctly unusual task for a civil servant and as the body itself was unique in the British Isles I think it right to devote a chapter to the Convention as seen from the worm's eye view of an official. Much of this next chapter has already appeared in the form of a longer article in *Blackwood's Magazine*.

Chapter 13

THE CONSTITUTIONAL CONVENTION

A s soon as it became clear that someone was needed to act as chief adviser to the chairman of the Ulster Constitutional Convention early in 1975, and indirectly as midwife to the Convention itself, the lot fell on me. I was the oldest living inhabitant in the Stormont village. While my colleagues had been hard at work over the years on the constructive functions of government—schooling, farming, industrialising and so on—I had been dabbling in what I was pleased to call 'structural problems' affecting local authorities, public boards and reorganisation of public administration. And, most important of all, my colleagues and superiors consoled themselves with the knowledge that if in the course of working closely with the Convention I fell foul of the members I would not be there to form a stumbling block in future, for the simple reason that I should be safely in retirement by the time they came to operate any new constitution to which the Convention might give birth.

With extraordinary speed and firmness the Westminster Command Paper no 5675 of July 1974 announced the chosen instrument—a wholly elected convention—complete with details of numbers, constituencies and the electoral arrangements. Given the continuing violence in Ulster and the general confusion created by the fall of assembly and executive, the timing of elections to the proposed Convention was a matter of fine judgment. The announcement came eventually in March 1975 and elections were held on Thursday 1 May, with final results (under the proportional representation system) not available till Saturday 3rd. A meeting of party leaders took place on Monday 5 May, and the Convention met in plenary session on Thursday 8 May.

Enough of history; now for the Convention itself.

The Convention was composed basically of members—seventy-eight of them—elected from the twelve Westminster constituencies. The political strengths were as follows: United Ulster Unionist Coalition (comprising the Official Unionist Party, the Democratic Unionist Party and the Ulster Vanguard Party together with two independent members who supported their cause) 47; Social Democratic and Labour Party 17; Alliance 8; Unionist Party of Northern Ireland 5; Northern Ireland Labour Party 1. On major issues the split was obviously going to be of the order of forty-seven to thirty-one. The Convention was given the use of the handsome Commons Chamber in the Stormont Parliament Building as well as a most comfortable and convenient set of party rooms with attendant services. Excellent security arrangements together with that extra boon nowadays—ample car-parking —added to the attractiveness of the Convention precincts in the conditions of present-day Ulster.

Who was to preside? There had been a lot of speculation on the choice. The act clearly stipulated that 'the Convention shall consist of (a) a Chairman appointed by Her Majesty and (b) seventy-eight persons elected . . .'. The chairman, selected and appointed in good time, turned out to be the Rt Hon Sir Robert Lowry, Lord Chief Justice of Northern Ireland. He therefore formed an integral, statutory part of the Convention. The very presence of the Lord Chief Justice put a stamp on the proceedings from the outset. He looked the part. A local cartoonist drew him in the presidential chair with the shadow of a high court judge clearly discernible over his shoulder. Convention members responded to his dignity and firmness with behaviour that—given the intensity of political feeling in Ulster and *pace* some English press reports—was exemplary. He was, needless to say, a master of procedure and dealt speedily, easily and commandingly with points of order, amendments, interruptions and all the trip-wires of public debate. He had seldom to admonish, but when he found it necessary to do so, he admonished with charm and wit. He displayed a further ability (which is rare in politics or public administration) of being able to foretell with extraordinary accuracy who in the chamber was going to feel obliged to respond to points made by particular parties or members. He was even able to foretell what an individual speaker was going on to say; and on some occasions mercifully saved members from themselves. The Convention members fully appreciated all these qualities in their presiding officer and were warm in their praise both public and private. Sir Robert Lowry's performance in the chair was the one subject which united the Convention and which could have secured a unanimous vote of confidence on any day and at any hour. Apart from his many other actions the chairman made a lasting impression on the members by welcoming them to the Convention in a series of no fewer than seventy-eight separate manuscript letters, a prodigious feat of diligent penmanship.

No deputy chairman was appointed and no discernible provision made by which either Her Majesty or the Convention itself might select a deputy to act in the unavoidable absence of Sir Robert. This was a glaring omission, for the existence of the Convention depended totally on the presence of the chairman. If he had been taken ill, the Convention could not have functioned. With widespread violence, assassination, kidnapping, not to mention countless bombs, bomb hoaxes, army road blocks and all the other well-known features of life in Ulster, the risks were very considerable indeed. Besides, the effect in practice of having no deputy to take his place was that Sir Robert Lowry had to sit in the presiding chair for many hours at a stretch. At the final session on 3 March 1976, for example, he sat for five hours and twenty-six minutes—a quite remarkable achievement of physical and mental endurance. May I add at once that he bore these burdens with immense good humour and delighted in meeting the demands of the chair. From the outset Sir Robert saw himself as 'the servant of the Convention'.

Now, like most other affairs in public life, the Convention did not operate without a great deal of staff-work behind the scenes. Being in line of succession to the former assembly and the former parliament, the Convention had the good fortune to inherit a ready-made, experienced and quite admirable staff. (I write with detachment because although a full-time salaried officer of the Convention myself I managed to play little part and could make no worthwhile contribution, alas.) First there was the clerk, R H A Blackburn, who held his appointment from Her Majesty the Queen and was in general charge of the administrative, financial, procedural and servicing arrangements. He enjoyed both the respect and the affection of the members and would have much to teach new clerks of devolved assemblies in other regions. He had two assistants, both experienced parliamentary servants also.

Before going on to describe the full range of parliamentary services that were made available I should at this point recall the problem of morale which afflicted the parliamentary staff. With the suspension of parliament in 1972 they felt unwanted; and substitute work had to be found for them, work that fell short of fully engaging their particular skills. With the creation of the assembly in 1973 and the power-sharing executive in 1974 hope rose in their hearts that an opportunity for using their skills would once again be open to them. The unhappy experience of those bodies and their eventual collapse represented a further set-back to the hopes of devoted staff. When, therefore, the Convention came to be elected and was offered the former parliamentary facilities, the understandable reaction of the staff was to believe that here at last was an opportunity to do a professional job and, in doing so, to serve the Ulster they so obviously loved. Dedication and zeal were the order of the day, to an extent that may not be understood or appreciated in London, Edinburgh or Dublin.

Seldom can any parliamentary or similar body have slipped into top working gear as quickly and smoothly as the Ulster Convention in May 1975. The Hansard staff, with their unusual skills, were straining at the leash and constantly astonished Convention members by producing each forenoon a printed verbatim report of the plenary debate of the day before, complete with impeccable grammar and splendid sentences that stood on their own feet. More difficult for Hansard staff, in some ways, was the recording of the rules committee which met on many occasions and which required some but not all of its proceedings to be taken down verbatim. More difficult again was the recording of inter-party talks towards the close of the Convention's life. This involved constant switching on and off as some of the parties were adamant about placing on the record their policy statements, their questions and their responses while others were much less insistent. Incidentally, the tone of the discussion in the inter-party talks (abortive though they turned out to be) was coherent and dignified and could well stand comparison with the level of such political agrument anywhere. Ulster is indeed a land of paradoxes.

Next came the library, with a small research facility added for the use of Convention members. Dining-room and refreshment facilities, constantly available, provided further opportunities for informal exchanges. The minor offices of parliament, e.g. the vote office giving out published documents and distributing Convention papers; the table office receiving notices of motions and other submissions; the accounts office paying members' salaries and—a great deal more complex—secretarial and travelling expenses; the security staff; the doormen who in Ulster quickly become characters, enjoying an informal and colourful relationship with members: all these warmed up the machine and oiled the wheels. Delicate microphones aided hearing in the chamber and a neat little closed-circuit television system throughout the precincts kept members and staff constantly informed of what was going on in the chamber. The public galleries were well filled for every one of the thirty-four plenary sessions, even for those which ran late into evening and night. Press coverage was fully adequate and accredited lobby correspondents had special status and facilities. Before the Convention met we went out of our way to have discussions with the BBC, IBA and the local company, Ulster Television, about the possibility of direct television or radio coverage and all three bodies showed every readiness to meet their obligations and fulfil their public duty as they saw it. A proposal to broadcast the proceedings live was debated in the early weeks of the Convention but turned down on a cross-party vote. The additional staff required for the particular needs of the Constiutional Convention were modest in the extreme. We had one information officer, Fred Corbett, who released information to the press and dealt with their queries; but he had no more positive function since the Lord Chief Justice had no desire or need 'to project an image' and the Convention (unlike a government or other executive body) had no policy of its own to put over to the public. This was therefore a sensitive role calling for delicate handling. And that is what it was in fact given.

As well as a private secretary the chairman had a 'chairman's office' consisting of Dr Maurice Hayes and myself. Our job was to stand by the chairman at all times, to advise him, sustain him and help him; we were also to help the parties and the members and we made a point of being readily available to them for informal consultation in the chamber, our rooms, the corridors or at home. We had vastly more informal and indeed private approaches made to us than formal requests for help.

Looking back, one can see that the Ulster convention was well organised, well served, well behaved but empty of any real content. The popular view is that it was a flop, a miserable affair, a pathetic non-event. Harsher critics will blame the loyalist members for being intransigent, humourless and ungenerous; the SDLP for seeking to be victimised; the Alliance for being wordy and woolly; the UPNI for deciding, once the election results were known, that the Convention could not succeed; the NILP for moralising. It is no part of my purpose here to examine political attitudes, still less to apportion credit or blame. It may, however, help if I try to convey some of the strengths and weaknesses of the Convention, if only as a friendly warning in case any other officials in the British Isles are landed with a similar situation.

Although it is common form to place the blame on the Ulster politicians, the matter is by no means as simple as that. Unlike the armchair critics, they were after all the elected people. They had offered themselves at nomination; they had devoted time, energy and money to the campaign; they had run grave physical risks; and they had eventually been chosen by the people. Some had to give up their jobs; some had to forego other chances of employment. Many had to contend with severe pressures on their families and on their private lives. All had to travel constantly, some for long distances and most of them through highly dangerous areas, often after dark. Violence made their work harder, as it was intended to do. Many were shot at, stoned or otherwise molested. Some, after making liberal or conciliatory speeches in the Convention, went home to find constituents bereaved by a shooting outrage waiting for them in the farm kitchen with the plaintive but menacing cry: 'That's not what we sent you to Stormont for.' Some of the worst acts of violence were thought to have been deliberately timed so as to prevent a promising move towards voluntary coalition from coming to fruition.

Again, in fairness to the members, they made matters difficult for themselves by adhering to their word—that is, by upholding the old-fashioned virtue of honouring their election manifestos and election speeches. Besides, the status accorded to them was ambivalent and totally unenviable. It must be understood that many had been members of the parliament of Northern Ireland or of the assembly; many expected to continue in public life and to seek election to any new devolved legislature. They found that constituents were coming to them with personal or constituency problems—pensions, jobs, housing, water, sewerage, roads, the closing of a factory and so on. Even those who did not cherish hopes of public life in future still found that constituents came to them with their problems nevertheless. Their inclination was naturally to take these problems to the Northern Ireland government departments with which they were familiar and which they knew were situated in the very same building as the Convention itself or near by, and try to get a reply for their troubled constituents. If the problem was big enough they would seek to lead a deputation.

The secretary of state denied them these facilities or granted them only in such attenuated form that they derived no political satisfaction from them. His reasons were impeccable in principle: first, that the Convention members had been elected to a deliberative body, not a legislative or executive assembly and that their one and only task was to try to devise a constitution; and second, that the public had twelve representatives in the House of Commons at Westminster and that it was the responsibility of those members to take up complaints with ministers there. This irritated Convention members enormously. They felt they were being treated as second-class citizens, disadvantaged by the very fact of having been elected.

The problem went much deeper, however. The members developed an unhealthy suspicion of the secretary of state and his motives. I considered this wholly unjustified but I knew that the suspicion was genuinely held and that, regrettably, it was repeatedly fed by a stream of informed but unattributed comment which appeared in the British newspapers. One small example which occurred in the early days of the Convention was the repeated forecast that the Convention was preparing to set up a series of subject committees to take evidence on such subjects as security, finance, machinery of government, human rights and so on. The members there and then resolved with typical Ulster 'thrawnness' that, whatever else they did, they would never set up subject committees (thereby unfortunately depriving themselves of much useful help). Again there were well-meant hints appearing in the British press that the Convention members ought to travel abroad—to Holland, Belgium, Switzerland and even Fiji! The outcome once more was that they steadfastly refused to move a step from Stormont (again denying themselves contacts and experience that might well have helped them).

The trouble was still more fundamental. An elected Convention had inherent weaknesses, no matter how fair it must have sounded in liberal English ears. To call a political election, with all that that entailed in party nominations, campaigns, manifestos, speeches, 'getting themselves on hooks' and so on, was simply to ask for a set of party-political responses. To offer them the parliamentary precincts and services, as I have described, compounded the error in as much as it led the elected members to kit themselves out with pseudo-parliamentary rules of procedure and with hallowed traditions from *Erskine May*. Divisions, motions, amendments, adjournments, hon members—'Will the Hon. Member give way'—and so on, were the common usage. The pseudo-parliamentary atmosphere—and I emphasise that it was all the more unreal because of the decision not to grant the elected members any status as constituency representatives—had the unexpectedly amusing effect of leading members into flights of heady language. At the peak of goodwill in the summer of

1975, for example, members promised (or, more accurately, demanded promises from their opponents) to act in a 'magnaminious' fashion. Later, when proposals were being rejected, they were not just turned down or discarded, they were 'consigned to obliviation', The outcome was preordained long before the first meeting, namely a parliamentary system with built-in tendencies and pressures towards prepared attitudes, set public speeches, confrontation, disagreement and majority voting. We had foreseen this risk and had rearranged the seating in a horseshoe formation; but this was a feeble defence against the enormous pressures for disagreement. In this respect Ulster is not so very different from Great Britain or any other country. The great issues which divide the community in Britain—industrial relations, levels of taxation, entry into the Common Market, the death penalty and so on—likewise divide parliament. They are settled not by universal agreement and happy hand-shaking but by confrontation, debate and vote. If—for some reason that may seem remote and improbable at the moment—Britain were to draw up a written constitution for herself, what would be the prospects for agreement and happy hand-shaking at Westminster? Why then were these expected of the Convention politicians in the much more difficult circumstances of centuries-old conflict and historical inevitability?

A further weakness in the political and parliamentary framework was that we had a sort of parliament without a government. Parliament normally depends on the existence of a government front bench, and on the flow of legislation, estimates and other government business which it brings forward and which creates the great bulk of the activity and the pressure. The Convention resembled a parliament with a hole in the middle. In the absence of anything resembling a government front bench, some other suitable initiator could have been devised—an 'interlocutor' or an *amicus curiae* who could have prepared proposals and put them to elected members to bite upon. What alternatives to the concept of a wholly political elected Convention could have been considered? I shall try to suggest some.

A nominated Convention—as in the case of the Irish Convention of 1917 under Sir Horace Plunkett—could have been tried. Admittedly no nominated body—however well it might manage during its sessions—could guarantee to 'deliver' the support of the electorate in the end. But, then, what guarantee can the present-day parties in the unstable conditions of Ulster give in fact? Similarly, the concept of a part-elected and part-nominated body could have had advantages. The presence in the chamber of even a small bench of independent, nominated men and women could have helped. They might not have been popular but their presence and their votes could have frustrated (or at least discouraged) the party-manoeuvring which increasingly went on, the temptation for one party to upstage another and for the other to retaliate by wrong-footing the first. And all the time the nominated members would have been free to table and expound a variety of practical proposals, uninhibited by election pledges, party discipline and so on. Yet another alternative would have been to have an elected Convention as a sounding-board in the background and as an instrument for legitimatising agreements reached by a small group of nominated political people who would have worked in a smaller, quieter and less public forum.

One of the many factors which bedevilled the Ulster Convention was the otherwise laudable urge of the loyalist politicians to secure 'open arrangements openly arrived at'. Largely a reaction against the methods employed by Her Majesty's government at Sunningdale, this urge inevitably led the loyalist leaders to try to do their difficult and delicate task in public debate; and it also led their back-benchers to insist that they should be allowed to see their leaders doing so. The combined effect of all this was to deter the parties from engaging in any worthwhile meetings of minds, on the grounds that their 'grass-roots would not permit them'. Or again we might reasonably have been given an expert commission of Ulster people from the universities, the professions and the public administration to work out a series of alternative draft proposals for all aspects of the admittedly intricate business of constitution-making; and then, for political guidance, to submit their drafts (complete with pros and cons on each) to an elected Convention who for most of the time could have been performing a useful service in supervising (and advising upon) the activities of the Northern Ireland government departments. In that way a treble benefit could have been gained: calm, dispasionate analysis of all the many possible forms of government; responsible political comment; and a gradual return to representative government.

As it was, there was astonishingly little attention given to the many alternative forms of government, constitution, legislature and executive. If the members were asked today, they would be extremely hard put to say why the idea of a second chamber in the proposed legislature had so little attraction for the parties;

or to give the pros and cons, as the parties saw them, of the seventy-five per cent voting rule in a divided community; or to explain why the American-type constitution has so much less appeal for Ulstermen today than it had for their ancestors two hundred years ago. And similarly with many other possible solutions to the constitutional problem. The members allowed themselves, for the many reasons I have sketched, to become obsessed in the early weeks with rules of procedure; and then as time went on, to become equally obsessed with party position and party advantage. For another thing, the level of party management in the bigger parties was disappointing. The parties made little use of their own party staffs. They showed a reluctance to make use of the chairman and convention officials in anything deeper than a procedural sense. Taxpayers' money generously set aside by Her Majesty's Government on an extra-statutory footing to enable the parties to engage outside independent experts of their own choosing was little used.

What was possibly most damaging was the determination of the main parties to lock their horns in combat over the sharing of seats in a cabinet—thereby carefully choosing the most difficult single problem in the book. We tried repeatedly to suggest that it would have been only elementary common sense to begin by negotiating on the simpler problems first and then to work up to the more difficult ones; but they insisted on starting their mountaineering training course by scaling the north face of the Eiger without troubling first to master the foothills. We also urged them—but with equally little success—to consider calmly and objectively where, precisely, power lies in a small regional administration. We thought we could identify ten or a dozen places, any of which would then have offered scope for participation and partnership between all parts of the Ulster community. But they preferred not to listen. Power-sharing in a (non-existent) cabinet was elevated to the dignity of a doctrine, as was the opposing unwillingness to entertain the very idea of power-sharing in a cabinet (that might never in practice come into being).

Now that it is all over and I am happily planting potatoes in my garden, how do I see the Ulster Convention from my worm's eye viewpoint? The Convention, like its members, was the captive of a political situation from which it could not escape. It was too much to expect of elected members that they should burst the chains of party attitudes and seize an array of new ideas and experimental forms. And how could they be expected to sign the peace treaty, with the war still raging outside the gates?

Part II

THE NATURE OF PUBLIC WORK

Chapter 14

WORKING AND LIVING CONDITIONS

Our working conditions are good. The offices in Parliament Buildings, Stormont are comfortable and quiet. Open windows let in fresh air rather than dust or noise. The rooms in Stormont Castle, though less spacious and less convenient, have the same advantages. And those in the new 1960s block at Dundonald House, though perhaps not so dignified as the offices of the 1930s, provide good accommodation too. All are set in the magnificent parkland of the Stormont estate. A morning walk up the Spender path, through banks of azaleas and potentillas, heathers and hydrangeas; a lunch-time stroll in the woods; parking in a capacious car park surrounded by trees, a few paces from the office; these are indeed attractive adjuncts to office life by any standard anywhere. And we have more than our fair quota of pretty girls in the service, as is widely recognised.

Many of us live nearby in the bosky suburbs of Shandon, Knock or Belmont or a mile or two further off in the well-placed little towns of Holywood, Bangor, Donaghadee, Newtownards or Comber in county Down. Journey to work, as the town planners put it, is a quick and pleasant affair. And being recalled to the office in the evening or at a weekend or on a holiday is no hardship. The civic amenities of Belfast—in happier times—are also at hand: a few minutes takes one to the libraries, bookshops, art galleries, other public offices and to the convenient shopping facilities of downtown Belfast.

There are still many further advantages in our working situation. Within the Stormont estate are the main recreational facilities, with extensive playing fields and a fine sports pavilion. Public transport comes to the door of the main building; the lay-out of the estate provides for a bank at the gate; doctors and dentists have their surgeries within a mile or so; there is a post office within Parliament Buildings; the ordinary needs of personal and family life can thus be met with a maximum of convenience and minimum loss of time.

Colleagues who have seen the manuscript of this passage have all begged me to qualify it. They point out with accuracy and justice that the inner rooms of Parliament Buildings are dark and the basement and fourth floor offices are unattractive; that many of our staff work in most indifferent, old and scattered accommodation in the centre of Belfast and elsewhere; that within the Stormont estate a lot of staff were condemned to work in temporary huts that were allowed to linger on for a disgracefully long time; and that, amongst those of us who enjoyed good offices there, many lived far off, sometimes in neighbourhoods of considerable political and social tension from which they had to emerge every morning and to the terrors of which they had to return every evening. I willingly record and endorse all those qualifications but I do so in this separate paragraph without spoiling what I still hold to be in the main a valid picture of attractive living and working conditions.

We share these facilities with our politicians because our main offices are accommodated on the floors above the two parliamentary chambers, the lobbies and the parliamentary rooms generally. The result is that contacts with members of parliament, senators, assemblymen and their whips and organisers have always been close, informal and easy. When I read in the world press of the two communities in Ulster and of the unbridgeable gulf which is said to exist between them, my mind flies at once to the forty years over which I have seen ministers, leaders of opposition, backbenchers, journalists and officials cooperating on easy terms in the give and take of the daily parliamentary round. It may have left us, officials, much more open to quizzing and pressurising by MPs on constituency matters than our London or Edinburgh colleagues are, but we were not the worse for that. Most of us formed happy friendships with members of all parties. I was once very nearly persuaded to buy a sheepdog from the Hon Member for mid-Tyrone, anxious to turn an honest penny!

Our conditions of service, slowly and painfully worked out under Whitley consultative machinery, are good. Sick leave arrangements are sound; annual leave is reasonable. If there are difficulties for senior administrators, they are of their own making. By this I mean that our people are so schooled in dedication to the public service, and so conscientious about turning up for duty, that when they do fall ill they seldom take the time off that has been prescribed for them by their doctor; and few ever take their full entitlement of holidays. This is a form of egoism; each man firmly believes that he is indispensable. It can, in itself, become a civil service disease. There are colleagues whom we have to urge to go away to bed or to take a week's holiday.

The predominantly non-contributory character of our pension arrangements seems fine on the surface; but it becomes a shackle that discourages some from leaving the service when perhaps they ought to, and discourages the Service from getting rid of some officers as promptly as it might. Successive acts of parliament have sought to resolve this problem by facilitating early retirements on certain conditions. With fewer young people nowadays regarding the service automatically as a lifetime career, and with the growing need for people to be recruited later and to move in and out of the service, the future may see a greater swing in the direction of a contributory pension scheme, on the lines of our present scheme for widows and orphans.

The Service abounds naturally in social and recreational clubs —sporting, artistic, musical and choral groups. I can recall in my first year in the service seeing a fine production by the Ministry of Labour Dramatic Club of that popular Ulster comedy that is seldom produced nowadays—*Thompson in Tír na nÓg*. And the only activity in which I achieved anything approaching representative status was in a service match against the Dublin service at chess!

So far as pay is concerned, let us be quite clear that no one enters the service with the expectation of making big money. Pay is modest and it increases by extremely moderate steps. Taking one thing with another, and considering the size and the limited resources of a mainly rural province it must be said that successive governments have done not badly by their servants. Pay is not generous; in times of inflation adjustment is painfully slow; but by and large it is not bad. The plain fact is that for senior civil servants pay is not a burning issue.

As with most people in the community, of course, civil servants cast an eye occasionally on their pay position in relation to that of others. Their work brings them into contact with practically all aspects of the working population. Their permanent position and their fixed salaries put them in an enviable position contrasted with small farmers, and one-man shopkeepers. School teachers also for long seemed poorly paid by comparison with officials, especially the leading specialist teachers in the grammar schools. It is in the bigger world of industry and commerce that the scales start being tipped the other way. How often has some salaried official, with a professional background and a lifetime of training and experience, found himself in the thankless position of keeping on the rails some businessman obviously earning two or three times his salary? It is the attitudes of businessmen at the margins that strikes us most forcibly. We see it at close range when they accept top positions (for the most part unpaid, be it said) in local authorities or in statutory boards and have a hand in the settling of the pay of their officials there: 'Why not make this salary up to the round figure? I don't like advertising this job at anything less than five figures; it looks cheap. Let us throw in a car if that will keep this fellow happy. I always like to see a sizeable gap in pay between a man and his deputy.' No one ever rounded up my pay scale. No one ever threw in a car to keep me happy. At the time such words were being spoken, for every pound I earned (gross, before tax) my deputy was earning 92p and the next rank below earning 88p—not much of a differential.

Businessmen often admit that our senior people are underpaid and that our clerks, messengers and doormen are badly paid, but there is in their view a tendency to overpay our middle ranks in between. Apart from all other arguments I consider that this reflects a failure to recognise and understand the inner nature of work within the service. While it may seem that the middle rank officer is well bolstered by his subordinates on the one hand and by his seniors on the other, and can therefore hardly go wrong, this is a superficial view. The inner ethos of the service impels each man, no matter what his rank, to discharge as much responsibility as he possibly can and to prepare as fully as possible any work which he must submit to higher authority. And in doing so he may find himself exposed to question and criticism in a host of ways that are comprehensible only to those who have had the experience.

There is another facet of relativity in matters of pay that is more telling than any mere making of comparisons. It is the matter of competitiveness in the open market. Whether you or I think that a grade of officers ought to be paid a few hundred pounds more or less is of small importance beside the harsh question: 'Can we recruit men at this rate of pay?' There is seldom a time when the service is not in difficulty in one field of recruitment or another. Over the last five years or so lawyers have been earning a lot more in private practice than they would be paid in the service; and the result is that they are hard to recruit and hard to hold. Architects have moved into the same class. Quantity surveyors have seldom been out of it! It is extremely

Parliament Buildings, Stormont. *N.I. Tourist Board.*

Stormont Castle. *Government Information Service.*

Stella, the author's wife.

J. F. Caldwell, Parliamentary Draftsman.
Belfast Telegraph.

hard for the service suddenly to increase the pay of one particular discipline just because it has happened to acquire a scarcity value in the market place; apart from everything else, it may lose it again!

Allowances for travelling, subsistence, removal and so on have traditionally been on the strict side, and rightly so. Perks were nonexistent. We get our official pay and that is all. We are not given shares in the company, or a bonus when sales are good or a hamper at Christmas. Whatever we earn is set out clearly and fully in the annual estimates and a lot of other publications. I shall have more to say on this in a later chapter where I shall be dealing with gifts.

The real return which we get for our work is job satisfaction. Although this may sound pompous I believe it to be immensely true. We are intimately bound up with our jobs, we are fascinated by them and the satisfaction we derive from doing those jobs is what keeps us going. What form does the satisfaction take? There is unfortunately no measuring rod; and there cannot be. Houses built, industrial jobs created, the infant mortality rate reduced— one would like to be able to use such indices to prove to oneself that one had done a good job but, as I shall explain elsewhere, life is not nearly so simple.

Hours of work follow basically the traditional nine-to-five pattern. Senior officers seldom get away till 6 or 6.15. Some make a habit of working later, but it is a habit, and a bad one. In times of stress anything can happen, and when your minister is engaged in parliament you may want to be in attendance till 9 pm, or occasionally later. But to stay in the office in the evenings when everyone else (including telephonists and typists) has gone is seldom a good practice. There is a lot of silliness talked about the value of long hours of work. Without analysing all the vagaries and subtleties of office life it is still possible to assert that some officials can make themselves appear, and actually feel, busier than they really are. They find it hard to accept the good advice of Lord Grey of Falloden to aim at 'resolute economy of irrelevant toil'. On top of all that it is important to understand when comparing Stormont with Whitehall that the social patterns are different. We follow for the most part a healthy provincial pattern of a tea-meal at six o'clock and an even healthier provincial pattern of spending some time with our families and children at around that hour. To keep onself busy in the office till 7.30 pm as a matter of regular habit may suit the London way of life; it suits ours rather less.

Lunching at a downtown club has played a much smaller part in our lives than in those of our London or Edinburgh colleagues. While the three best-known Belfast clubs, the Union, the Ulster and the Reform, were still operating and while the ministries were still housed in the city centre, some senior officers were club members and thus regularly met leading businessmen in that setting. With two of those clubs dropping out and with most of the ministries moving away to Stormont in 1931, the practice largely died out. A pity, perhaps, as it is good for administrators to get to know leading businessmen on an easy footing and to learn of their frustrations at first hand. It can of course be embarrassing for administrators in a small region to be involved in casual conversation about planning appeals or the compulsory acquisition of land (when as often as not they are *sub judice*) or about other departmental business which they know of but are not free to discuss. All the time, of course, membership of church bodies, social clubs and sporting organisations, with even wider contacts, was and still is the order of the day, but departmental business does not raise its head there in anything like the same way.

The basic nine-to-five pattern is not just an accident of history or a stale custom. Some officers might well prefer to start earlier and finish earlier. There are some who like a variable lunch-hour. But this seldom works well amongst senior people. One has to be in the office to fit in with other people; that is part of the job. Flexible hours will have but limited appeal for senior administrative people. Even if one were free of commitments and even if one could do one's essential daily job in an hour or so, or even if one thought one could work more efficiently at home, one would still have an obligation to attend at the office. Every officer is the repository of a great deal of experience and knowledge; this is public property; it is his duty to be in the office as a matter of course and to make that experience and knowledge available to others. Even one's very presence can be useful. I remember when I was leaving a particular block of work in the field of social service, a leading woman voluntary worker thanked me and said she was sorry I was going. Believing this to be an empty formula, I countered by saying that there was nothing for which she needed to thank me, and that I had never been able to do anything for her or her organisation. 'Ah' she replied 'But you were always there. That was the great thing.' An easily earned tribute. On another occasion an up-country county planning officer spent the best part of a day with one or two of us, simply running over his problems and rehearsing with us the pros and cons of various courses of action he was thinking of taking. At the end of the day he was profuse in his thanks, and when we protested that we had done nothing he was adamant that the very opportunity of talking his problems over in a coherent way with a couple of more or less sensible (and wholly impartial) people was a rare benefit indeed.

Events in Ulster since 1968 have been so hideous and conditions so difficult that it is becoming hard to recall the lovely conditions of working and living which we in the service used to enjoy and may one day enjoy again. One aspect which it must be hard for office workers in London or Birmingham to appreciate is the shortness of the distances in our position and the quick, easy access to the sea, the countryside, the hills and the many delightful amenities. When conditions are good, the escape from Stormont in the evening is enviable. Two or three minutes takes an enthusiast to his golf course, or twenty minutes has a yachtsman on salt water. To those with the eye and the ear to comprehend, the signs in the month of May that rouse the angler are unmistakeable: the telegram arriving with those cryptic words— 'the fly is up'; the quick request for a few days' annual leave; the speedy departure; the couple of hours' run by magnificent roadways to Ulster lakeland in county Fermanagh; and then the bliss of air and scenery and solitude doing whatever anglers do in those lovely places.

Although I was not a golfer or a yachtsman or an angler I had my own pleasures and indulged in them to the full. Let me recall one weekend typical of many in the happy days we used to have.

Home from work on a Friday evening at 6.15, a meal and off with some of the family to Bangor, a good centre for amateur drama, where a festival play is being put on. Twenty-five minutes there and twenty-five minutes back. Saturday morning is devoted to taking a bunch of Wolf Cubs to camp on the Ards peninsula (using the opportunity to gather some seaweed to fertilise my vegetable garden). Saturday afternoon sees a representative game of rugby at Ravenhill with Ulster playing the All-Blacks; we leave home at 2.35, run over in ten or twelve minutes; park at 2.50 and are on the terraces in time for kick-off at 3 pm; home by 4.50. In the evening we go to the Queen's University Film Society where I am chairman but have mercifully light duties and can enjoy three films in contentment—again a matter of twenty minutes there and back. On Sunday morning we go to the picture borrowing group—again a matter of twenty minutes—and bring home some painting of doubtful value drawn in a lottery. On Sunday afternoon there is time for a run to Slievenaman in the Mourne Mountains; one hour takes us to the foothills and in another fifteen minutes we are walking up to Slieve Lough Shannagh. Home by six, with time (if still awake) to look over some papers for Monday morning.

For most of us, whatever our specialised interests, it is probably the easy access to the country that appeals. Most of us are only second-generation Belfastmen; we still have the *glaur* of the farm-yard on our boots. The magnet is the countryside—the heather-clad hills, the marginal farms, the long fuchsia hedges, the wet black bog, the bog cotton, the friendly word by the wayside: 'Och sure it's a brave step' or 'It's a soft day'; the brown water in the streams, the big gateposts, the cry of the whap, the perfect golden, empty strands—these are the things that bind us to Ulster and that make our working and living conditions so enviable.

Chapter 15

THE WORK ITSELF

It is the work itself that matters. The nature of the work of the Northern Ireland administrator is what I am trying to convey in this book.

The way in which the work is done has changed since I entered the service. The pace has increased. The pressure has increased. Public interest in the substance of our work and in the way we do it has intensified enormously. And the publicity that surrounds our activities has increased out of all recognition.

The essence of the job has not changed. It still is to advise ministers, to get decisions from them and to carry out those decisions. What has changed most significantly is probably the approach, that is to say the shift from the relatively negative approach of waiting till a problem arose, or a situation presented itself, to the much more positive approach of going out to identify a situation and tackle it before it became a problem. A number of things have conduced towards this shift in public work. First there was the war; then the welfare state, the assumption by the state of responsibility for service over a wide range of personal needs; next I would list the Matthew-Wilson innovations in regional affairs under which government accepted a new range of obligations in physical and economic planning; the troubles have motivated successive governments in Northern Ireland to penetrate further into the social and political fields, in an effort at winning the hearts and minds of people and wooing them away from supporting violence.

Many of the forms of administrative work have remained the same—parliamentary questions, motions, bills, estimates, ministers' correspondence and so on.

Deputations have always featured prominently in life at Stormont, that is deputations sent by local councils, statutory boards, trade unions, trade associations, professional bodies, the churches and other special interest groups to make some request or present some case to a minister or his department. Negotiations about receiving them, preparation of the subject matter, briefing the minister if he is personally involved, recording the proceedings, handling the publicity and arranging for the follow-up action, all form part of the daily work. It is widely accepted that the ready reception of deputations and the easy access which they enjoy are one of the real benefits of devolved regional government. Comparable bodies in Great Britain do not have the chance of discussion with ministers and senior officials to anything remotely approaching the same extent. And it is beyond question that this has over the years served to maintain at a high level the quality and effectiveness of our administration; we have little chance of being allowed to get out of touch. A senior officer of the old Dublin school once said to me when as a very young man I was urging that some deputation should be received, 'You people receive more deputations from the six counties in a month than we in Dublin used to do from the thirty-two counties in a year.' I did not take it as the rebuke which I think he intended to convey. The accuracy of his statement is fully borne out by the annual reports of the old Local Government Board for Ireland which obligingly listed the names of the few deputations received.

Admittedly deputations are often overdone. While some have a genuine purpose and directly or indirectly achieve some aim, many, alas, are quite futile. Many come merely for the sake of appearance and to impress the folk back home. Almost all take about twice as long as they need do. Many are quite unnecessarily aggressive, displaying that unattractive face of Ulster public life whose features are intransigence, awkwardness and downright rudeness. I always found it difficult in each case to decide how much of this was natural and instinctive and how much was contrived in order to enable the deputation to relate afterwards how firm they had been with those officials up at Stormont. As well as that, deputations are all too often used as an easy way of gaining publicity for a complaint that could more properly and more effectively be pursued through one of the many statutory channels for the redress of grievance. These, alas, are little used.

Inspections by departments, on the other hand, have declined in importance and in intensity. It used to be that practically every aspect of administration was buttressed by a thorough-going programme for the inspections of the field-work—schools, hosptials, factories, refuse dumps, public lavatories and so on—followed by the rigorous pursuit of defects discovered. Now regarded as bureaucratic and interfering, inspection in the old style has largely given way to various gentler forms of advice, consultation, conference, working party and so on. I am far from sure that this is for the better, for there are few things as useful to a department as a regular flow of information and assessment based on the objective findings of experienced, qualified inspectors; and few things as reassuring to a public anxious to know how their money is being spent in practical terms.

To be clear, it is not that the inspector from Stormont knows best, or even that he knows better than the man he is inspecting. He would not make such a claim; nor would I. But by the very nature of his job, moving constantly from place to place, the inspector cannot help being in a position to make comparisons that are not so readily open to the busy man on the spot, confined as he is to his own pitch. This is best understood if the inspector is seen as reporting to the management committee or board of governors or other lay body in charge of a hospital or a school or a residential home. What they want to know is—not whether the inspector can catch their chief officer out in some particular —but to what extent their institution measures up to generally accepted standards; in which respects their work is good and in which respects it could be improved; and generally whether compared with other comparable bodies, they are providing a comparable service. Viewed in that light, and conducted with courtesy and commonsense, inspection can still be a valuable public service. I would like to see it revived, intensified and elevated to the level of a parliamentary activity.

Committee work has grown enormously. Partly designed to secure the widest range of up-to-date advice and partly to secure the participation of a wider circle of people, the advisory committee has come to influence administrative work very greatly indeed. I once counted in our department at least eight committees of this type: on the Ulster countryside, nature reserves, wild birds, rent restrictions, abandoned dwellings, the Lagan valley country park, the Local Government Interim Staff Commission. It falls to our staff to help organise the work of those bodies, to provide them with basic information, and to act as secretariat.

Looking further into the substance of the work one sees that it is the reconciling of interests and of clashes of interest that lies at the heart of much administration. It is easy to draw up a scheme. It is easy to establish procedures and in nine cases out of ten those procedures will see the work through; but in every tenth case, so to speak, there is a difficulty that calls for high level attention, experience and skill.

Let me try to convey this in two different ways. Most work in the established fields of administration flows in at the bottom of the pyramid whether it be applications for social benefits, licences for bulls or grants for the improvement of private houses. A hundred may be received and the office will be organised so as to settle expeditiously some ninety per cent of those at a given level (which we generally refer to as executive level). Ten per cent will present awkward points of principle or of law and need closer administrative attention. The advice of lawyers, or accountants or other specialists may be needed. Out of this ten per cent, eight or nine may be discharged in that way, with the result that only one or two in a hundred will reach the most senior officers of any well-ordered department. Those may still contain problems of law or procedure; they will almost certainly also embody a point-blank conflict of legitimate interest or priority. This is at the heart of administration.

A small episode in my own experience may serve to illustrate the same point in a different way. (Administrators are so closely bound up with their work and discuss it so seldom with people outside the service that they come to take its intricacies for granted; it is only when they meet some independent assessment that they come to appreciate the importance of aspects that they are accustomed to treat as everyday and commonplace.) I gave a talk one evening to a sixth form club in a grammar school. The subject was 'Town and Country Planning: Negative or Positive'. I took the simple line of summarising a number of planning cases I had been dealing with in the previous few days. Inserting fictitious names and places I set out the pros and cons of permitting a bookmaker to open a betting shop in a residential street —motor traffic, pedestrian traffic, men hanging around from race to race, existence of a public house at the street corner, the effect on the street life and on the family life of the immediate neighbours, all set against the perfectly legitimate aim of the promoter to open a properly licenced business and to meet a real need of real people in that very neighbourhood. I then went on to give the conflicting considerations for a public house, a noisy bottling plant, an odorous car-spraying plant, a factory promising much-needed jobs for men but emitting a noxious effluent into a trout stream, and half a dozen other similar cases. The schoolmaster's remark at the close remained in my memory: 'I was surprised to find such human material in planning: I thought it was all to do with procedures.'

Compulsory acquisition of land features largely in the work of most administrators today, and again the legal and procedural components, though important, are seldom as difficult as the interests that conflict: the need for a housing scheme as against the needs of the farmer; the needs of today as against the needs of the future; the alternatives open to the public body and their readiness to explore them; the alternatives open to the farmer and his readiness to explore them; and so on. One of the great new factors nowadays is the desire of the public and of various interest groups to participate in public business. The modern administrator accepts all this to an extent that his predecessor of even twenty years ago would never have foreseen. Third parties are freely heard at public inquiries, and even before the stage of public inquiry is reached, there are frequent consultations with groups about proposals or plans that may conceivably affect them. In town and country planning in Northern Ireland, for example, every application for planning permission to develop land received by the department is sent to the local elected council for its observations, and it is also published in the local newspaper so that anyone who wishes may make representations. This is of course all very popular but it is not widely understood that it involves more administration and more paper work, and it inevitably means delay. The administrator today is therefore constantly waging a battle on the one hand to ensure publicity and public participation, and on the other hand to free the developer (be he public body or private person) to get on with his development.

Legislation under a devolved system of parliament and government is also affected by modern publicity in a perhaps surprising fashion. Departments here have always been anxious to exploit their devolved powers by promoting legislation designed to suit their precise regional situation. Notable examples include the setting up of the tuberculosis authority, the General Health Services Board, the Housing Trust, the special care bodies for mental deficiency, the arrangements for amenity lands, industrial training, and much else. All of these were either peculiar to Northern Ireland or embodied certain distinctive features. But differences, especially small differences, are hard to sustain in face of the flood of modern publicity. Press, radio and television pour out material based on English or English and Scottish law. Citizens here find it confusing and tiresome if they are constantly being told that our law is different, and that such and such a promise made in a full-page advertisement in the national newspapers does not apply. Imagine what chaos there would be if every here and there our laws on social security benefits differed from those in Great Britain; if contributions were higher by a few pence and, dare I say it, if benefits were lower. I suggest that it would be quite impossible to administer such a scheme. My point is that in most fields different laws, though not impossible to administer, add greatly to the difficulties of the administrator. I nevertheless consider it worthwhile making the attempt to use a devolved constitution to shape legislation to local needs. Rubber-stamp or copycat legislation has little to commend it and much to condemn it.

Another of the complications of our modern administration is the plethora of supervisory bodies within the government circle; or, in a word, too many bosses. It used to be that a department recognised two bosses, its minister and the Ministry of Finance. Nowadays it has to answer to a great many more. The modern cabinet plays a more positive role and makes constant demands. So too does the Prime Minister's Office. The old Ministry of Finance has two distinct manifestations now—the Treasury side and the separate Civil Service Department looking after staffing and management affairs. The Ministry of Community Relations (as the keeper of the conscience in matters of good practice in religious and community dealings) had to be satisfied as well while it was in existence from 1969 till 1975. Then there is the Parliamentary Commissioner for Administration (the Ombudsman), while for good measure we have in Northern Ireland a Commissioner for Complaints as well; and although his sphere of action is that of local authorities and statutory boards, there are certain points at which his investigations can impinge on departments. We now have, on top of all that, a Human Rights Commission. Under the Stormont parliament we had a committee of parliament examining and questioning us upon statutory rules and orders. That has now been replaced by a further personage, the Examiner of Rules, who performs much the same function and reports his findings to parliament. And all the time we have our trusted old faithful, the Comptroller and Auditor-General, advising and reporting on us to the public accounts committee of parliament. I have to add yet another body, presently in mothballs, namely the consultative committee of the assembly, provided for under the Constitution Act of 1973. Under direct rule we must add the Northern Ireland Office in its Belfast and its

London manifestations. Quite a list. I recognise the need for each one in turn; what I cavil at is the sum total in relation to the burden which their existence and their activities impose on government departments. We are in danger, quite serious danger, of spending more time telling what we are doing than in actually doing it. In that context the institution which I would most seriously question (after the Ministry of Community Relations, which has been wound up) is the office of Ombudsman. I do so for two reasons. First: his published reports and other statements have confirmed what everyone knew already, namely that the standard of administration in our departments was extremely high and that there was nothing for the public to worry about. Second: I am concerned about the deeper point, namely that the value of his office in correcting the very few minor discrepancies that are revealed (any bigger flaws that there may be are either put right by departments themselves in the ordinary course or are uncovered by members of parliament) is trivial in comparison with the time and the effort entailed. Deeper still is the long-term effect which such a system must inevitably have on departments, by inducing them to indulge in yet more recording on paper of trivial aspects of a case, telephone conversations and so on when they would be better employed out on the job. It all leads inexorably to further cautiousness in the pursuit of consistency, at a time when departments ought to be striking out on new and more imaginative paths.

Does our service lack imagination? Is it always staid and conservative? To the extent that it is possible to answer this—and one cannot go very far because public business nowadays is an amalgam of parliamentary, ministerial, advisory and publicity influences—I would say that lack of imagination is not one of the shortcomings of the service. My recollection of thousands of office discussions, of working parties and of memoranda over the years is that there is no shortage of bright ideas in the service or of unorthodox thinking. As I see the problem, the need for more imaginative thinking (in the sense generally assumed) is not as great as the need for realism and for getting things done. This is the true sphere of the administrator and it is here that the greatest effort has constantly to be made.

In the service, one of the besetting sins is that of allowing the best to become the enemy of the good. The modern administrator is concerned to put up to ministers the best solution to a problem that he can devise. He draws on many sources, he brings in many professional disciplines. He balances interests. He tries to arrange for the long-term view to prevail over the short-term. The result is all too often that the advice he tenders is too complicated, too abstruse, too refined. A simpler, less ambitious proposal might often fare better. The more conscientious the administrator, the more anxious will he be to see his problem from every angle. This is particularly true at the third and fourth rank in our departments, where information is abundant and where expert resources are at hand. The task of the most senior officers can often consist in pruning proposals to manageable proportions. This position, taken together with the serious inadequacy of the service in conveying its work in comprehensible form to the general public, results in that depressing but all too valid aphorism, 'The outturn of government work is seldom commensurate with the quantity and quality of the civil service input.' The service itself is entirely to blame. No one else is to blame. Ministers most certainly are not to blame. There should be lessons included in all civil service training courses especially designed—whatever the general title or content of the course— to train administrators to select the most workable, not to chase the perfect solution every time, to concentrate on what can be done and to present it clearly, simply and cogently.

It is not that the modern administrator is remote or inexperienced in the direct handling of practical affairs. A few examples will illustrate this point more effectively than any protestations from me. Every department has naturally a certain amount of high-level policy, administrative and legislative work to do. But all have nowadays direct managerial responsibility as well. Agriculture has forestry and drainage, big services employing many manual staff, using heavy machinery and so on. Health and Social Services has the huge cash benefits machine to operate, with thousands upon thousands of claimants expecting their payments. We in Housing, Local Government and Planing had to manage the whole of the planning service on direct drive at the same time as we supervised and handled indirectly the work of the Northern Ireland Housing Executive. And there are countless other examples in the departments. One officer may have to switch from administration (indirect) work one week to executive (direct) work the next week. Any one officer may have to discharge both types of work more or less simultaneouly. This calls for considerable flexibility of mind.

There can be few professions so experienced as ours in viewing a problem from every conceivable angle. Town and country planning provides me with the most convenient examples, but every department has plenty of examples of its own.

A characteristic case might be a proposal arising in the department to revoke a valid and perfectly proper planning consent previously given. Normally a consent is firm and unchangeable; but conditions in the surrounding neighbourhood can alter and can make it necessary to consider revoking the consent so that the developer shall not go ahead with his project. Let us say it involves building a public house. The professional town planners report that circumstances have changed and that on grounds to do with road traffic and road safety it is no longer right to let the public house be built. These views have to be confirmed or otherwise by specialist road engineers. Next one has to ascertain the present position and find whether the developer has in fact started work. This will involve an inspection. Then one must confirm that the department has clear legal power to do what is recommended. There is the personal factor to be considered; the developer is entitled to know the intention and the arguments. Next there is the legal procedure to be watched and carefully followed. Revocation is a serious business, and even though this is a relatively small case the approval of the minister will be sought. The developer by now will probably have incurred some expenditure on architect's fees, quantity surveyor's fees and possibly some understanding with his builder. He is sure to expect to be compensated. How much is the compensation likely to be and on what basis will it be assessed? If we proceed, there is the risk of challenge in the courts and we must prepare for that contingency. At the very least the developer will appeal against our decision; we must be ready to defend our action. The public will be puzzled, so we shall have to be ready to explain the facts. The developer may, or may not, have the support of the elected local authority; so also may the neighbours, with the result that there is a need to carry the local council with us. The member of parliament is certain to be approached either by the developer or by the neighbours, and is likely to raise the matter in parliament, because revocation of a good and valid consent is indeed a matter of some public concern. I would describe this as a fairly typical case of average weight that any of us might have to deal with. Let us just note how many different angles are necessarily involved: planning, road engineering, procedure, law, land compensation, finance, personal relations, public relations, diplomatic relations with the local councils, politics and parliament.

Administrators anywhere would recognise such a pattern as

familiar, but we here have still further angles to take into account. The member of parliament may be a Stormont Member, or a Westminster Member, or both. Again, during times of political unsettlement, dealings with members of parliament can become extremely delicate. There have been times when some members refused to recognise ministers and insisted on dealing with officials only. The instructions to us were of course to decline to deal in this fashion and to make certain that all members' business was referred to ministers. This is easy to honour if it is only correspondence that is affected. But what if the dissident member telephones? Am I to refuse to talk to him, even though I know him very well and he is telephoning from the lobbies a few paces from my office? How should we carry on our business with a local council that adopts a resolution spurning our minister, refusing to send a deputation to see him and insisting on sending the deputation to us as officials?

There seem to be no limits to the complexity of the demands made on our senior administrators. Let us take the little matter of the title of our political heads. Long referred to and accepted as 'ministers', they came to be known in the 1974 Assembly as 'heads of department'. While the title of 'minister' was still occasionally used in everyday parlance, we had to be extremely careful to adhere strictly to the constitutional title of 'head of department', as that formed part of a whole new terminology to which considerable importance was attached. When the 1974 Executive collapsed and direct rule was brought in again, we were very ready indeed either to adhere to the new title of head of department or to revert to minister; but it was a little hard to accept that by a strange quirk of the new 1974 constitutional arrangements the title head of department which we had been so assiduously applying to Mr Hume, Mr Napier, Mr Kirk and others now applied to us! Permanent secretaries had suddenly— and without any political intention or implication—to accept for ourselves the very title which we had been foremost in applying to our political masters. One could scarcely call it a routine existence.

In trying to explain the extraordinary degree of flexibility demanded of us I have strayed from the main theme of this chapter—the work itself. I wish to emphasise once again the essential character of the work—to advise ministers, to get decisions from them and to carry out those decisions. Now those decisions are not always moving in the direction of creating, expanding and increasing; and neither is our work. It is often imagined by people on the fringes of public work that an administrator's job is to build more houses, more factories, more hospitals and so on; and there is disappointment and annoyance when he is seen not to be doing so. This all arises from a profound misunderstanding. The housing administrator's job is not to build houses; it is to carry out government policy in relation to house-building. Mostly that does in fact mean building (or helping to get built) more and more houses; but often it does not.

A few examples will make the point abundantly clear. An official may be engaged on administration of the railway system; he may advise ministers that sections of the system ought to be closed; if ministers agree, it then becomes his duty to close those sections and to put as much skill and thought and energy into that—apparently negative—action as he would put into the building of a new track. When the Ministry of Community Relations was being abolished the permanent secretary of that ministry was actively engaged in what was for him the distasteful task of dismantling the very department which he had so enthusiastically created, disposing of the staff which he had painstakingly built up, and seeing that the many projects in hand were properly assigned to successor departments. And the same type of task falls to all of us each time economy cuts are decided on by ministers. Officers who a month earlier were busy devising ways of expanding their services must now devise ways of reversing or slowing down that growth. Each time I read in the newspapers that the Chancellor of the Exchequer is expected to 'cut public spending' or 'apply a touch of the brake' or 'take some heat out of the economy' my mind runs to a group of administrators at Stormont who will have to seize that very proper policy decision (which the Ulster public have probably not noticed) and apply it in a dozen different ways to curtail services which most people in Ulster expect to see constantly expanding.

There is no limit, I repeat, to the demands made on the flexibility of mind and attitude of senior civil servants. These demands reached a peak in my case in 1969 and again in 1973. Most of my colleagues have had similar experiences in their careers but these two episodes will serve as examples.

In 1966 I was given the personal assignment of preparing the ground for the reshaping of local government, a major political and administrative reform. I worked intensively on the project and became personally identified with it. Taking guidance from ministers from time to time, I pushed the business ahead to the stage of the White Paper of 1967, setting guidelines for a new local government that would have a wide range of functions and strong powers. Between that white paper and the second white paper (which did not appear until July 1969) I took the chair at no fewer than 125 conferences, meetings, committees or deputations, all designed to take the proposals further in the same direction of an efficient, all-embracing local government system. Then during the visits in August and October 1969 of James Callaghan, Home Secretary, it became clear that those proposals had no future. They were to be disrupted by a major decision to take housing out of local government, and what is more, the remnants of our local government proposals were to be thrown into the melting pot. This was for me a galling experience. And when ideas began to emerge for conducting yet another study, to abandon the proposals I had worked on so intensively and so long and to devise a different and clearly a much weaker local government system, I felt like throwing down my pen and suggesting that ministers should allocate someone else to the new and different task. But when I was asked to do the new job, I agreed. I went through mental agonies; but it was clearly up to me to reverse engines and to put the same effort into moving in the new direction as I had put into moving in the old. The new direction turned out to be the Macrory reforms which we saw through to a conclusion by 1 October 1973.

The date 1 October 1973 brings me to my second bitter experience in having to undergo a tergiversation that strained my mental and emotional system to the limit. We were immensely proud of the Ministry of Development which had been created in 1964 and had reached its climax on 1 October 1973 when we assumed direct responsibility for a further range of executive duties. The need for the closest of team-work was imperative and we redoubled our efforts with conferences, working parties, exhortations, hospitality, transfers of staff and every device we could think of. For my own part I did little else in 1972 and 1973 but work to blend this body of talented professional and administrative officers into one team, in order to provide the public in every corner of Ulster with the best service we could by October 1973. Within a few weeks we learned from the radio that the ministry was to be split in two. I was eventually allocated to the new Housing Department and had the unpleasant duty of having to go to my colleagues and tell them to forget all that I had been saying for the previous two years and to regard themselves no longer as one team but as two. It fell to me to initiate the splitting of the private office, the accounts, the personnel branch, land acquisition and a great deal else. The emotional strain of having to demolish what had been so carefully built was considerable.

Although I have now in this chapter described a great many aspects of the work, I am afraid I have still not quite managed to convey the type of day-to-day situation which creates immediate pressure on a senior officer and imposes an inescapable strain.

A decision whether or not to accept a building contract is fairly typical of the situation I wish to describe. A contract under one's own control may have its problems but these are as nothing compared with giving or withholding approval to a contract about to be placed by another body, say a statutory board. The issue is likely to reach you as one of great urgency. The board, anxious to push ahead and show results, will be pressing for a decision. There will only be one valid tender. If it is rejected, or if a decision is delayed, the building firm is likely to withdraw. The job will then have to be readvertised, new tenders obtained and the risk of serious delay faced. On the other hand the tender price is extremely high and will set a new floor for all future tenders of this type; the builder has attached some punishing conditions; your quantity surveyors are doubtful whether he has the resources to finish the building in anything like the time he has stated. And to complicate matters the security forces advise heavily against building at all in the particular district at this time, believing that the outcome will simply be to create yet another area of sectarian confrontation. And it is extremely doubtful whether in practice the builder will be able to get possession of the old properties on the site as they are currently occupied by squatters. It is now Friday and the minister faces a parliamentary debate on Tuesday on a motion accusing the government of slowness and indecision.

The reader may well ask at this point why the official need worry himself personally. Surely a problem of this difficulty ought simply to be left to the minister himself to decide? This misses the point entirely. No official would fling a problem like this to his minister without preparing it fully, sifting the essentials and presenting the final issues to the minister along with his own advice. And, secondly, no matter whether it is the minister or the official who actually takes the decision, the official will have to live with the decision, placate the statutory board, face the problems created and so on. There is no escape.

Chapter 16

APPROACHES TO THE WORK

Every civil servant worth his salt is sensitive to the popular charge of slowness and delay and he is constantly struggling to push his work ahead and to disprove the charge. On the whole it is probably right to say that the charge is valid. Government work is slow and would be improved by being discharged more briskly.

Of course there are reasons for the apparent slowness. The problems put to a government department are for the most part difficult ones. An answer is generally being sought that will commit the government—that is, the state—to money, or to a legal consent, or to some future action. Government is one entity, and just as the principle of collective responsibility governs behaviour in cabinet, so also does it govern the actions of the various branches of government. None can act in isolation from the others. Planning affects roads, roads affect housing, housing affects employment, employment affects education and so on. All are governed to some extent by consideration of finance, and the treasury division of the Department of Finance keeps a tight rein on the spending departments. Then, all actions of government are accountable to a degree that no other activity of society is—through the minister to parliament, through the accounting officer to the Comptroller and Auditor-General, through the permanent secretary to the Ombudsman, not to mention all the other supervisory bodies listed in the previous chapter.

I find it helpful to see action by a government department in three different time-scales.

From hour to hour and minute to minute we operate as fast as anyone I know of. The principal sitting down to dictate letters and memoranda concerning a pile of files before him will operate fast. The officer in attendance on a minister receiving a deputation will be forced to move quickly in composing the press statement which may have to reach the radio and television studios in a matter of minutes. A frequent experience for us is (I am speaking here of the system under the former Stormont parliament, with cabinet sitting in the Castle and ministers walking up from there to Parliament Buildings where the Commons sat and where most of our offices also were) to meet our minister coming from cabinet at one o'clock with fresh decisions (or more usually decisions with qualifications and conditions added) affecting a parliamentary question he is to answer at 2.30 or a statement he is to make after questions at 3.15. It falls to us to digest the cabinet decisions, take the minister's wishes, dictate or write a statement and have it ready for the minister's approval, for copying and for release within an hour or so. I am quite certain we do this as rapidly as anyone could in the circumstances.

Emergencies also stimulate speed in the service. Each time there is a threat of petrol rationing an organisation to manage the administration is set up within two or three weeks. A major industrial strike in the same way evokes an immediate response in the form of emergency arrangements formed within days to safeguard essential supplies and services. The public, for very good reasons, hears little of those arrangements. It is hard to convey the feeling of what happens in such situations but the fact is that they bring out the best in civil servants so far as speedy practical action is concerned. They leap to action, they cut corners, they work regardless of hours. It has something to do with a feeling of release from humdrum, day-to-day, normal duties that take so long to produce visible results. It has something to do also with a feeling of being able to help with something important and dramatic. It has something to do with the heady atmosphere. Be the explanation as it may, the fact is that the administrative adrenalin flows and that results appear in surprisingly short time. A good recent example was to be seen in the setting up by the secretary of state of incident centres to help monitor the Provisional IRA ceasefire of Sunday 9 February 1975, nine p.m. The decision to set up the incident centres and to staff them with civil servants (and of junior rank at that) was taken on Monday 10 and announced in the House of Commons on Tuesday 11. By Wednesday 12 they had been formed and manned and by Thursday 13 all of them were operational.

Where we fall down is in the time-scale of weeks and months and in the discharge of tasks that call for deliberate, concerted action by more than one department. The preparation of a booklet to which several departments contribute, the final clearance of a memorandum affecting other departments, the printing of a leaflet, the erection of a building, the creation of a new staff post, the recruitment of staff—these and similar matters take an unconscionable length of time. We know this only too well and are more frustrated by it than anyone outside the service could possibly be.

When it comes to matters that have to be judged in the time-scale of years our record improves again. Given the realities of the parliamentary and political system our methods show real results in reasonable time. We used to be able to get a bill through all stages of the Stormont parliament in about four months (without asking for standing orders to be suspended or for other extra-ordinary measures to be taken). From the stage of advising our minister on the need for new legislation, securing the policy decisions from cabinet, arranging for the money, both capital and revenue, getting the legislation, setting up the administrative machinery, appointing committee or board members right through to the appointed day, as we call it, could be as little as twelve months. It is in retrospect that the pace is fully appreciated. One day I can see motorway traffic moving on land which a year earlier the farmer with a shotgun was refusing to give up. By 1955 the Tuberculosis Authority, with all modern aids, had conquered the problem of tubercle that ten years earlier had seemed insoluble. In the summer of 1964 some of us were giving evidence before the Lockwood Committee on the development of all forms of higher education and on whether or not there should be a second university. By October 1968 the first students were in their lecture rooms at the New University of Ulster in its new buildings on its beautiful site at Coleraine. By 1 October 1973 the multifarious problems of legislation, finance, rating, staffing, accommodation, records, systems and instructions for the monumental Macrory reforms that had seemed insurmountable in early 1972, when the Stormont parliament was suspended, had in fact been surmounted. This is not the place to argue whether more could not have been done or whether much does not still remain to be done in all fields of public work; the point here simply is that in the perspective of time the government service can and does show a rate of progress that stands up to criticism.

Another relevant aspect of timing is the choice of the right moment to do things that have been carefully thought out and prepared. How often is a sound and proper departmental action or announcement spoiled by happening to coincide with some other event that captures the news or seems to contradict the action or in some other unfortunate way reduces its value. Civil servants find timing a most tricky matter. Ministers are much better judges as their minds are attuned to popular feelings and reactions. A good minister will feel in his bones that such and such a day is not right for the release of some announcement that the department is pressing him to make, or will see advantages in bringing forward something that the department would rather spend more time refining and polishing.

Timing is of course but one small aspect of the whole wide and deep subject of government publicity. Confining myself to the viewpoint of the administrator I can say that this is probably the approach to public work which has changed most over the last couple of generations. My recollection from my early years is of departments blandly taking decisions and making announcements with little regard to the impact on the public other than that arising directly from the content and merits of the matter in hand. The needs of a participating democracy have, since the 1950s, demanded much more attention; the public have hungered for more information; press, radio and television have tried to satisfy those appetites. And ministers have thought it increasingly important to influence public opinion. Within departments this has led to the appointment of press officers or information officers with a noticeable proliferation at the centre of affairs.

In many ways the press officer, being a card-carrying journalist, is a great support to the administrator. With his journalistic skill he will help a branch with the wording of an explanatory leaflet and see that neither technical jargon nor legal niceties blur the message. With his familiarity with the trade he will know which newspapers or journals are the most suitable for advertising aimed at a particular readership. Again he will know on which days of the week the provincial papers go to press and what the deadlines are for the bigger papers and for radio and television. In the reverse direction he will do something which busy administrators wrapped up in their own speciality cannot find time to do, namely to read in the press the reactions of small local authorities, public bodies and so on and be able to advise the administrators of public attitudes which they would do well to take note of. With his professional standing and knowledge he will relieve the administrators of a burden in organising a press conference or in looking after foreign journalists. To do all those jobs properly it is essential, absolutely essential, that the press officer be in the confidence of the senior officers and feel free to approach any of them with advice. This is not so easy for the administrator to accept as may appear on the surface, because the press officer is after all a journalist, he trades in news, he mixes with working journalists and editors and he is therefore extremely vulnerable to pressure and is a possible source of leakage of confidential information.

At this point the danger begins to arise. Is it perhaps part of his job to let out judiciously chosen snippets of information in advance? Should he try to influence the newspapers in the way they present government information? Should he have a word in the ear of an editor? Should it be part of his duty to protect the political reputation of the minister? I have been involved in all those operations directly or indirectly and the more I saw of them the less I liked them. I now believe that they are positively harmful both to good government and to healthy democracy; and not only in Northern Ireland. The press are perfectly capable of forming their own opinions. Good ministers do not need protection and bad ministers do not deserve it. The process is insidious, self-inflating, and harmful to truth.

Mind you, the press have a lot to answer for. The tendency which they have to seek out the froth rather than the meat of a problem, their practice of referring to some slight and honest difference of opinion as a row (when what the province needs is rational discussion and peaceful argument) or to a trivial discrepancy as a blunder—depresses the administrator just as much as it does the more perceptive reader. But administrators suffer in other ways as well. Journalists are prone to telephone administrators at home at night and then either dramatise some trifling comment or else blame the department for being unhelpful. Another trick is to telephone an officer about some complicated matter and then a moment later telephone a second officer about the same matter, receiving naturally a slightly different wording or a different emphasis. To the journalist all this makes better copy than the content of the matter. In that situation administrators nowadays heave a sigh of relief and say 'Go away and talk to our press officer'. Clearly there is no golden rule and there is no finality with a free press in a democratic country but it is surely not beyond the bounds of reason for government and press to move towards a new concordat under which government would relax its efforts at influencing the press in return for more responsible treatment of departmental business.

One other side of publicity in the administrative sphere lies in the promotion of general literature such as yearbooks, annual reports, *Ulster Commentary*, official histories, 'Facts and Figures' and so on. These can be of considerable value, especially in a region too small to sustain a publishing industry. Whatever shortcomings such literature may have, it is nevertheless there on the record for all to see and, if need be, to criticise. Other developments in my time, to which the government press officers contributed greatly, were Festival 71 (to mark the fifty years of parliament and government in Northern Ireland), the Ulster Weeks in British cities (to promote exports and tourism), the Ulster-Scot links with North America and the Ulster Folk Park and Mellon House in County Tyrone. This is admirable work.

Another of the attitudes to work that has changed greatly over the years is the shift from individualism to group and committee work. This is probably more marked in our service than in that of other countries for we were until twenty years or so ago fiercely individualistic. Keen officers looked on it as something of a slight if one suggested that they might combine with another branch of the same ministry, to say nothing of combining with other ministries.

Within each department there have been big strides towards consultation and joint action. There is little formality about this; as I hope to show later on, the service is not greatly given to methodology but prefers ad hoc and commonsense ways of doing things. The circulation of papers; the circulating file of letters issued; the working party; joint and simultaneous decision-making in matters that affect two or more branches: these and other simple systems have brought about changes within each department.

Between departments the changes in this direction have been even more marked. Inter-departmental committees abound. It is not enough that programmes have to be jointly prepared, they must also be jointly monitored. Before I saw the light and withdrew from these worthy endeavours I found myself serving on no fewer than six interdepartmental committees at one time: the steering group that monitored the implementation of the Development Programme 1970–75; the steering board that supervised the carrying into effect of the Macrory reorganisation; the Growth and Key Centres Committees that fostered the development by all departments of the agreed growth towns and key centres across the province; the Legislative Programme Committee that advised ministers and the leader of the house on the progress of departmental business coming before parliament; the Official Advisory Committee that was trying to look ahead and foresee some of the administrative problems likely to arise beyond the immediate horizon; and the Civil Service Commission—a permanent body in a very different category and responsible for recruitment to the service and for standards of entry. I found it all fascinating. The servicing was of a high standard, the discussion stimulating, the realism reassuring—but I was having no time to do any work of my own.

This is of course the danger. And there are still amongst us a few diehards who reject the whole concept, prefering to keep their heads down and get on with their own jobs. But direct rule has given an enormous impetus to interdepartmental work as the British ministers and officials understandably seek to acquaint themselves not only with the problems of departments but with the problems that cut across departmental boundaries and in particular those that may affect security and the responsibilities of the Northern Ireland Office in one way or another.

I have said that we are not greatly given to methodology. This is certainly true in any formal sense. We do not use the terminology of the modern business world and I suppose that business consultants would find our methods, our files and our organisation charts distinctly old-fashioned for the most part. (I know I am doing some departments an injustice here but I must abide by generalities if I am not to end up by writing an encyclopaedia and a boring one at that.) Our methods are essentially pragmatic. We tackle the problems as they come. A motto forced on us by hard experience is *solvitur ambulando*. With our teamwork in the office, our informal meetings, our habit of popping one's head into a colleague's room, our need to bear finance in mind at every turn, our centralised personnel (or as we say, establishment) arrangements, our habit of taking other people with us before we take a major decision, I suppose one could say that we practice corporate management; but we would be loath to make any such claim. We read our specialised journals; we attend our conferences; we submit ourselves to training courses (even the most elderly of us) both here and in Great Britain; and we make ourselves familiar with the terminology of modern office methods—accountable management, management by objectives, programme budgeting, programme evaluation and review technique, network analysis. All these and many other techniques are being absorbed and tried; some of my colleagues are more optimistic about their usefulness in the public service than I am; I am quite ready to be proved wrong. One of the techniques which we have found of undoubted value is JAR—job appraisal reporting which has already shown itself to be of real service to all concerned. A training course which was of lasting value to me personally was concerned with rapid reading, a really useful trick.

Fulton, that is to say the report of the Prime Minister's Committee on the Home Civil Service that reported in 1968, has had little relevance to our service even though it was taken up energetically by our civil service management department and closely studied by departments. Several of the principal themes put forward by Fulton simply did not apply here. One for example was his concern over the rigid separation in the British service between the various horizontal grades—clerical, executive and administrative—together with his recommendations for overcoming the problem. But we have no such rigid separation in Northern Ireland, and never had. Ours has been, par excellence, *la carrière ouverte aux talents* with plenty of free movement from one grade to another by promotion on merit. The great number of men who started as boy clerks and rose to occupy the highest positions in the service testifies to the adage that every junior clerk carries a permanent secretary's carpet in his briefcase!

Another of the windmills against which Fulton tilted was the exclusion of professional and technical officers in the British service from posts of administrative responsibility. Again the point had already occurred to us for we had been accustomed right since 1921 to have professional experts moving into administrative posts when able and willing to do so, particularly in the Ministries of Agriculture and Education where many distinguished cases had occurred. There are some lesser aspects of this problem, such as giving the professional expert (who is basically an adviser, inspector and researcher with us) a greater measure of managerial responsibility in his own field of work, and these are being pushed ahead rapidly nowadays. I support this trend but I should not be inclined to go much further than that, as our professional men have become scarce in recent years and hard to replace; and I am happier to see their valuable experience and talents devoted to their speciality rather than to the filing of correspondence, so to speak, and the tiresome details of land acquisition and superannuation with which we, trained clerks, have to occupy ourselves so much.

The third of Fulton's principal themes—indeed the one to which he gave precedence—was an attack on the traditional concept of the amateur generalist in administration and a plea for the training of administrators in a field of work, thus building up an experience and competence in that field. I suppose I show myself to be obscurantist when I say that I find this a foolish and dangerous doctrine. I believe profoundly in the value to governments of a body of all-round administrators, from any academic background, experienced over the years in several different fields of administration, capable of absorbing, leading, judging and balancing, and of advising not so much on the specialised problems (there are plenty of people to do that) but on the ultimate issues which ministers have to decide: yes or no, today or tomorrow, firmly or gently, things or people. I am simply revealing my own prejudices at this point and betraying my own upbringing; but I did promise to be truthful.

As in any other trade or profession the tools of the trade are essential to the workman and familiarity with those tools is a great help. We too have our tools to help us clear a path, build a bridge or open up new fields of public work. These had to undergo a change under direct rule and, as I have described elsewhere the mental readjustment which we succeeded in making, let me try now to list the changes made in the tools of administration under parliamentary government. I speak entirely as an administrator, with no thought of politics or religion. It had been our duty to submit certain documents to the Governor for signature; one day he disappeared. Certain types of legislative orders had to be approved by the Privy Council; one day it too disappeared. Where we had a parliament we found ourselves working to an Assembly; and where we had had two legislative chambers we found we had but one. Bills and acts of parliament, the very pith and substance of so much of our work, gave way to Measures. Hansard became merely the Official Report. Cabinet became the Executive, prime minister the Chief Executive Member. The title of ministry with all its overtones of service and of caring gave way to Department with its suggestion of bureaucracy. Ministers became heads of departments, parliamentary questions became questions, hon members became assemblymen, MPs MLAs. Where there had been one member for each constituency, we now had to deal with several assemblymen representing each constituency under proportional representation. Several of them might write or speak to us about the one case; and the etiquette of informing a member of a forthcoming visit or official function in his constituency was transformed into a baffling conundrum. Just as we were getting accustomed to the handling of those new tools, the changes of May 1974 threw us back very largely on the old tools again—or on some of them at any rate.

As Alexander Pope wrote:

For forms of Government let fools contest
Whate'er is best administered is best.
For modes of faith let graceless zealots fight
He can't be wrong whose life is in the right.

Corny sentiments no doubt, and threadbare poetry, but the
thoughts have nevertheless sustained some of us throughout the
vicissitudes of our careers. A well-known saying by a good friend
of ours at St Andrew's House in Scotland used to keep our spirits
up: 'It's the quality of the administration that counts at the end
of the day'. Lest I get carried away by these comforting sentiments, let me repeat again the sobering aphorism which a shrewd
and experienced observer once formulated: 'The outturn of
government work is seldom commensurate with the quantity and
quality of the civil service input'.

It would be both wrong and misleading to leave the impression
that the Northern Ireland service was a solemn place, peopled by
hard-faced puritans responding only to the stern voice of duty. It
is in fact a friendly place enriched by good comradeship and good
humour. In the early years there were outbreaks of warfare between certain sections, with learned men bombarding one another
with verbal abuse quarried from the recesses of their literary
vocabularies, but the decline of the eccentric and the extreme
pressure of business have swept such antics from the scene. As
is only to be expected amongst intelligent and conscientious men,
sharp differences of opinion can arise over the proper course of
action to follow, advice to give to a minister and so on. And there
can be healthy conflicts over the distribution of business between
departments in situations where interests coincide such as food
hygiene (a Health matter) in relation to milk factories or abattoirs
(an Agriculture concern); or in the control of water supplies
where Environment have the responsibility for water purity and
where Agriculture have the responsibility for drainage and for
fisheries. These differences of opinion are inevitable; to surrender
an important statutory responsibility to a department with other
interests and other priorities is no small matter. My point is
imply that such differences no longer lead to acrimony and do
get resolved eventually in the interests of efficiency and economy.

Office parties never featured prominently in the Stormont life.
They flourished for a time in the 1950s and early 1960s but declined again under the influence of the Don't Drink and Drive
campaign. A modest tea or drinks session to celebrate a retirement
is generally as much as we stretch to nowadays.

I miss the office parties for one thing and that is the doggerel verse which they elicited. The most successful line of humour was that which deflated civil service pomposity or ridiculed our more obvious weaknesses. Of a permanent secretary to the Ministry of Health and Local Government the bard of the day sang in a quavering tenor:

> He builds our houses, mends our drains,
> Makes war on all diseases,
> And cir-cum-loc-u-tor-ily
> Each public board appeases.

Another contribution ran:

> When Ministers begin to grouse
> At awkward questions in the House
> When civil servants face distress
> As odd disclosures in the Press,
> We look for stuff of fitting size
> For pulling over people's eyes;
> We then recall the golden rule:
> There is no substitute for wool.

It will not have escaped notice that my reference to colleagues are in the masculine. We have few women in the senior ranks and none at all in the permanent secretary or deputy or under-secretary grade. I think this a great pity as I am sure the quality of the service would benefit. I am not aware of any conscious prejudice against giving women administrative responsibility but for some reason that perhaps the sociologists can explain, rather few enter the administrative grades, few stay and fewer still reach positions of real authority. The fact that we retained the marriage bar much longer than in Great Britain was a big factor. By 1974 we had two women assistant secretaries so perhaps some signs of grace were beginning to appear amongst us.

Chapter 17

WORKING WITH MINISTERS

The essence of the senior civil servant's job is to advise ministers, to get decisions from ministers and then to carry out those decisions. This book is not about ministers or politicians; it is about civil servants, but no account of their working lives would be complete without some picture of their relationships with their political heads.

To be clear—we are speaking of elected political men and women who accept appointment as ministers or parliamentary secretaries in charge of departments, who may be in parliament for a term or two and may then drop out again, and who may hold office for a period before returning to the back benches or to the opposition. The precise titles and terminology may change with changing constitutional forms but those essentials remain. The distinction with which I am concerned is of course between those political ministers on the one hand and on the other the permanent career officials. I may suggest some lessening of the distinction or rather of the separateness as I go on but the distinction has to be made clear at the start.

For the clerk in some outlying office and even for the middle-rank officer at headquarters changes of minister have little or no effect on the daily work. Nor have they for most of the specialists or technicians. For the more senior professional and administrative officers on the other hand the politics and personality of the minister mean a great deal, first because they come into frequent contact with him and second because of the nature of their job as I have repeatedly tried to summarise it. A permanent secretary in Northern Ireland will see his minister on three or four days of the week, on average, often for half an hour or an hour but sometimes for a great deal more. They get to know each other really well. And the same holds good for other senior officers in varying degrees and in varying ways.

Let me plunge in at once and refute the rumour that departments like having a weak minister whom they can easily influence and win over to their point of view. There is no satisfaction in such a situation and, worse still, if the minister is weak with his department he will be weak also in cabinet, weak in parliament and feeble when outside interests catch him by the throat. This is of no use to a department. It suits a department a thousand times better to have a strong minister who can make up his own mind and can defend his decisions before all comers.

Ministers differ greatly in the ways in which they prefer to be briefed and advised. Some enjoy reading a file or a memorandum while some prefer a discussion. Some like to have a discussion paper first and then to talk about it while others prefer to argue a subject out with their advisers and then ask for a definitive paper that embodies the agreed line. Senior officials for their part have a lively concern to make sure that no relevant facts or points of view are kept from the minister no matter how distasteful. Even when clearly advocating one firm course of action a good official will add, 'Of course, Minister, I must warn you that our planners (or our engineers or whatever) are not happy about this course and I have therefore brought along the chief planner to speak for himself and his colleagues'.

Departments are not pressure groups. They are corporate and statutory bodies charged with a wide range of duties. It is part of their duty to understand the political position and the personal wishes of their minister and to advise him to the best of their ability. There is a strong desire in every department, with its immense store of knowledge and experience, to persuade the minister to read the documents, to listen to advice and then to make up his mind. Whether he acts on that advice is entirely a matter for him, and the department of course regards him as free to reject their advice, to take advice from other quarters and generally to make up his mind as he thinks right, but they undoubtedly believe they have a duty to present their advice to him and to persuade him at the very least to apply his mind to it and to come to some decision. The really bad decisions that I can recall were all taken by ministers without advice and not by ministers acting either in line with or contrary to advice which they had received and weighed up.

Indecision by a minister soon makes itself felt in a department. Delays occur and the stream begins to back up and soon the upper reaches of the department overflow with undecided issues. Once decisions are taken on leading issues, business starts flowing again. Political indecision is quickly reflected in departmental hesitation and accusations of civil service shilly-shallying. We bear this cheerfully because we (and few other people) understand the background to it.

The reasons for indecision can be very real. The minister may be waiting to carry out further consultations or to win over other interest groups before he settles an issue on which some of the interests may be clamouring for an immediate settlement. He may have made up his own mind but been unable to carry the Minister of Finance with him. Both may be of one mind but cannot get clearance from a cabinet that is giving priority to some other matters. Or again the government as a whole may be awaiting a debate in parliament or party conference or some other major turning point. We know all these situations. We accept them because it is our duty to help make the system work and we know better than most people how difficult it is to operate the bigger and more controversial aspects of departmental business within the party political and parliamentary system. We like to have time with our minister to get to know him, to learn his problems and his wishes and to take his mind. This all helps to make the flow of business easier and smoother. There would be little advantage —and much disadvantage—in the department constantly bombarding its minister with proposals which he found it necessary to reject. Embarrassment, awkwardness, delay and bad feeling would be the inevitable outcome. The Queen's business is facilitated rather by a flow of submissions which, within the perimeters of law, finance and other departmental considerations the department can conscientiously advocate and the minister is likely to be able to accept and to promote politically. There are finer points of judgment involved in deciding to what lengths such sensible courses ought to be taken and at what point the department should refrain from pushing any further its very proper recommendations. And moral judgment can be called for if the department considers that the minister is proposing to act improperly. The department's duty is to advise and to persuade but not to pressurise, much less to prevent a minister from taking a particular course. That would be to exceed its duty. After all in the sort of position we are considering political judgments are involved and civil servants are out of their proper sphere. And the numbing thought is that, great though their knowledge of a situation may be and detached their thinking, it is always possible that their judgment of politics or of timing or of public morality may quite simply be faulty or incomplete. Every senior official can recall the many occasions on which he had to respond to some suggestion from his minister by saying, 'Yes, Minister, that is all very fine but. . .' This sort of response was all the more necessary from us under prolonged conditions of one-party government. The inner problem of course lay in the divided nature of the Ulster society, and ministers would forcefully remind us that they had to carry their policies against critics opposed not only to the government but to the very existence of the state. Advocacy by officials of particular courses that were unwelcome to ministers under the Stormont parliament had therefore to run the gauntlet twice over, once in the ordinary sense of being unpalatable to ministers as party politicians, and again in the sense of appearing to put ministers in the impossible position of encouraging the enemies of the very constitution itself. Still it was our job to do so and we did it in various ways that we thought realistic and effective, certainly not in ways that were uselessly idealistic or quixotic. After all we were practitioners in a real world, not philosopher kings in some ideal platonic state.

Once the minister has arrived at his decision, it then becomes our decision immediately and without question. For within the system there can be only one policy and that is the minister's, even when he has gone totally against departmental advice. It is well known and widely acknowledged that in such circumstances civil servants are not found going around complaining that the minister has overruled them. This attitude of acceptance perhaps reflects an unusual human reaction but the reasons for it are pretty plain. First, civil servants are schooled to respect and to implement the constitutional rule of ministerial responsibility. Second, they are (in a case such as we are considering that may well have taken weeks or months to settle) mighty glad to get a decision at long last. Third, in a complicated case requiring the minister's decision and causing him (as we are postulating) to go against his department, the arguments are never wholly on one side; they are more likely to be balanced in the proportions of fifty-one to forty-nine. And fourth, we are well aware that our advice, though sincere and well-informed, may not always be what the minister's political instincts tell him is best.

At the beginning of this chapter I drew the elementary and obvious distinction between a minister and an official in order to point the way clearly towards the difference in their roles. The minister's role is essentially political; the department needs his help in (amongst many other things) interpreting its work to the politicians and the public and in interpreting the wishes and

The Northern Ireland Cabinet in session, Autumn 1958, with Arthur Kelly and Cecil Bateman in attendance. *Belfast Telegraph.*

The County and County Borough Sanitary Officers 1951; a most dedicated team.

Ministry of Commerce officials at a routine meeting with their Dublin counterparts, 1971. *Lensmen.*

A meeting to review progress, 1973. From the left: the author; Chairman of the Ulster Countryside Committee; Secretary of State; Chairman of the Nature Reserves Committee; Departmental Minister. *Dept. of Environment.*

reactions of the politicians and the public back to the department. The image in the popular mind of a minister coming in to his office in the morning, sending for his staff and instructing them to prepare such and such a bill or scheme needs to be corrected. It may happen occasionally but not very often. Most bills and schemes arise out of the facts of a situation and brew for a long time. Inspection of factories week by week may be piling up evidence of, let us say, risks to the health of workers in an industry handling radioactive material. That evidence may be shown to an advisory committee. The report of that committee may very well raise legal issues concerning interference with exports and imports. Common Market directives could be involved. It is only when all these matters have been examined and sifted that the outlines of a proposition to mount a parliamentary bill can be framed. While this process is going on the minister may have changed two or three times. In the end the minister of the day must decide whether or not to sponsor the bill and must then steer it through its many political hoops. Once in a while a bill arises from purely political sources, from an election manifesto or a conference resolution and it then becomes the job of the department to provide the minister with advice on how to go about the task. But even in such circumstances the idea seldom comes to the department as a total surprise. The idea may well have been argued within the department and the weight of opinion against it may have been greater than that in favour, and so it has rested in a file in a cupboard until the new political impetus is manifest. It does not often need to come to that. It is part of the job of senior administrators to know what the pressures on their minister are and even to foresee what they are likely to be. In the course of day-to-day discussion with him they will be able to gauge how seriously he rates various political pressures, the opportunities for political gains and the time factors involved, and in the light of all that, they will be able to meet his needs without his having to formulate them. Things have come to a pretty pass when a minister has to instruct his permanent secretary.

It follows that the minister's job is not to sit at his desk all day. That is more the job of the official. It generally proves to be sufficient in practice if the minister devotes say half his day on average to the department, devoting the rest of his time to cabinet, parliament, his party, his constituency and the special interests falling within his field. Ministers in Northern Ireland lead a busy, hard life. Successful cabinet building generally results in ministers from different parts of the country being appointed. They think it right to continue to live in their constituencies even though this means a great deal of travelling every day. Add to this the constant demands made upon them for speaking at evening meetings— again in far-flung places—and their working day becomes long indeed. Add again the enormous exposure to publicity which they undergo—much more than in other places—and the day looks truly over-full. I formed the view early in my career that ministers had an extra gland in their make-up, a superlative energy gland. Often when, as private secretary, I would help my minister in the morning with a pile of letters, see him off to cabinet, be with him when acting as host at an official luncheon, breaking off at 2pm to go and take questions and a bill in parliament (coming out in the middle to receive a constituency deputation) I would be mighty glad to get away home at 6 o'clock. He would be setting off at that hour for a meeting in Castlederg, the most of a hundred miles there and a hundred miles back. I, too, have heard amusing stories about the easy lives that ministers lead but like most stories about public life there are generally second- or third-hand. Without a single exception every minister whom I served directly—from Billy Grant to Don Concannon—was a worker. I may have been lucky.

I found one little wartime episode amusing and illuminating in the context of the differing attitudes of ministers to office work and to outside political and popular contacts. It fell to me to accompany the Minister of Public Security on a visit to Banbridge urban district council. He had most diligently studied the files and memorised all the relevant figures. On entering the town hall he asked to be shown the ARP room and started at once to check the number of stirrup-pumps, turning to me and saying a little sharply, 'I understood that there were eighteen here, but I can only find sixteen.' By chance I was the official escorting another minister visiting the same council a little later. As we entered the town hall he greeted the first councillor he met with 'I am afraid Glenavon didn't play too well on Saturday,' the next with 'I see you've been elected to the co-op committee; be sure you keep down the cost of burials'; and so on with each councillor in turn. It is not hard to guess which minister made the greater impact, whatever other qualities they possessed.

Having in my early years served as private secretary to several ministers I was particularly sensitive to the actual ways in which ministers receive their briefings. Departments are generally so concerned to advise their minister comprehensively, with all the facts and all the arguments for and against, that they tend to produce lengthy and very detailed papers. For a busy man hurrying from one meeting to another this can be a burden rather than a help. For myself I always preferred—rightly or wrongly—to öffer my advice in the most terse form, generally in manuscript (rather than pile typescript upon typescript), often simply in the form of a word or two in the margin and frequently using coloured pencil so that when under pressure at a meeting the Minister could be reminded of a fact or a figure at a glance. There are obvious risks in this method, but I believe they are worth taking because nineteen times out of twenty it is more important for a minister to get one or two simple messages across than it is to deal exhaustively with every aspect.

There is also the matter of de-briefing, if I may use that word. Officials, needless to say, do not accompany ministers to cabinet or to meetings of ministers or to party meetings and so on. They therefore do not know what happens nor what the prevailing atmosphere is. It is helpful to them in preparing for the next stages to have some idea of the feel of the meeting and so it is useful to see their minister afterwards and get an account from him of decisions or arguments or developing attitudes that affect their work. It can also be useful to him. Where a really good relationship exists, a minister will often wish to unburden himself to his permanent secretary in the sure and certain knowledge that he has a sympathetic, if critical ear, and a completely discreet tongue.

One striking confirmation of this belief occurred in December 1973 when the office arrangements were being worked out to implement the power-sharing settlement and to help get the 1974 executive started. For a number of reasons that seemed sensible to me, I offered to stand down from my existing post, to act as permanent secretary of two departments and therefore not only to manage two departments but to report to two of the incoming ministers. The first minister to whom the proposition was put rejected it out of hand not because he feared inefficiency or anything of that sort but because he would not, under that plan, have the exclusive services of one permanent secretary. As he put it, 'I could not see myself able to relax and to confide in my permanent secretary if someone else was confiding in him as well.' In a negative fashion this illustrates one of the best aspects of the relationship that can grow up between a minister and his own chief adviser.

All our prime ministers have from time to time appointed parliamentary secretaries to departments and have experimented with countless different ways of using their services, for example as assistants to ministers in the bigger departments, or in the departments with the heavier load of outside visiting or of parliamentary work, or in a joint capacity in two separate departments and so on. In theory this all sounds splendid. It should be of help to a busy minister to have some practical relief or to have a political colleague with whom to discuss departmental problems in some intimacy. It should be of use to the prime minister in balancing his administration. It should be of great help to a young politician to come in, learn the business of government in a subsidiary capacity and earn his spurs. But looked at through the eyes of the departments the number of occasions when the arrangement worked well was rather small. It was often extremely difficult to make the system work at all. Deputations coming to see a minister insisted on seeing the real minister and were not content with the carbon copy. Local bodies arranging a public function greatly preferred the prestige of a cabinet minister. It was difficult in political terms for a minister to sit still in a small House of Commons and leave it to his parliamentary secretary to handle a bill or a motion when members obviously wanted to get at the minister himself, sitting there in full view and within a few feet of them. I am not saying that the idea has to be totally rejected. It is possible to imagine a situation with fewer and therefore larger departments, headed by a minister supported by one or possibly two assistants or parliamentary secretaries specialising in the work of particular divisions or branches of the department under his guidance. Some such scheme (provided it was seen to be needed in order to carry a real burden of work) might serve most effectively to secure political supervision of all the work of a department and to facilitate the task of answering for it in a local parliament or assembly especially under power-sharing or partnership arrangements.

For the ministers must answer to parliament for every single action taken in their name. Daily we see ministers arise and give replies to parliamentary questions about obscure and detailed matters which they could not possibly have handled and decided themselves. In an ordinary Stormont department there could well be a hundred decisions taken each day; in the field of social security there might well be a thousand. Everyone realises that the minister could not know about each one, much less have done anything effective about it. The reasons underlying the tradition are deeply rooted in the parliamentary system and are concerned with the control by the legislature over the executive and the granting to every member of parliament of the right to question ministers about everything that is done in their names. Departments, well trained to the system, make great efforts to ensure that decisions are taken in a way that can eventually be explained and defended by their ministers.

But is this really a healthy system? Is it in the best interests of parliamentary democracy for all of us to go on pretending that ministers decide every housing contract, every application for a licence, every decision to rent an office for a government department? And is it worthwhile maintaining the vast system of records and reporting which are necessary to support the myth?

I inclined to the view many years ago that such an edifice was on balance unhealthy and hardly worthwhile. I formed the simple proposition that the minister should answer for those matters (and in particular those aspects of certain matters) which he really controlled and which everyone could see were in his power to control. I am thinking of policy, the broad allocation of finance, programmes, priorities (of very real importance, this) and new legislation; he should decline to answer for a mass of detail which it was patently clear neither he nor any one human being could effectively master and control. This latter type of work—let us call it executive as distinct from administrative work—could, I felt, be entrusted to specialised bodies unconcerned with policy or politics and free to get on and do their job without having to look over their shoulder all the time to see how their activities were being received in high circles.

The weakness of the case, I could plainly see, was that once the executive group were freed from answering to the minister, they would be answerable to no one.

The idea was touched on by the Fulton Committee in 1968 when they recommended the hiving-off to specialised bodies of certain types of government technical services and procurement or purchasing. Macrory gave some pointers in the same direction in 1970. The idea was much more fully worked out in a comprehensive study of the public services in the Irish Republic produced by a committee headed by Liam Devlin and published in Dublin in 1969. This study recommended the creation of small policy departments attached to ministers, and, quite separately, of large executive departments subject to law and to government policy but not answerable to ministers from day to day; and the Devlin report carried the concept right through in terms of the actual functions of all the public offices in the Republic. I under-

stand that the idea is still alive in Dublin and experiments are
being made to put it into practice.

The solution to the problem of answerability has of course
arrived independently in recent years and is to hand in the shape
of our two Northern Ireland watchdog institutions, the parliamentary commissioner for administration (the Ombudsman) and the
commissioner for complaints, not to mention the Human Rights
Commission, the Equal Opportunities Agency, the Fair Employment Agency and the whole growth of modern supervisory bodies.
Under modern arrangements we have the worst of all worlds:
busy and overburdened ministers attempting to answer for executive detail, a cumbersome support system to enable them to do
so, the Ombudsman arrangements applying both to our administrative and our executive work, senior civil servants distracted
again and again and again from concentrating on policy by the
need to supervise detail, striving to combine the roles of administrator and manager. Admittedly the arguments are not all
on one side as there is a respectable case to be made out for the
value of ministerial intervention in individual cases and for the
ventilation of grievances on the floor of parliament, but do not
let us delude ourselves into thinking that it is this alone that
makes for good, humane administration. It is not. Too often it
is the shadow rather than the substance that is examined at such
pain and expense.

Chapter 18

PAPER

A^s excessive reliance on paper work is one of the weaknesses of the service I propose to devote a chapter to the topic.

The orderly and responsible conduct of public business naturally demands a system of written records. Information received, requests made, decisions given, these and the countless other minute-to-minute transactions are best put on record. Memories are fallible; passing information by word of mouth can lead to results every bit as strange as those in the old parlour game where the military report 'Send me reinforcements, I am going to advance', ends up as 'Send me three and fourpence, I am going to a dance.' Stranger things have happened. There is little to equal the contemporary written record, especially when, as in the service, it is also initialled and dated as a matter of the firmest discipline. Information and instructions can therefore be reliably handled and a whole system properly built upon them. The receipt of papers is similarly recorded so that anyone can see at a glance when exactly papers were dealt with, when they were referred to others and so on. This referring of papers in a public office has very considerable importance because fundamentally each officer attracts responsibility once he handles a set of papers; he carries less responsibility if he has merely been told of a problem but has not actually handled the documents. When any investigation or inquiry has to be undertaken the question 'Did you refer the documents to your departmental solicitor?' becomes very relevant indeed. Paper records have of course the further value that they can serve to inform others who are not directly involved but who would benefit by knowing.

And of course recording on paper is one of the basic planks of our tremendous edifice of answerability which I constantly stress. With the possible exception of the banks there is no trade or profession with anything approaching the civil service in its need for paper records that will serve to answer the subsequent—I was almost going to write, posthumous—demands of parliament, the comptroller and auditor-general, the Ombudsman—I hardly need go through the whole list of public guardians once again. All have an insatiable appetite for facts, figures, dates and expenditure, exhumed from the past.

There is—or there can be—an added advantage in putting a proposition on paper; it can serve as a discipline in clarifying the proposition itself. Anyone who has had the task of recording a confused committee meeting will understand. As Francis Bacon put it, 'Reading maketh a full man; conference a ready man; and writing an exact man.' Frequently a point is reached in an office discussion when agreement seems to have been secured and someone wisely says 'I will go off and dictate a rough draft. It will be good to see how this all looks in cold print.' It is a salutary test to apply.

All very good, but the trouble is that the service is disposed to take paper work to excess. There are some of us who delude ourselves that by committing an instruction to paper we have solved a problem. There are some who derive a sensuous enjoyment from taking a sheet of virgin foolscap and starting to pen a memorandum, whether needed or not. Most memoranda and minutes are too long. The virtues of brevity and clarity are tremendously underrated in the service. Many officers, even with years of experience, succumb to the temptation of putting on paper all that they know about a topic and the result is too often a hefty memorandum made up of solid blocks of close typescript. In contrast I recall that once when I wrote to a friend in the British diplomatic service for advice about going to the USSR on holiday he replied giving me a complete set of guide-rules on one side of a sheet of Foreign Office octavo notepaper and in clear manuscript at that. Learning from this and other examples I used to try to keep my memoranda, minutes and letters as short and clear as possible even at the risk of sounding staccato and appearing brusque, as I know I did appear to some of my colleagues.

So much has been written on the subject of officialese or civil service jargon that I do not propose to go into the subject here, apart from recording that civil service writing has become a great deal simpler and more direct in recent years and that most of the stiff old legalistic formalism has gone. As in other aspects of life there are of course fashions and trends in office language; we are now on a wave of dismal economic influence under which we identify areas, operate at the interface and compose alternative scenarios, making planning assumptions, measuring input and throughput and so on. Doubtless that will give way to other influences in time. I think I can already sense that the sociologists may be taking command, for I noticed recently in a paper placed before me the suggestion that we were facing, in Ulster, the problem of alienation, that is to say the process of withdrawal of attribution of legitimacy from the established social norms. I hope that is quite clear.

Our Northern Ireland service has been less given to the excessive use of paper than the Great Britain service, I should say. We have been able to measure this since direct rule because the British officials seem to have a much more highly developed sense of team-work and cohesion than we have. It seems to be an act of faith with them to circulate copies of minutes, of meetings and of memoranda to the widest imaginable circle of officials. This has been made easier by the widespread use of the photocopier. The outcome is lavish distribution, and the trouble is that people at the receiving end face the unwelcome burden of having to read and handle all this documentation. The photocopier has become something of a menace by making the copying and circulating of papers too easy.

Letter writing presents special problems of course and much attention is given to improving the quality and the clarity. Organisation and methods branch has done wonders. I propose here to touch on only one aspect and that is the phenomenon of the angry letter. When a conscientious officer finds his department being unfairly attacked or a colleague being unreasonably criticised there is a strong temptation to send the aggressor a pretty tart letter putting him in his place. This is always a mistake. I know; I have been guilty of the practice myself; but midway through my career I saw the light and became a reformed character. Angry letters do no good. They annoy and they produce a thoroughly unfavourable reaction in the very person whose actions and attitudes one is seeking to influence. Composing such a letter may provide a release of feeling; it may well be a splendid piece of prose; but the wisest course then is to lock the letter in a drawer and read it again when feelings are calmer. Wise is the man who tears up in the morning the letter he dictated the previous evening. The best letters may well be those that are never sent. It is no part of our job to scold or upbraid other people. As we used to say at the foot of every official communication, 'I am, Sir, Your obedient Servant'. That is our role, even though that precise formula has been dropped from daily use.

Work in a government office is sometimes stigmatised as 'pushing bits of paper around', and at times it can certainly feel like that. But the bits of paper have their purpose, and pushing them around has its purpose. I am going now to describe five bits of paper that could well have fluttered down on to my desk one day when I was permanent secretary of a busy, complex department. None of them will be in the least startling or unusual but they may illustrate something of what paper work is about. To be clear, many documents are for me personally to act upon, and of course I start many myself. I am confining myself here to examples of papers which have to be 'pushed around' for others to act upon.

The first is a letter from the Secretary to the Cabinet telling me (as he is telling all permanent secretaries) that a parliamentary motion criticising the government for delay and neglect in promoting public works west of the Bann is to be taken on Tuesday 12, that the prime minister proposes to make the major reply immediately after the mover, that he wishes to have from departments an up-to-date summary of actual facts and figures and that he will need to have the material by Friday 8 so that the PM may work on it over that weekend. That letter conveys a lot. It would have been possible for the secretary to have telephoned all of us but that operation could well have occupied two or three hours whereas he was able to dictate that short letter and have it typed and issued within forty-five minutes. And the likelihood is that he would not have found many of us at our desks; some were sure to be at meetings, or up-country or in London. The letter was therefore the most efficient medium. It calls for up-to-date facts and figures, which I do not have personally and which it would be most unwise of me to try to muster on my own. The information is in the relevant subject divisions of the ministry. All I have to do is to mark the letter out to precisely those officers whose help I need (and to no others) and to set a time-limit for their submissions. I do not need to compose an instruction or to transcribe the prime minister's wishes. It is all there.

The second bit of paper is a letter to me from the comptroller and auditor-general saying that he is dissatisfied with the explanations which my department have supplied to him on an intricate matter of superannuation and compensation, and giving me the opportunity of commenting before he reports the matter to the public accounts committee of parliament. He is right to come to me personally because I carry the personal responsibility for all our expenditure. He is a parliamentary officer and holds the trump cards; it is therefore up to me to respond fully and to do so personally. The subject is so complex that I must have help from the experts. Again the simple and efficient thing to do is to send his letter to them, show what I need and set a time.

The third is a complaint from an individual alleging maladministration by the ministry and conveyed by the parliamentary commissioner for administration. The accusation is that in disposing of a small piece of land surplus to our needs (but which we had acquired compulsorily as part of a bigger take) we had offered the land back to the original owner but when he declined we had sold it to a neighbour without making sufficiently searching inquiries to find whether any relative of the former owner had any desire to purchase the land from us. The commissioner proposes to investigate the whole affair and he offers me the chance of setting out the facts as we know them. Again I am responsible, again I do not know the details and again the sensible course is to give his letter and the complaint to a named officer and ask for a statement of fact. It will be a tedious business to reconstruct at this late date all the negotiations, discussions at the farm gate, telephone calls and so on but it has to be done. The sooner started the better. So let us push that bit of paper out, too. I have two thoughts in my mind—fairness to the individual who complains and protection of the ministry's good name; but so will my staff and there is no need for me to start preaching to them. They are as sensitive as I am on such aspects and simply wish to get on with the job in the knowledge that they have nothing to hide or to be ashamed of.

The fourth is merely a carbon copy of a letter from the Ministry of Health and Social Services to the parliamentary draftsman instructing him to prepare legislation conferring new minor powers on local authorities in connection with food handling and good hygiene on the public streets. Their permanent secretary merely wishes to keep us informed in view of our interest in local authority work in general. We do not question the policy; we want to give the ministry all the support we can but question whether it is wise to complicate the statute book by further amending legislation. It might be possible, and just as effective, to advise local authorities to use their existing power to make bye-laws for good rule and government, a power that has never been fully tested. It was sensible of the Ministry of Health to let us know and between us we may be able to find a neater and more acceptable solution. I send the bit of paper first to our local government branch and second to our solicitors.

The fifth is another battered looking and rather crumpled carbon copy of a letter to London by one of my deputy secretaries on the subject of aerodromes; he is offering to go to London on Monday morning, returning the same evening; he makes a valuable point about an aspect of the United Kingdom responsibility for navigational aids (which I am afraid I had not fully appreciated); he asks nothing of me, merely wishing to put my mind at rest. How welcome. I shall push this bit of paper back (he is out of the office all day, locked in trade union negotiations) with my grateful thanks scribbled on it. To read and clear this copy letter takes me three or four minutes but it spares me hours of work and hundreds of miles of travel. The business is pushed on without my having to lift a finger.

Chapter 19

FOUR PRINCIPLES

There are four basic principles which govern our behaviour and cause us a certain amount of concern in the management of our offices. Two of them show signs of changing with the changing times but the other two are totally immutable.

Anonymity is the first. Every civil servant is trained to act as an anonymous official and to eschew publicity. He is part of a bigger affair; his office or ministry is the corporate entity and he learns to subordinate his personality to it. Traditionally the official letters concluded with an indecipherable signature. Although signatures nowadays are generally more legible and recognisable, the basic suppression of anything approaching an ego in correspondence still remains a strong feature of civil service life. Getting one's name in the newspaper is an achievement that attracts more criticism amongst one's peers than admiration. Unusual situations give rise to exceptions as for example the threat of an epidemic of foot and mouth disease when the chief veterinary officer of the ministry of agriculture would make statements to the press in his own name or speak personally on radio. The constitutional reason for anonymity is of course the total responsibility of ministers and the maintenance of the strict role of the civil servant as confidential adviser.

In the past twenty years or so the Northern Ireland civil service has been imperceptibly emerging from under its carapace of anonymity, abandoning its back rooms and coming out to explain its work to the public it serves. Our staff are easily accessible and the hunger of the press and radio for live personal material has been increasing by leaps and bounds. So too has the desire of clubs, societies, community associations and local authorities for firsthand, reliable information about matters that affect them. The work of town and country planning has turned strongly in the direction of public participation and this immediately involves our planners in meetings, exhibitions, discussions and so on. As they appear in person and become known and talked about, the cloak of anonymity is withdrawn. Public inquiries also demand personal appearances. In the same way every other department has also been gradually drawn into consultations, seminars, and public participation exercises to an extent that causes their previously unknown officers to become known.

A further step away from anonymity occurred in 1973 when departments took over the direct management of many services for which local authorities had previously been responsible and along with that task took on a statutory liability to consult with the local authorities about programmes in their districts. Local authorities meet in public, with the press present, so that our officers became known far and wide. And we wanted them to be. Rather than organise our business so that all decisions would be taken at Stormont itself we deliberately and with our eyes wide open delegated authority in many matters to professional officers living and working in the areas affected; and we encouraged them to make themselves known to their public so that the public would feel they were dealing with named individual men rather than with faceless officials. This has worked well. So also has the new arrangement we devised for placing in the area of every elected local council a development officer to act as liaison officer. Again we went out of our way to introduce these men to the local newspapers and to encourage them to make themselves known within their bailiwicks and to be ready to speak at Rotary clubs, young farmers clubs, chambers of trade and other local groups.

I am sure that all this is to the good, even though there are serious pitfalls. No official should pronounce on policy or make statements about new departures in policy. Nor should he become involved in controversy or argument. But it is not always easy to draw the line between information and discussion on the one hand and on the other hand policy and controversy; and there are plenty of hostile and articulate critics around who will make certain that the line is blurred. What is more, an official may be extremely well informed and fully capable of dealing with his technical subject but not quite so alert to the pitfalls of public debate. In a word he can drop a brick. Ministers find this hard to accept and even harder to explain under parliamentary scrutiny; no matter how liberal, helpful and well-intentioned the administrative arrangements which we make, the minister remains answerable for every single one of our actions. I feel sure nevertheless that we have been moving in the right direction and that this is one of the ways in which we perform rather better than our colleagues in the United Kingdom service.

The second principle governing official behaviour is the principle of the confidentiality of all government business, amounting in many cases to outright secrecy. The basic reasons with us in Northern Ireland have less to do with protecting the interests of the state than in Great Britain where clearly a great deal more of official business has to do with national security. We have, unhappily, a whole field of police work, crime and subversion that understandably demands the utmost secrecy; but that is in a special category. I am concerned much more with the confidentiality of ordinary administrative work and the reasons why a high degree of reticence must be maintained. The first reason is the need to protect the sources of information and the legitimate interests of persons and companies. Much of our information falls into that category, a great deal more than is commonly understood —applications, requests, entreaties, personal and family circumstances, internal affairs of business firms and so on. Clearly these must be protected and the work of protection imposes a requirement of absolute confidentiality. This is most scrupulously observed. The second reason lies in the very nature of our relationships with our ministers which I have already described many times over. The advice we tender is confidential and must remain so. Public business is difficult enough already without adding the complicating factors of the advice given to a minister, what use he made of it, whether he accepted or rejected or modified it and so on. If these matters were left open to public comment a huge and totally nugatory dimension would be added to the conduct of public affairs in a parliamentary democracy. The effect on officials would be bad; they would start looking over their shoulders to gauge the impression their advice was making on parliament and the public. And the effect on that advice would be deplorable; unless they are absolutely free to speak their minds in strict confidence and to present their advice—palatable or unpalatable —in a fearless manner then the whole system suffers drastically.

Most of us have been aware for a long time past that the secrecy which surrounds our work nevertheless had its serious drawbacks. Like secrecy anywhere it provides the atmosphere for mistrust and for rumour. Disappointed clients can readily come to believe that the cause of their rejection was neglect or prejudice if not downright corruption. I have many times in the past wished, as I closed a difficult and controversial case, that I could have displayed the file for all to read somewhere in Donegall Place for the purpose of demonstrating the enormous amount of care taken over even the most trivial case as well as the punctilious regard for fairness and impartiality.

But changes have taken place in that respect also. The reports of inspectors at public inquiries have now for a number of years been made available to the parties. Plans and schemes are made available at the stage of preliminary drafts. In 1974 no fewer than four alternative routes being examined in the department for building a contentious new road at Knock, Belfast, were explained in a leaflet and made available to householders in the area and their comments invited. This links up with the trend away from anonymity described above and typifies a trend towards more open government that is as welcome to officials as it is to the public. I support it entirely but feel obliged to say that it is shot through with practical difficulties, contains within itself the seeds of misunderstanding and complaint and adds substantially to the burden of official paper, manpower and above all delay, none of which the public relish.

We come now to two principles of administration which stand firm and unchanging: impartiality and incorruptibility.

Impartiality and fairness in the handling of public business are of course such obvious requirements that it is unnecessary to describe them or trace their development. Quite simply they represent the embodiment in administrative practice of the rule of law. But there are some aspects affecting senior administrators that may be worth mentioning. Political impartiality is an absolute requirement of senior civil servants. We may not take any active part in politics. In practice this is hardly an onerous restriction as few of us would have the slightest desire to do so even if the rules permitted us. The test comes rather in the other direction, that is to say in the impartiality with which we advise and serve our ministers of different political backgrounds. Any possible doubts there might have been about our ability to make the necessary adjustments while still preserving utter impartiality were thoroughly dispelled in the course of the extraordinary constitutional and political changes of 1972-74, when we served in rapid succession Ulster Unionists, Westminster Conservatives, the Power-Sharing Executive, and Westminster Socialists; and within the power-sharing executive some permanent secretaries had to advise and serve Unionist ministers, some SDLP and some Alliance, while some of us served all of them simultaneously. Few senior civil servants have undergone stiffer tests in the fire of political impartiality. In practice all this presented us with rather less trouble than the standing requirement on all officials in the British service to ensure that the records of one set of ministers are not made available to an incoming or subsequent set of ministers and that the confidential actions and attitudes of the one set are not made known to the others.

The aspect of political impartiality which in practice caused us most concern was the task of holding the service together under the strain of those political and civil disturbances which affected the working lives of all our staff. Amongst the hundreds of disturbances from 1968 onwards there were, remarkable to relate, only four which seriously threatened the work of our offices. The first was that associated with the introduction of internment in the autumn of 1971; the second followed the suspension of Stormont and of the constitution in the spring of 1972; the third was the episode in January 1972 known to many as 'Bloody Sunday'; and the fourth was the Ulster Workers' Council strike in the early summer of 1974. The background in all four cases was a huge outburst of popular feeling, a gross polarisation of the people, a call for a general strike, barricades, suspension of public transport, all accompanied by varying degrees of pressure, intimidation and violence. It was physically impossible for some of our staff to get to work; it was awkward and even dangerous for others. And of course it was not to be expected that every single civil servant would be totally immune from some degree of emotional involvement. Although the workers' strike of 1974 was by far the most widespread, it was the internment demonstrations of 1971 which threatened to affect the civil service most seriously for the simple reason that it was associated with the initiation of the rent and rate strike, corrosive in any society but utterly abhorrent in an ordered community such as the civil service. We managed to weather all four with surprisingly few wounds. In retrospect I believe that the very success of the service in holding together, keeping up morale and maintaining the efficiency of our services in face of the most appalling strains and stresses has served to conceal the serious threat which the troubles have posed to the conduct of civil administration. On several occasions the country showed some signs of approaching an administrative breakdown but I doubt whether London appreciated the fact.

At the other end of the day-to-day administrative scale, that is to say in the fair and impartial treatment of individual applications for grants, subsidies, permissions or licences, a very different problem arises. I am thinking of the inordinate amount of time and meticulous care that is devoted to ensuring absolutely fair and uniform treatment of cases, particularly of cases which present unusual, awkward, or anomalous features making them hard to bring within the rules. A law of diminishing returns begins to apply beyond a certain point and it is doubtful whether the undoubted fairness eventually achieved fully justifies the exceptional effort spent on such cases. I would be hard put to find a civil servant willing to draw a line and leave such cases to chance and I would be slow myself to suggest the adoption of any rough and ready rule of thumb. But I do draw attention to the problem because of the increasingly heavy deck-cargo of accountability and answerability that we carry.

The fourth and last principle which I need to stress is the principle of incorruptibility, the principle that puts every emphasis on personal integrity in the discharge of duty and prohibits entirely the acceptance of gifts, bribes, inducements or rewards in any form. The rules of our service are absolute. They are as firmly applied and as willingly accepted today as ever they were and they are frequently restated by the Ministry of Finance for the guidance of all of us. In the modern world of business hospitality and of cultivated public relations, this repeated insistence is more needed than ever it was. At a meeting of officials once a Ministry of Finance man held up a nasty cheap little vest-pocket diary costing about twenty pence and said 'If absolutely obliged, you may accept this', adding 'But you may in no circumstances accept this', holding aloft a rather decent looking desk diary that must have been worth fully seventy-five pence.

All this is very well, but what does an officer do in practice if he is performing his duty by making himself known to professional and business men in the world in which he works, visiting factories, receiving visitors, facilitating incoming industrialists and so forth? Their methods are not our methods. They make a practice of offering gifts at Christmas to their associates, they entertain freely and most lavishly by our spartan standards, they send book tokens in the form of Christmas cards, they enjoy giving samples of their products. They seldom set out to bribe; they simply wish to show friendship or appreciation and they do so in the coinage to which they are accustomed. We must refuse. I once heard the permanent secretary of Commerce declare, in tones that were meant to be heard far and wide, 'I wish it to be known that any business firm that offers gifts, inducements or hospitality to any member of my staff will find its path harder rather than easier from then on.' But refusal can be embarrassing and can be misunderstood. It calls for presence of mind, firmness and tact to refuse a small and carefully chosen gift suddenly offered at the close of a happy visit and intended for one's wife. We do not all possess those qualities in the same degree; we all have our vanities and our frailties. I can only hope that we have acted sensibly and that we have done our best, within the real world in which we work, to live up to the high standards we have set ourselves. Perhaps some of my colleagues are like myself in this way, and find it hard to say no in the face of kindness.

Chapter 20

SATISFACTIONS

A s I go about the Province and see a fine stretch of road, a handsome bridge, a well-placed housing estate or a busy health clinic I am tempted to take a pride in it and to mutter to myself 'I signed the contract' or 'If it had not been for my intervention the land for that scheme would never have been secured'. The warm glow of satisfaction at such visible reminders of one's work for the community soon fades, for obviously the signing of the contract or the deal over the land was but one item in a long process to which many others contributed. And had I not been on the job someone else would have been and the project would have been completed just the same.

Besides, there are all too many visible reminders of one's failures as well. I wince every time I see a stiff, suburban-type two-storey house sitting square on the skyline of a beautifully rounded County Down drumlin; a modern housing estate jammed in between a railway siding and a grit mill; a huge ugly concrete farm building with its foul effluent flowing gently into a trout stream. I was associated with those and many more and I failed to get them stopped or diverted. The documents may even bear my signature as it may have fallen to me to consent, directly or indirectly, to those monuments to the victory of short-term commercial or political gain over long-term community and human values. Administration, like politics, is the art of the possible.

Again, browsing in a library I sometimes stumble on a section in an act of parliament which I devised, pushed through my seniors, persuaded the minister to endorse and cajoled the draftsman to include in the bill. Even though the sentiment may seem jejune today, a feeling of satisfaction remains and is intensified by the very anonymity of the printed page and by the knowledge that not more than three or four people know that it was I who was responsible. Even they have probably forgotten.

Equally there are whole statutes staring out of the page at me that I should rather not be reminded of, well-meaning attempts in that forlorn cause of trying to make people good through the medium of legislation. A clear example is the litter act of 1960 making it a criminal offence to drop a bus ticket on the street. Through the late 1950s I argued in vain against introducing legislation in the absence of real, hard public opinion for clean and tidy public places. Far too few people in Ireland cared about these things to justify the passing and the enforcement of punitive legislation. I therefore argued in favour of holding back until there was a public clamour at the doors of Parliament Buildings. The local authorities on the other hand were contending that as every country had a litter act we must have one, too. It is fair to say that seventeen years after the passing of that act the amount of litter is about seventeen times as great as before the act.

Looking back from retirement I should dearly like to be able to claim some signal achievement and describe how I changed the course of history. This is simply not possible. All I can say— and I do so in order to indicate to younger readers some of the inner satisfactions of the job—is that for me, as for all senior officers, there were certain episodes in the administrative history of the Province that I recall vividly, in which I invested a lot of hard work and much of myself. The first was, surprisingly, an arrangement that regulated the conditions of night-workers in bakeries in 1938; another came later that year with the launching of the Northern Ireland Council of Social Service; the tuberculosis authority in 1946; the concept of a distinct statutory welfare service in 1946, separate from the medical services and different from the arrangements then in force in England; the creation of the modern public health environmental services in 1948–1950; the housing act of 1956 dealing with slum clearance, the start of the slum clearance programme and the nursing of the earliest practical schemes (which were far away to the west in Omagh rural district); setting Robert Matthew to work in 1960 on the daunting Belfast housing and planning problem; our ambitious regional plan and the first of our area plans (for Ulster Lakeland in Fermanagh in 1963) under new legislation and, naughtily, sometimes even without legislation. Incidentally this illustrates one of those matters which officials see differently from outside critics, namely the alleged neglect of the area west of the river Bann. This has always struck me as a fallacy. Every department gave as much attention to areas, problems, local councils and other local bodies in counties Fermanagh, Tyrone and Londonderry as it did to those in Antrim, Down, Armagh or Belfast, allowing for the disparity in population. The western part had only about one fifth or so of the total population. Indeed departments probably gave more than a fifth of their thinking to the western parts as there was usually much less local initiative there. In the richer, more populous and more go-ahead eastern parts there was always far more locally generated drive, private and commercial as well as municipal. A tour of the west will suggest to any impartial observer that a greater proportion of capital invested there is public capital than is the case elsewhere: roads, bridges, hospitals, schools, clinics, libraries, police stations, court houses, agricultural colleges, forests and forest parks, advance factories. That certainly was how we saw matters.

The list of episodes above illustrates one other relevant aspect of this study of job satisfaction. Most of the episodes occurred when I was a junior or middle-rank officer and none of them after I became head of a ministry. This prompts me to try to explain something of the ranking system in the civil service and to relate it to the question of getting satisfaction from the work.

As in every calling, experience, knowledge and the esteem of one's fellows bring advancement and some form of promotion. Because of the high degree of answerability needed in the public service as well as the need to organise and control sizeable numbers of staff, there has to be a hierarchy. As in the army, the ranks are sharply defined, named and respected, to such an extent that the 'perks' attract very understandable mirth—the size of the desk, the thickness of the carpet, the hour of arriving in the morning and so on.

As we are concerned in this work with the administrative group or grade of the service, let us start with the lowest rank in that group, that of assistant principal or administration trainee as it came to be called. Recruitment is mainly from outside, direct into the service, at around the age of 22 to 28. The competition is intended for honours graduates and there is some scope for bright, up-and-coming young people already in the service. The rank is essentially a trainee rank, involving some attendance at training courses in Ulster or in England; but of course in the civil service training is largely made up of practical training on the job. The young man or woman will be under close supervision, will be transferred from branch to branch and will be given some difficult work to cut his or her teeth on. The trainee is likely to find himself secretary to an office committee or to be devilling on the preparation of a bill. He may also after a year or two be made private secretary to the parliamentary secretary or eventually to the minister. This is especially good experience and training. Not only does it give him the flavour of political work and the feeling of his minister's many outside contacts but —what is relevant to the problem we are examining just here— it gives him a bird's eye view of the whole ministry and also a glimpse into other ministries. His parliamentary secretary or minister, in their capacity as MPs, will receive from their constituents a stream of complaints, queries and requests affecting the work of other ministries and the job of the private secretary is to pursue those complaints into those other ministries and obtain the facts and figures on which his minister can then base his reply or frame some course of action. Were the young trainee not to become a private secretary to a political chief, he would run the risk of being (at any one time) confined to one section of one branch of one division—say the improvement and conversion section of the private enterprise branch of the housing division.

Similarly, when he is promoted, as his superiors hope he soon will be, to the rank of deputy principal he will be in charge of one limited and defined block of work—say, building schemes at voluntary intermediate schools, or animal health or tourist development or acquisition of land for trunk roads—perhaps one thirtieth or fortieth part of the work of his department. He will know his subject thoroughly but he will have little chance of seeing many other sides of the department's work unless his duties impinge on them. After say five years or so and after proving that he is an all-round administrator he may become a principal. His view then becomes wider and his contacts with outside bodies more frequent. The next rank is assistant secretary and is the first statutory rank, that is one recognised by law as competent to commit the ministry. Above that come a very small number of posts of senior assistant secretary and deputy secretary, concerned largely with policy and political matters. The permanent secretary is in charge of all.

Alongside and mingling at various points are the professional men and women, the architects, the forestry workers, the school inspectors, the factory inspectors and a great many other cadres; but let us concentrate for the sake of clarity on the lay administrators.

Now, as an officer is promoted up through the ranks he gains more pay, more standing, more scope, more authority, rather better working conditions, and freedom from petty restraints on attendance, timekeeping and so on. Whether he gets more rewarding work is another matter. Amongst the reasons for doubt is one which has been explained earlier, namely the arrangement by which the more straightforward cases and the more successful and happy projects are cleared at the lowest possible rank, with the result that the only practical cases which reach the senior officer's desk are those that cannot be solved easily or quickly, or have gone off the rails or are going to result in an action against the ministry in the high court.

But there is a deeper reason. At some point—in my experience it was at the level of principal, though it may have crept up to assistant secretary today—conditions conspire to let the man or woman do some really constructive work. At that point the officer is in actual day-to-day touch with the problem, be it farm improvement or teachers' pay or registration of companies. This is his only job. He is at home with it and confident about handling it. He knows the outside interest groups and the personalities involved. He goes to the Ministry of Finance and argues his case for money. He deals with the minions of the comptroller and auditor-general who come raiding his files. He prepares instructions for Parliamentary Draftsman. He is secretary of the relevant advisory council. He attends in parliament when his minister has business there. He will be sent to training courses and will attend conferences on behalf of the ministry. I have no hesitation whatever in saying that from the point of view of creativity and sheer satisfaction at being totally immersed in positive work, I was happiest in the rank of principal from 1944 till 1953. Others may not have had quite the same experience and may put it a rank higher or a rank lower but most will at least recognise the inner feelings I am trying to convey.

By contrast the permanent secretary covering the whole of his ministry's thirty or forty recognisable services can concentrate on few of them and can specialise in none. He has to keep switching from one to another as they demand attention from him in turn. Trying to keep abreast of developments he has to read a lot of paper, mostly at short notice. Generalising (for men and methods differ) a permanent secretary is expected to be on call at all times and bit by bit he becomes a prisoner in his office. Often when, as a permanent secretary, I would be standing about waiting to catch my minister or being told that the secretary of state's plane from London had been delayed so that he could not see me till late evening, I used to envy my principal officers their solid, planned working day.

There are of course some satisfactions and to a certain extent an administrator reaps what he puts into his work. The very opportunity to take a view over a wide range of functions—in Finance for example the permanent secretary oversees not only treasury work and government accounts but also charities, public loans, savings, public works, ordnance survey, valuation and rating, registry of deeds, land registry, registration of births, deaths and marriages and other matters—can in itself be stimulating to the creative mind, as can the job of combining different services, with different disciplines, into a harmonious public service. Close contact with ministers, often leading to mutual regard and lasting friendship, can be enjoyable. The special task of inducting a young minister, new to public responsibility, can be particularly onerous but correspondingly satisfying.

A special satisfaction for a permanent secretary, with his considerable power to make postings and promotions, lies in spotting talent and bringing on the most promising young people. The elaborate arrangements worked out in consultation with the staff associations under Whitley Council look after the promotion of men and women of normal quality and ability. Then the routine people, the nine-to-five people, the lazy dogs and so on will find their own level. But a permanent secretary is always on the look-out for really bright young men and women, with constructive minds that can be counted on to turn into gold any subject they touch. It is partly a matter of using their abilities to the full, of rescuing them from comparative drudgery and putting them onto constructive tasks before they grow old and tired; but it is also a matter of reaching across the generation gap and harnessing to evolving policy work young people in tune with the spirit of the times. The various official terms 'accelerated promotion' or 'starring' are but tokens of the recognition of excellence which gives the permanent secretary particular satisfaction. No training manual, no computer, no network analysis will tell the permanent secretary how to achieve such a coup. It takes flexibility of mind to spot the promise in youth, skill to get him through the hoops of official procedure and courage to stand up to criticism in a system that understandably places much weight on seniority.

Yet another satisfaction of a very different sort springs to mind. Apart altogether from pressure groups and business organisations, there come to notice from time to time non-profit-making bodies that would founder without some special encouragement. Examples have included the Northern Ireland Council for Orthopaedic Development, the Abbeyfield Housing Association and the famous Belfast Linen Hall Library, all of whom have testified to the help they have received and the happy relationship which they have enjoyed with government departments. It is much easier for a department in a small region to go out of its way to encourage such a body than for a big national department. The staff probably know the leaders of the voluntary body and know the quality of their work. They can advise them on how best to present their affairs, on how to apply for available financial aid and on pitfalls to avoid. To be involved within the ministry in such an encounter and to see it through to some successful outcome is most satisfying. Trust, on both sides, is the keynote.

One of the many problems in any big office is the degree of contact which the most senior man should maintain with his junior staff, his clerks, his typing pool, his messengers and technicians. It is mercifully not a severe problem at Stormont because there is a welcome air of informality and a noticeable lack of stuffiness about rank. But the problem does exist in the form of keeping in touch with the wide base of the pyramid. Some permanent secretaries take pains to go round the general offices and make themselves known, believing that in doing so they are giving encouragement to the bulk of staff who seldom meet the senior people and that they are helping to build good morale. I found this an embarrassingly selfconscious exercise. On the few occasions when it happened to me as a junior I was covered with confusion as for example when HE The Governor, the Earl Granville, insisted on coming round all our offices in 1950 and speaking to each of us about our work. I took the view very early in my career that the staff have no wish to be patronised in that way. They are adult people, with families, church connections, many of them active in St. John Ambulance Brigade or the police reserve, with their own ideas about public affairs. Besides, morale building is a job all up and down the line and should not be thrust on the most senior man with his many other burdens. What I always did consider worth doing, from my earliest days of responsibility, was to ask officers coming to see me about difficult items to bring along the clerks or executive officers who had been doing the groundwork, in the hope of making them feel part of the business of decision-making. I found this most useful to me and, I believe, satisfying to them.

Royal Honours are amongst the pleasanter rewards of the job, especially nowadays when there are fewer of them as the range of recipients in the population at large has been so greatly and so rightly widened. Those most often conferred on civil servants have traditionally been the MBE in the middle ranks, the OBE in the more senior ranks and the CBE at the top. The Imperial Service Order comes occasionally to officers with long service in particular situations. The secretary to the cabinet and the head of the service have been awarded knighthoods. Even in the present age of informality, the practice of awarding honours without public or private justification and under rules that remain impenetrable still has the fascination of the inscrutable. It is another of the many popular misconceptions that honours come as a matter of routine to all officers in certain ranks. This is wide of the mark. I can think of many senior officers, the overwhelming majority of all whom I worked with, who although men of great ability and industry, ended their careers without any such recognition. The system is widely criticised today as being old-fashioned but it was that very old-fashioned quality that intrigued me when in 1968 I was made a Companion of the Bath, an order which had been created in its original form by King Henry IV in 1399 and revived in its modern form by King George I in 1725. Those who have the letters CB after their name are thus tiny links in a very long historical chain.

One of the unspoken privileges of being a general administrator in government work is the opportunity which he gets of working with a range of different professions and of seeing into their professional organisations. Negotiating with a prestigious professional body can be tiresome, for you quickly find yourself up against a well-informed, well-disciplined pressure group. But looking beyond that stage to the further stage of friendship and confidence the insight into their methods is enlightening. My first experience of any consequence was one of the most testing, when as a young principal I found myself in 1947 helping to prepare for the national health service and having much to do—outside the office more than inside—with the medical, dental, pharmaceutical, optical and nursing professions. My closest and happiest associations came next with the public health inspectors and then the social workers and almoners. Later it was with the architects, the highway engineers, the water engineers, the structural engineers, the lawyers, the accountants and the chartered secretaries. The town planners went so far as to make me an honorary member in their jubilee year of 1964 (and followed this up by also honouring in 1966 those redoubtable public men, the Rt Hon William Craig MP and Mr Neil Blaney TD). All the professions, I found, were generous both in the way they revealed to us in confidence their internal problems, their hopes and fears, and also in the way they extended friendship and entertainment to us.

Allowing myself for once the luxury of a rash and sweeping generalisation over the vista of thirty years I would say that in all they did the architects were the most stylish, the highway engineers the most assured, the public health inspectors the most selfless and the town planners the most far-seeing.

Chapter 21

LOCAL AUTHORITIES AND STATUTORY BOARDS

So far I have written almost exclusively about the civil service, viewed public affairs through the eyes of the service and referred repeatedly to 'we' and 'us' and what we have managed (or more often, perhaps, failed) to do. To some extent this is a type of shorthand writing that when transcribed includes the public services in the widest sense as well as those in private and commercial life who work with them. What senior civil servant, however able and however dedicated, can 'improve the hospital services' without the active participation of a whole line of people from the area health board chairman to the hospital matron to the manager of the building firm to the man with the wheelbarrow? I could not attempt to deal with all the relevant agencies within the compass of this book, but there are two which so closely affect the work of the senior civil servant that they must be mentioned and their role assessed, namely the elected local councils and the whole range of nominated statutory boards. Once again, I disclaim any political interest or intention, and confine myself strictly to the working arrangements in the context of all that I am seeking to convey.

By local authorities I mean the elected local councils and in particular those which existed before the Macrory reorganisation of 1 October 1973. I consider it more useful to put on record something about those seventy-three councils which have disappeared rather than about the new twenty-six which now operate but which have still to establish their identity and their character.

They took the form of county boroughs, counties, borough, urban and rural districts. In the six counties there were thus two tiers of local authority, namely the county council and, at the district level, the borough, urban and rural district councils. We did not have parish councils in Northern Ireland. All were independent, elected, statutory bodies voted into power by their electorates and answerable to them.

Traditionally the local authorities all had special links with, and looked generally for guidance to, one central department: the Ministry of Home Affairs in the twenties and thirties, then Health and Local Government, then Development, recently Housing, Local Government and Planning, and now Environment. But they had also official contacts with other ministries as well, for example with Commerce on matters concerning harbours, tourism and gas supply, with Education on educational services, with Health and Social Services on health and welfare and so on.

In some contentious situation critics would often say to us, 'Why don't you tell your local offices what to do? Why don't you instruct them?' There were two fallacies here. The councils were not our local offices; they were in no way branches of the ministry; they were, as I have said, independent, elected bodies answerable not to us but to their electorate. Admittedly there were many items of business in which they needed to secure the statutory approval of the department or a grant of money or a sanction to raise a capital loan. But it was not open to a department (save in very rare circumstances governed by law) to instruct them or to 'tell them what to do'. Therein lay the problem.

The problem consisted in establishing the best possible working relationship with the local authorities. On the one hand they were, I repeat, elected independent bodies manned by councillors who were public figures in their own right, whereas we were anonymous, salaried officials. There was a limit therefore to the distance we ought to go, or could go, in persuading or influencing them. On the other hand we were acting for ministers, for government and for parliament in carrying out public policy; it was our duty to translate public policy into effective action.

There were a host of methods adopted: ordinary correspondence, circular letters, deputations to the ministry, visits to council or council committee meetings, conferences, discussions with the three local authority associations (covering the counties, the municipal authorities and the rural authorities), the associations of officers of various categories and then also contacts with the many specialised bodies in local government dealing with education, libraries, health, welfare, water and so on. And there were also countless individual visits and consultations going on all the time.

With local government officers relations were extremely close and cordial, granted a few pardonable exceptions. They were loyal to their councils and always advocated their causes. It was only when a council was hopelessly divided or had lamentably failed over a long period to come to any decision on a difficult issue that a worried official might let it be known that it might not come amiss if the ministry were to intervene and settle the issue for them. Certainly when consulted about proposed legislation designed to confer some new function on local authorities, the advice of the official was always in favour of recommending ministers to make the function a mandatory one rather than a permissive one that would inevitably lead to endless debate and misunderstanding.

With the elected councillors our relationships were naturally a lot more variable but on the whole they were close and harmonious, especially in the country areas. I am well aware that they often found us legalistic, parsimonious and slow in our methods. There were undoubtedly many points of political friction, especially with the more extreme unionist councils. That our relationships survived all those difficulties is really a tribute to the councillors, for however argumentative and critical they might be they were undeniably anxious to cooperate with us in the last resort and, despite all ups and downs, I cannot recall a situation in which they refused to work with the departments, even when some of them were claiming loudly to be alienated from the system. They embodied and reflected the Ulster situation as a whole—divided, contentious, voluble and yet hard-working, competent within limits and surprisingly effective. And it must be remembered that their financial resources were extremely limited for they enjoyed only a minor share of the meagre resources of a far from wealthy Province.

We certainly kept close to the local authorities and they to us. All our senior officers with responsibilities in the local government field were familiar with their particular sections of it. This was always so, right from 1921, but as things worked out in the 1960s I had especially good opportunities, with the result that a point was reached at which I was able to say that I had stood in every town hall, county hall and council office in the Province and was on personal terms with every mayor, chairman, town clerk and chief officer. There can be few government officials in the British Isles who could make such a statement about local authorities in their territories. I make this little point for two reasons: first as a matter of historical record and second as an indication to young people entering the public service that work is not by

any means confined to desk work and to paper. The councils were
certainly most hospitable. They constantly invited us to functions
and our memories are filled with recollections of the ceremony to
celebrate the thousandth house built by the Magherafelt rural
council, of the generosity of the Belfast water commissioners, of
the elegance at the Bangor town hall, of the splendid accommodation in the Antrim and Londonderry county halls, of the friendliness in Enniskillen, of the ferocious debate between the Macrory
review body and the Strabane urban council (who were determined to put all the blame on King James the First), of the many
happy times in Limavady urban and rural, of the late nights at
(and following) functions in Ballymena and so on and so on. But
no account of relationships with the councils would be complete
without a reference—and a sincere word of thanks—to those ineffable twin councils, Newry No 1 and Newry No 2, whose annual
dinners tested the stamina of the most stout-hearted Stormont
official: a sumptuous meal, a tremendous company of individual
characters, a bottle of whiskey between every two diners and
another under each chair, speeches, songs and more speeches.
Once when I was trying to make myself heard I had to contend
throughout with a rival speaker who had a message to convey and
was determined to get it across in the presence of so many
Stormont officials. The awful secret can now be revealed that that
particular dinner was held at a famous hostelry 'outside the
jurisdiction'. The covert object of the whole exercise was to ensure that the councils in their promotion of housing, water,
sewerage and all other local services extracted the maximum per-
missible (or impermissible) amount of government grant from the
department, and the subtlety of course was that we knew that they
knew that we knew that inner truth.

The local government system stemming from 1898, from 1878
and indeed from 1854, had by the 1960s totally outlived its day
and had to go. The services and all the problems associated with
them had far outgrown the system.

With such manifest difficulties—structural, political, sectarian,
administrative and financial—inherent in establishing and in
operating a local government system in Northern Ireland it would
seem attractive to try to meet the needs by conferring traditional
local government functions on nominated statutory boards instead.
To a certain extent this is possible, and has in fact been done, but
only to a certain extent, for there are equally great pitfalls along
that path also.

We are speaking, to be clear, of boards, authorities, commissions or other legal entities created by act of parliament and authorised to acquire land, engage staff, place contracts and generally carry on executive business. They are managed by a committee of persons appointed by the responsible minister.

The first pitfall lies in the choice of members. To begin with, the minister may not have much effective choice because the act of parliament, reflecting the needs of the situation, may require him to accept names put forward by relevant interest groups or at the very least to consult with them in the selection. Then to the extent that he is free to go out and select people of his own choosing, public considerations will limit his choice. He will have to bear in mind the importance of having members from different parts of the Province; he will have to balance town and country; protestant and catholic; he will probably need to include at least one woman and a trade unionist; he will not want all the members to be from middle-class business or professional backgrounds; and will need to have some regard to age so as to avoid a preponderance of elderly members. A minister often finishes up by searching frantically for all those qualities in a young working-class Roman Catholic married woman from west of the Bann! The interaction of these considerations upon those touched above —the requirement to accept nominations from interest groups— can become most complex for it can still further limit the minister's effective choice and sometimes force him to appear to make selections he would not otherwise wish to make. The struggle between efficiency and representative quality goes on all the time.

Assume that the members have all been appointed. Knowing that they have been appointed by the minister the first thing some of them will do, being Ulstermen, is to adopt an attitude of antagonism so as to demonstrate just how splendidly independent they are. Next, they find it hard to accept the restraints of public accountability. Often this is not their fault for they have accepted nomination on a vague sort of understanding—justified or not— that they have been asked to run the particular service as if it were a business concern. How often have ministers, speaking at the first gathering of nominated members of a new board, narrowed their eyes, clenched their teeth, stuck out their chin and assured the new and unsuspecting members that they would be expected 'to act as hard-headed businessmen'. When they find that this is not quite so, they become aggrieved and working relations with the department become more difficult. It would be salutary if all appointed members could be advised before they take office, 'You are being asked to operate an act of parliament. You will depend on the taxpayer for all your capital and (depending on the particular service) some of your revenue. Your expenditure and your actions will have to be justified to parliament—in one way or another and to varying degrees according to the items. In so far as you possess commercial experience and acumen, splendid; these can be most useful in carrying out those of your actions which have a commercial content. Otherwise please remember that you are being asked to provide a statutory and public service and that I am answerable to parliament.' Having worked closely with a great number of both categories over forty years I have always found that appointed members are prone to take themselves much more solemnly than elected members and to be far too easily offended. The slightest action by the minister or his department which fails to meet their wishes or even to conform to their stereotype of propriety is the immediate occasion for taking exception, or taking umbrage, or threatening resignation. The chairman who cannot stand politicians; the one just man; the member who affects to despise the civil service; the member who finds himself frustrated in his well-meaning efforts at reforming the world through his participation in, say, the gas board: these must be unhappy men who really ought to find their fulfilment in other and less onerous spheres of activity; or perhaps they are civic adolescents who have still to grow up.

But there are problems associated with statutory boards that go a great deal deeper than the temperamental tantrums of a few unfulfilled members. What is the proper field of a statutory board in a small Province like Ulster? In what ways is a statutory board a more suitable administrative instrument than a government department or an elected local authority? The report of the Macrory review body tried to answer those questions and drew a broad distinction between technical services—such as electricity, harbours, gas, fire-fighting and so on—which (once the policies and finances have been settled) can with greater advantage be entrusted to an independent board not answerable to ministers for its day-to-day activities; and on the other hand social services which are of obvious concern every day of the week to politicians and public representatives generally, and which ought preferably therefore to come under direct political and popular control. The fact that we departed radically from that analysis in Ulster in relation to health, personal social services, education and housing is a measure of the unusual conditions that obtained in 1972 and 1973. This would justify a full examination in itself but this is not the place.

If all the various types of tribunal and advisory committee are included in the reckoning, then there must be several hundred statutory or public boards and committees operating in connection with government work in Northern Ireland; of these possibly about seventy are executive bodies exercising decision-making and financial powers. This is a large number in a small Province and apart from anything else their number and complexity deserve a special study in themselves.

Quite apart from that, there is the position of the considerable number of staff whom those statutory bodies employ in totally independent and separate groupings. These are neither civil servants on the one hand nor local government officers on the other. They fall some where in between. Not only does this present problems in settling pay and conditions of service but it leaves to a large extent unsolved the deeper problems of the loyalties of these officers, their *esprit de corps,* their transferability, their evolving methods and traditions and their long-term futures. The practicalities in terms of recruitment, pay, pension and so on have in fact been tackled and dealt with; but the deeper problems remain. The concept of one unified Ulster public service, which the Cameron Commission in 1969 recommended for consideration in paragraph 231 of their *Report* (Cmd 532), may be a long-term concept but nevertheless represents one possible method of securing the highest performance right throughout all public bodies in this Province, on the strict condition that the underlying problems of standards, traditions, discipline, impartiality and so on are thoroughly understood and honestly faced.

Chapter 22

A DAY IN THE LIFE OF A
PERMANENT SECRETARY

My wife, dear girl, gets up first and starts the household going. She brings me a glass of orange juice. As I arise and move about, the radio is on and I vaguely absorb 'what the papers say', 'the religious message' and the local news. A political speech, a poor fellow murdered and left dead in an alleyway, a huge 300 lb bomb exploded in Castlederg devastating the council offices, a girl tarred and feathered by the IRA. What was that about the council offices? Devastated and documents scattered. That affects me. We must do something about that. We must send the general inspector along to see if he can help. And it would be good for morale if the minister could visit. No, he is tied up all day today. Maybe the parliamentary secretary could be got hold of at home and persuaded to make the journey. I'm sure he would want to go. A stroll up the garden to see whether the British Queens are showing through yet. Breakfast. Post. Some letters but none from any of the boys. All to much caught up in their own affairs to think of writing. How I hate it with all five of them away and the house empty. I must get to the office. Stella will run me up in the car. Here we are at nine-fifteen. Be sure to telephone the builder about repairing the roof. Yes, sure. In through the security check, bag searched, pass shown. I'll walk up the stairs instead of waiting for the lift. Good morning. Newspapers. Lovely sight but I have time to glance at the front page of the Belfast morning papers so as to check whether the minister has got himself involved in any controversy. One or two letters. Nothing of importance. Yes I shall dictate replies to these. I like to get my dictation done early in the day. Minister going off to cabinet. Must catch him and make sure he is briefed on that business about the Belfast corporation contract. Difficult case. Back again. Meeting with officers of housing division about rent policy. Good discussion. Real meeting of minds. What a pleasure. Costs, interest rates, rationalisation,

Caldwell Hoey and Ronald Green with Eileen Lyons on her retirement before her marriage.

Austin Currie, young radical Minister for Housing, Local Government and Planning, 1973.

Dick Rogers. *Joe Furphy*.

The unmistakable figure of L. G. P. Freer, making a presentation.

Paddy Shea. *Belfast Telegraph*.

deficit, rebates. We can't wait for events to happen. We have a
duty to act. How will Finance take all this? Will our own minister
wear it? How will he sell it to his colleagues? Yes, all right. We'll
do a paper. Must be ready by Friday. If someone does a draft I'll
look at it on Thursday evening. Back to my desk. A planning
appeal about a bungalow for a retired farmer. What a lot to read.
Inspector's report as long as your arm. Verbatim evidence, sheets
and sheets of it. All seems sensible. Inspector's advice is clear and
firm. Branch have analysed the whole thing. Assistant secretary
recommends granting the appeal. Why didn't he go ahead and
clear it? Well, there are third party interests involved. Including
an amenity society. But the development is pretty trifling. Always
the same story. The smaller the more tricky. Branch has handled
well. All right. Approve and initial. Little do the public know
what trouble we take over these cases. I wish we could publish the
whole file. Anyway they will see the Inspector's report. I'm glad
we brought in that rule. Yes? Who wants to see me? Joe Smith?
All right. Show him in. Principal officer, competent, intelligent,
too intelligent maybe and too conscientious. Unhappy. Always
unhappy. Always worked up. Thinks he is not appreciated. I
don't value his work, is that it? Look here, man, this is not a
nursery. Snap out of it. Forget about these imagined slights. Get
on with the job. We all think well of you. Do you want a change
of work? No? All right. Let's forget about it. Actually he thinks
he is indispensable. Have to let him talk. What a time he takes.
Why is it that the really good people never complain? What
next? Parliamentary question? The minister wants all the draft
replies before 1 pm. Why am I seeing this at all? Did I not say
that assistant secretaries were to clear PQs direct with minister
and leave me out of it? Ah well, I see. He is being gently coaxed
into promising legislation on further compensation arrangements
for blighted property. Hardly, I think. We'll have to look into this
much more deeply. This is a crazy system under which a PQ can
be tabled on Tuesday afternoon, reach us on Wednesday and
have to be answered on Thursday. I'm dying with hunger. Where
are my sandwiches? Good. Marmite and two peanut butter. I
love Stella's brown bread. A handful of nuts and raisins. I wish
she wouldn't include this messy yoghurt. And I hate fruit in an
office. It smells. Time to read the report on Ballymurphy. Grim.
Phone call? There is a Mr Bill Jones ringing? Says it's personal.
I doubt it: but I'm too weak to turn him away. 'Hallo. How are
you keeping, John? How is your good lady wife? And the boys?
I often see you walking with that wee red-headed rascal. Oh he

is married now is he? How time flies. Well it's just a wee personal thing I wanted to mention. I have gone in with a few of the fellows to form a company and we are trying to open a petrol station at Ballymuck. You know, Murphy's old place outside Ballymena, on the Ballymoney Road. We're having difficulty with the planning officer. The usual lot of red tape, you know. He is putting up some sort of fatheaded objection about the thing being on a busy crossroads and opposite a primary school and just a hundred yards outside the speed limit. You know the sort of fiddling objections these fellows put up. I'm sure you would see the thing in a sensible light. What about coming out one day to the Royal Majestic and have a bite of lunch? Can't manage? Too bad, but maybe you'd have a look at that planning case and drop me a line. Love and kisses to Sheila.' It's two-thirty already. I must get down to drafting that paper on local government election dates and their effect on the council services. The business is becoming desperately urgent. Where shall I start? What now? Would I ring the Whips Office about a date for taking the motion on the Fermanagh draft plan. Why can't the politicians settle all that themselves? Oh, it depends on the date of our forthcoming public inquiry. True enough. I must ask about that. I must start the paper on local election dates. Phone again. A man from Whitehall. Do we wish to be included in a bill they are preparing that will suspend the statutory requirement for planning approval to urgent shoreline oil installations. But we have none. True, but the need might arise any day and pretty quickly at that. Arguments for; arguments against. Yes, yes but aren't you rushing us rather? 'Quite, but the papers have to go to the cabinet committee tonight. Sorry you weren't consulted earlier.' Obviously London forgot about us till the very last minute. Out of sight out of mind. No use blaming this poor man; he is the one who apparently did remember us. I am quite sure we don't want to be included in your bill. But I must consult Commerce for they have a big interest. Could I ring you back in half an hour. Get me Robinson in Commerce. At a meeting, is he? Try to get him out. What next? No time to start that paper on election dates. Will have to take the files home and write it there on Sunday. That's the usual solution. Who's there? Road branch? In they come. Keen types. Don't waste time. Know what they want. Designation. Land, consultant. Big clash of interest over housing scheme—local opposition growing. Strict budget. What a price! Two million pounds. Can't get myself accustomed to these frightful sums of money. All right. Go ahead. Keep in touch with London about supply of steel. It is certain to become even scarcer. Right. A meeting down town at the Town Planning Institute. Pleasant prospect for a change. Wait a moment. Commerce on the line. They fall in with our idea. Better legislate on our own if we look like getting an oil strike, that is if we need to legislate at all. I don't think we do. Our procedures are good. Must ring back to London. Poor way to do business. Merely advice at this stage. Our ministers will be consulted in due course. I hear you. It will be too late for them to do anything effective by then. Right. Off we go. What? Ministry of Finance have called a meeting of all permanent secretaries to shape our reactions to a London draft paper on a new aspect of control of expenditure. Urgent. Five o'clock. Can hardly skip it. For any sake, Alison, phone the Planning Institute people and put in an apology. That's about the third meeting in a row that I have missed. They will think I'm a poor fish. Now for Finance. What's this, Gordon? Draft material for the minister to use in his speech on the supplementary estimates. Can't he look after himself? Yes but he asked us to give him the facts and figures about the Transport Holding Company's superannuation scheme. Could you clear it now please. We must get it into the minister's bag for this evening. All right. All right. Off to Finance. Good meeting. Everyone cooperative and realistic. Finish 5.50. Back to clear up. Away by 6. Lovely evening. Beautiful light in the sky. No car. No harm. Will walk down home. My goodness, I never rang the builder. I forgot completely. In at 6.25. Mayor of Ballypatrick was ringing. Seemed all worked up. Dear dear. All right, I'll ring him now. Don't make it long, supper's ready. All right. Yes Mr Mayor. Row brewing up in the council tonight over the new sewerage scheme. Some councillors very angry. Mayor thinks he can stave off trouble if he can assure them that the minister will receive a deputation. All right, all right. Tell them that. I'll explain to minister. Thanks a lot. Must have you along to Ballypatrick one of these days, John, and have a jar together. Supper. Lasagne. Delicious. Baked custard. I have *The Times*, the *Irish Times* and the *Guardian* home with me, but no time to read them this evening. Have to go and take the chair at the Inst Board of Governors. Good reports about the school. Splendid results from scholarship exams. Outstanding feats in swimming and life-saving as usual. But some bother over requests from outside bodies to use the school premises in the evenings. Security difficulties galore. Finish early. That's what I like. No point in letting them blether on till midnight. Home at ten. Hot milk and honey and rum. Phone call. Riot in Lenadoon.

Big trouble. People being driven out of their homes. Can we organise emergency services? Of course. Automatic. We ought surely to be practised by now. Sit down. TV. Minister on late-night programme. My goodness. He doesn't know about Lenadoon. I ought to have phoned him. My fault entirely. Another day gone and nothing done.

Chapter 23

ALL THE WORLD AS MY PARISH

Although our work and our working lives were largely confined to Ulster itself, they were not entirely so.

Our position as a government exercising devolved powers within the United Kingdom required us to keep in constant touch with Her Majesty's Government in London and with the departments there. To a certain extent—as for example between our Cabinet Secretariat and the Home Office—the relationship was a formal one arising from our constitutional links with the Home Secretary and our position under the crown. To a certain extent —as for example between our Ministry of Finance and the British Treasury—the formal relationship merely symbolised a host of day-to-day negotiotions of a severely practical nature concerning income and expenditure. In other instances our departments acted in an agency capacity—as for example the Ministry of Agriculture for its principal (in some respects) the Ministry of Agriculture, Fisheries and Food, or the Ministry of Commerce serving from time to time as the agent or representative of the Board of Trade or other London departments in the field of industry and commerce. Again, in a very practical sense, our works branch acted as the building and property agency for various United Kingdom departments at different times: the Admiralty, the Post Office, the Department of the Environment and so on.

On top of all that, we needed to keep in touch with departments in London in order to be up to date on a host of practical matters such as standards, research and the practical lessons from applied research. It paid us to do so. The large and well-endowed British departments had of course great resources for research and investigation; we could not afford to duplicate their establishments; and it was therefore only commonsense to make friendly arrangements for taking proper advantage of their knowledge, experience and facilities.

Beyond all that again, it was necessary to keep in touch so as to be abreast of new policies and new legislation. Nothing was more humiliating than for one of us to be telephoned by a newspaper-man in Belfast a few minutes after some departmental announce-ment in London about housing or hospitals and not to know what it was all about or even whether it applied to us or not.

All the relationships which I briefly summarise have meant work. They involved active efforts to establish working relation-ships with officials in London; keeping abreast of the frequent changes in personnel that occur there; corresponding by letter or by telephone, teleprinter or mufax (a machine for copying docu-ments electronically and transmitting them over a distance), or by visit to London. These things do not just happen by chance. Relationships have to be cultivated.

We found our London colleagues almost invariably helpful. We found them highly intelligent, well informed, courteous and most understanding. There were, looking back across the years, just two difficulties. For one thing, each of us in our small world in Northern Ireland would be responsible for perhaps five or six subjects whereas our London colleague would be specialising in only one of those. Put another way, in order to consult fully upon all my subjects I would be forced to get into touch with perhaps five or six opposite numbers. That meant a lot of traipsing around Whitehall, but no matter. The second difficulty concerned the universal problem of the centre and the periphery. So long as we brought ourselves actively to the notice of our Whitehall col-leagues, they were most helpful to us and most confiding. Often we have come away with copies of extremely confidential material essential to a proper understanding of a policy or a problem. But out of sight, out of mind. Once we disappeared from the scene, those same officers tended quickly to forget about us. I do not blame them in the slightest. To them the relationship was un-necessary and generally unrewarding.

Not always unrewarding, I think. While we were for the most part cast in the role of a subordinate group seeking help and advice, there were occasions and there were indeed whole fields of work in which Whitehall was glad to learn something from us. I can recall several of these: the whole field of veterinary research and animal health control; industrial training; private enterprise housing subsidy for letting and for owner-occupation; the R-licence system for newly qualified car drivers; and our highly suc-cessful arrangements for combating tuberculosis after the 1939-45

war, which were of particular interest to the Scots. I shall return
to this in a moment.

I found the London visits stimulating, but then I did not have
too many. On average I might have gone twice a year. For many
of my colleagues in other departments—in Commerce and Agriculture for instance—the visits were so frequent, so lengthy or
organised at such short notice that they became a heavy chore.
One of our regrets was that the traffic was so much in the one
direction; we seldom managed to persuade our London colleagues
to come and see us over all the years.

Relationships with Edinburgh were particularly happy since
they were frankly on the footing of mutual advantage and were
devoid of any constitutional or hierarchical element. Besides, they
benefited from the added spice of common experience which we
affected to suffer at the hands of London and, what is more,
Scottish envy at our immunity from direct Treasury control as we
had our own Ministry of Finance. At any rate it was on those
lines that the office banter ran. For some ten or fifteen years after
the 1945 war those of us who worked in our Ministry of Health
and Local Government enjoyed a particularly close and fruitful
relationship with St Andrews House. The balance of advantage
fell clearly on our side, for they had at that time a particularly
brilliant set of young senior administrators: Douglas Haddow,
Norman Graham, George Pottinger, R P Fraser, J H Maginness,
George Kelly, Bob Grieve and a whole bunch of bright, energetic
and imaginative men. (Pottinger came to grief much later as a
result of the Poulson scandals and was convicted; but this does
not expunge the memory of his better days and his distinguished
service. Nor do I wish to disown him.) Unlike the London officials
these men were perfectly willing to come over and see our
methods for themselves. Genuine though their interest in us was,
their Scottish upbringing prevented them from indulging in any
flattery or fine words. I was once foolish enough to fish for a com-
pliment when three of them came over specially to study our
Northern Ireland Tuberculosis Authority, a unique body; but the
only response I could elicit was 'TB is bad with us, so it is a case
of any port in a storm'.

With Wales we had few contacts. We met their officials sometimes in London but beyond that we had not a great deal in
common. The great scholar-administrator Goronwy Daniel once
visited us, but his interest at that time was confined to methods of
teaching our variant of the Celtic language.

With Dublin the relationships were extremely easy and

friendly. Some of us had straightforward cross-border business to settle, for example the running of the Belfast-Dublin railway, the Dublin freight train to Derry for Donegal traffic, the bus services that cross the border every day, the road freight licensing system, notification of infectious diseases, animal health, the hydro-electric scheme at Ballyshannon and later the main interconnector for the two electricity systems, the Foyle Fisheries Commission, and many other practical affairs. As well as that, we exchanged visits for the purpose of learning of new developments. And we frequently met at conferences. My colleagues and I will unashamedly confess that we thoroughly enjoyed our Dublin visits. There was without question an informality, a ready understanding, a shared sense of humour, and a friendliness which made our official dealings easy and pleasant; but it is right to add that the exigencies of the political situation imposed constraints from time to time. We thought highly of them as officials; and, if it does not seem patronising, we thought they advanced rapidly from the stage-Irishman image of a leisurely and antiquated bureaucracy in the early years of the Free State to the highly professional public service which they soon became. I prefer not to ask what they think of us! But once again my regret is that they did not much more often come North over all the years. I did a little count recently and I reckon that I must have paid about a hundred visits to the South, during my lifetime, in holidays, in attendance at rugby internationals, in visits to the theatre and in official journeys. I question whether my opposite numbers have been to the North once, twice, three times, four times?

The other great apparatus for getting out and about was attendance at professional conferences, one of the very, very few plums in our truly spartan lives. In the departments in which I worked, we made a deliberate point of sending a couple of our officers to each major conference, one a professional man and one a lay administrator. I am absolutely sure that this was a wise policy for a small provincial government and that it paid handsomely in terms of understanding, breadth of outlook, contacts and the spread of a tiny bit of enlightenment in the world concerning Ulster. I myself attended with the sanitary inspectors at Bridlington, the municipal treasurers at Torquay, the planners at Cambridge, the port medical officers at Newport, Monmouthshire, the public health doctors at Harrogate; my colleagues in the office had similarly privileged encounters with the dentists, the nurses, the architects and so on at some equally delightful places.

Apart from the intrinsic interest of these conferences there was one other attraction for us, namely the challenge of trying to persuade the professional bodies to hold one of their conferences in Belfast. And we certainly managed to do so. We had the pleasure of entertaining the doctors, the dentists, the town planners, the architects, the chartered surveyors, the highway engineers —to mention only a few in those fields with which I was concerned. The members of these bodies seemed to enjoy their conferences in Ulster; we were part of the United Kingdom and yet so different, the reception facilities at Stormont (both outdoor and indoor) were unparalleled, and above all, the personal welcome was warm and genuine. I used to study this particular aspect. When one went to a conference in England there was a formal reception by the mayor and mayoress and the president and his lady on the first evening; *et praeterea nihil,* if I do not sound ungrateful. Once at Torquay, in a detached mood and free to look at the scene dispassionately, I noted that throughout the whole conference not a single person from the association or the municipality addressed me, spoke to me or in any way connected with me. How different at Stormont! The hosts were invariably pleased to have the visitors, they made them welcome, they asked where they came from and tried to establish links, they took them to their homes or offices. I believe we can do the conference business in a happier and more personal way than most countries do—save possibly the Irish Republic who surpass us all in the arts of entertainment.

The Northern Ireland Agent in Great Britain, with his office first in Cockspur Street, then in Lower Regent Street and finally in Berkeley Street, provided a focus for some of our work in London. He did not in any way stand between us and the authorities there. Rather did he provide ministers and senior officers with a useful base, with office facilities, with accommodation for press briefings and for receptions. My brother Harry is now in charge of this office, where he is concentrating on industrial and commercial development.

I have set out our various extraterritorial activities systematically here in order to show how each of them arose; but of course the pattern was not always so clear. There were countless activities that took us out of Ulster spasmodically, from the Ministry of Labour official in my early days going to the Birmingham labour exchange to arrange for Birmingham job vacancies to be notified to our out-of-work men, to the sophisticated activities of our industrial promotion men calling nowadays on British firms pointing out the sites and labour resources available for expansion in Ulster.

Our work also took us abroad. Our industrial development officers comb the continent of Europe with considerable success. Our veterinary staff tell their European counterparts of their methods for eradicating brucellosis in cattle. I myself was lucky enough to be able to undertake several missions, all of which I found stimulating and thoroughly enjoyable.

In the early 1950s I was invited to a World Health Organisation seminar at Mégève in the Haute Savoie, where I had to explain, in French, the workings of the new British national health service to experts from some twenty different countries. Later I took part in working sessions of the public health committee of the Western European Union. It is due, in a minuscule degree, to my diplomatic prowess that, when you are today carried across the English Channel on a stretcher, the stretcher will fit equally well into an English or a French or a Belgian or a Dutch ambulance! On a rather grander scale was our work on the housing and town planning committee of Economic Cooperation in Europe, run by the United Nations in the Palais des Nations at Geneva. This had the real flavour of international diplomacy: splendid chambers, national name cards on green baize tables, strictly worked out placings that included the USSR, the Eastern countries, some fifteen other European countries and the USA, and that fascinating service of simultaneous verbatim translation into two or three languages. I feel constrained to add, in truth, that it achieved as little as most such conferences do. It fell to me to lead the United Kingdom delegation but, alas, we became bogged down with interminable bickering over the way in which housing statistics should be published, with each country holding out for the form of presentation which showed it in the most favourable light: numbers of dwellings as against numbers of habitable rooms, urban housing only as against all housing, and so on.

There arrived for me one day out of the blue an attractive invitation to travel to Frankfurt-am-Main to deliver a paper to a symposium of German bankers, builders, architects and lawyers. The subject matter was—just wait for it!—the rent restriction laws in Britain, possibly the most intricate code of law in the statute book. And I was being asked to deliver it in German. And my German has all the innocent charm of the schoolroom of the pre-Versailles era. But to make up for all those daunting difficulties the arrangements were superb: hospitality by a large German bank, meeting in a delightful spa at Bad Homburg, and transport everywhere by the directors' Mercedes. I was invited again a couple of years later; this time I was to speak on the British new towns. These tolerant people asked me for yet a third time; now it was to be on the subject of slum clearance and redevelopment. All this took place in the early 1960s and even then it was easy to discern the widening gap between their rapidly rising standards and the halting progress being made in Britain. Years later the whole episode was recalled to mind when I was made an honorary member of the West German Institute for Housing and Town Planning in a ceremony on the romantically beautiful Godesburg at Bad Godesberg. I cannot fully express my appreciation of the kindness and generosity of my German friends. I had known Germany and the German people since 1934. My three visits to Bad Homburg in the 1960s had therefore depth upon depth of interest and enjoyment.

There were other visits to Europe as well. One of the most instructive without any doubt was a study trip to Denmark and Sweden, to see hospitals, libraries, town halls, museums and so on. These I found staggeringly beautiful. For people engaged in municipal and public development work in Britain a study visit to Denmark or Holland is, in my view, more rewarding than any other foreign visit. Sweden is less helpful, I find, because of the exceptionally high standards that are for the most part plainly beyond our reach. The Latin countries are so different from Britain in make-up and in outlook that the British visitor must find it harder to learn from them. I have no hesitation in urging that many of our public officials should be sent on study visits to northern Europe and that the money would be well spent.

My wife joined me on several of these journeys, and she and I managed privately to get to Italy, Greece, Israel and Russia to see other things for ourselves. We went many times to Germany and paid sentimental journeys to places I had known as a student there forty years earlier. It was in the course of all these travels that I built up a collection of some sixty dictionaries and grammar books, for I enjoy puzzling out a few phrases in the language of each country visited and fitting together some patterns of vocabulary and of syntax.

To sustain the rash claim in the heading of this chapter I must now hurry on to tell how the Northern Ireland civil service touches even the American continent.

Commerce keep a representative in New York to look after our industrial and commercial interests. Our information staff visit occasionally in order to work up certain specialised aspects of information and tourism such as the Ulster-Scots influence on the history of the United States, helping the genealogical societies there; the long list of presidents who stemmed from Ulster, the Mellon connection, and so on, form a fruitful field of interest to Americans with a longing for historical roots. And of course many of our specialist officers had been to conferences in the States and some had taught there. I myself had never been and had no thought of going, until suddenly one day the whole scene burst open for me.

On a Monday, at lunch-time, I was asked by the Cabinet Secretariat whether I would be willing to set off for Washington on the Wednesday morning. The Foreign Office could use someone with an intimate and objective knowledge of Ulster in order to help the embassy there with preparations for a set of congressional hearings on the Ulster question starting on the following Monday; and to answer questions from a number of congressmen who—wisely, in the embassy view—wished to inform themselves on the facts before those hearings began. After I had decided to go, I was told that I should in the course of the Tuesday be able to collect some dollars at the bank down-town; get a visa at the American consulate, and have myself vaccinated at the doctor's surgery. On that same Tuesday I was chairing an interview board all day; and it was one that I did not wish to drop as it affected the careers and prospects of senior men in local government who were being badly upset by our wholesale reorganisation under Macrory. In the interstices between interviews I managed to complete all my obligations under international travel regulations!

Wednesday saw Fred Corbett and me arrive at Dulles airport in a blizzard and complete a long day with talks with our embassy officials. My first engagement next morning was unfortunately the all-important one of a briefing session with congressmen on Capitol Hill. This was something of an occasion. Our embassy colleagues swirled us around the great Congress buildings, transported us from one section to another by underground train, no less, and finally landed us in a roomful of representatives. The building was to my taste vastly overheated; my vaccination was itching madly; I was not quite orientated after the transatlantic flight; I could not, for the life of me, tell the difference between a Republican and a Democrat in front of my very eyes; and there I was striving, with all the in-burnt conscientiousness of the trained administrative civil servant, to answer the questions fairly, accurately, objectively. Quite a day.

His Excellency the Ambassador called the embassy staff together so that I could harrow their feelings with tales from the Ulster battle-front. And then there followed something which I had often heard about, namely the stream of pressing invitations to come and talk to groups of interested people in Washington: the *Washington Post*, the *Washington Star*, an assembled bunch of mid-western editors, a religious seminary (including an unmarried father whose baby howled incessantly in his arms in the noisy canteen where we were talking), a tourist trade association and so on. The tales I had heard as a child from emigrant relatives were borne out: fresh, interested people, anxious to learn, most hospitable and generous. On Saturday morning I took a run out of town to see what proved to be a place of ineffable beauty, George Washington's home at Mount Vernon, Virginia, overlooking Chesapeake Bay. That evening I left for home, determined to be clear of Capitol Hill, Washington and the American continent before the politicians and witnesses began to arrive on the Monday for the congressional hearings. My job was finished.

Chapter 24

THE COMMONWEALTH AND BEYOND

When my permanent secretary, L G P Freer told me in 1953 that he was nominating me for a course at the Imperial Defence College I had little idea of what a treat was in store. I had heard of the college and I realised that it was the top military academy in the commonwealth; but that was all I knew in my ignorance.

The course ran for a complete year, from new year till Christmas. The college occupied a handsome building in a London square. There were sixty of us. Most were soldiers, sailors or airmen, from the United Kingdom forces or from those of Canada, South Africa, India, Pakistan, Australia or New Zealand. And the college had begun to admit students from the USA as well. Most, as I say, were servicemen; but there were a few civilians as well, from the diplomatic service, the colonial service, the world of aeronautical research and telecommunications; I suppose I could be said to represent the social services and social administration. The essential point, in personal terms, was that we had all come straight from jobs of great intensity and pressure. General Mike West had been commanding the Commonwealth Brigade in Korea; D A Kendrew had been winning his fourth DSO; others had been in charge of ships, air stations, embassies, research units and so on at the peak of their active working lives. We were around forty years of age, and the ranks were roughly those of brigadier, air commodore or naval captain. Suddenly we were students in the leisurely setting of library and lecture room, with no responsibilities to anyone and with no pressures whatever upon us. The change was enormous. For a time we actually felt guilty at having nothing to do, as it seemed. The feeling soon wore off, I am glad to record.

The pattern was the familiar one of selected themes, lectures, problems, seminars. But a vast difference between this College and others was soon to be secerned.

A theme would run for several weeks, for example racial problems in America, defence problems in south east Asia, economic problems in western Europe, political problems in the emerging African states. Each day a different lecturer would arrive and speak on the theme as he saw it. We might hear, in a typical sequence, a foreign ambassador in London, one of our ambassadors abroad, a Harvard professor, a trade union leader, an archbishop, a permanent secretary, a company director, an American journalist, an army chief and so on. Each theme was therefore attacked from a different angle each day. The subject matter was turned round and round for possibly three weeks. We soon found a pattern appearing. The better lectures, the brighter and more attractive lectures, were given by the freelance or independent operators; but when it came to answering questions they had not so much to contribute. The people carrying responsibility for command or management may not have sparkled in delivering their set talks but stood up a great deal better to the searching questions which this lively company put to them; they had experience under their belts and that always counts. The question and answer sessions were fascinating. A group of active people, from various disciplines and differing countries, with nothing else to do for the moment but make up the subject, could extract a great deal from every lecturer. Seminars, too, were revealing. Here services, disciplines, countries, races and religions were pitted one against another in attempts to solve insoluble problems. Another unusual pleasure lay in the opportunity between lectures and seminars to drop into the library and read an article in one of the great array of learned journals which the college took. One might read of the colour problems of America in a Pakistani journal, of the Australian economy in a South African off-print, of a Soviet administrative failure in an Indian monthly.

But the outside visits we made were possibly unique. We carried out a constant stream. All were immaculately prepared. We were briefed in advance. When we got there, we were given top-level treatment. Under those matchless conditions we visited many of the key institutions of Britain. Another highlight was the industrial tour. In the spring of the year it was customary to send the students out in carefully arranged batches, one to the midlands, one to the north-west and so on. One party always went to Ulster and dined out on travellers' tales for years afterwards. I was sent to the north-east of England and spent a useful week going down coalmines, watching glass-blowing, breathing the hot air of steel furnaces and so on. And we did all this in the constantly changing company of men from all over the commonwealth. Each experience we had, each novelty we saw, each new idea put to us was tested not only by ourselves but by the companion we happened to have with us at the moment—a Canadian soldier, an Australian diplomat, an Indian airman. Leaning over the new balcony in the stock exchange one day and looking down on the hectic activity on the floor, my Muslim friend vouchsafed to me quietly, 'Of course you know usury is forbidden by the Koran?'

One highlight eclipses another. The foreign tour each summer surpassed all else. In my year we had a choice of three. Some went to America; some to Europe; I picked the middle east and was glad I did. This was a wonderful experience. About twenty of us set off, stuffed full of information about what we were going to see. We had our own plane and here was our itinerary: Malta, Egypt, Cyprus, Turkey, Baghdad, Bahrein and the Persian Gulf, the islands in the Indian Ocean, Aden, Somaliland, Uganda, Kenya, Northern and Southern Rhodesia, Sudan, Nigeria, Gold Coast and Libya. We were received in each place by extremely well-informed people who placed their knowledge and experience at our disposal. Admiral Lord Mountbatten and Kwame Nkrumah spanned the spectrum as I look back now. We had never been so well informed about world affairs in our lives previously; and we were not likely to be so well informed ever again.

What were the benefits of this experience?

First I am bound to put the fact of being free of responsibility and pressure for a year. I said earlier that we all came straight from hard, pressing jobs. And when we left, we quickly became caught up in hard pressing jobs again; for months and for years afterwards I watched the columns of *The Times* and saw my colleagues becoming commanders in chief, First Sea Lord, head of the diplomatic service, director of telecommunications at the Post Office and officers of similar standing—and, I knew, with similar burdens of work and worry. To be free for a year, to study, to listen, to read, to learn was heavenly. Next I must list the sheer value of information and of knowledge of the workings of the commonwealth. Then there was the inestimable advantage of learning to see a problem from every angle. How often men and women of real ability, energy and goodwill make a contribution to affairs that is ruined by their total inability to see points of view other than their own. I seek to make no political or moral point here; I am dealing in the most elementary terms of ability to take a problem, even one that is pressing on one's own interests, and turn it round a few times to see how it must appear to others.

One learned other lessons as well. One got an insight into the military mind; the soldiers gained some insight into the mind of the administrator and the diplomat; we all gained a fresh understanding of the American concept of the old world; one was admitted to a freemasonry that embraced a good part of the world and that in a modest way vindicates my little claim (with Charles Wesley) to 'look upon all the world as my parish'.

Part III

PAST, PRESENT AND FUTURE

Chapter 25

A VARIETY OF MEN

While the civil service is part of the machinery of government, has to do with formal business, and is shaped by many constraints, it is still composed of individual people and, as shown in various chapters, I am anxious at all times to bring out this personal and human element. Having both outlined the broad development of the service in part I and analysed some of its principles and methods in part II, I now turn to the question: What are the qualities of the administrative civil servant?

It would be easy to draw up a fine-sounding list of qualities: intelligence, hard work, imagination, courage, persistence and so on. A more realistic approach is to look at some of the men who in fact made up the service in our time and see what qualities they actually possessed. That is the approach I now adopt in the hope that it may illuminate what has been said in the earlier parts and, within a personal dimension, draw together the various aspects of the whole story. Before I start on this risky enterprise let me make it clear that I do not seek to write the obituaries of my colleagues nor presume to offer any balanced appraisal of their characters, but simply to record the qualities that were relevant to their place in the service and at the same time perhaps record something of the variety of men. And as the observer of the human condition, Honoré de Balzac, wrote, '[Men reveal] *les défauts de leurs qualités.*

Brilliance. Our wartime lives were dominated by William Angus Boyd Iliff, an extremely bright, energetic, almost electric person who loved to shock us all with his vivid language and his irascibility. After a lengthy discussion on some intricate subject late one evening, he would come back to the office next morning with a complete memorandum, telling us that he had done it on the strength of a bottle of whiskey and a very beautiful typist. Our service could not hold the restless Iliff who went off to the middle east as a financial adviser and eventually became vice-president of the World Bank.

In Eric Scales we had the complete Dubliner. A classics graduate of Trinity College, son-in-law of the provost, debonair, charming, he made everything look easy, from dictating a minute on the legal powers of the Home Guard to singing 'Cockles and Mussels'. L G P Freer was a triple-first from Trinity, and a man of immense authority, but so reserved and restrained that his influence in the service was never as great as it should have been.

Strong personality. By far the greatest influence in my direct experience was Ronald Green, a Lurgan Quaker who came into the service as a boy clerk and became a permanent secretary. Here was a man of drive. Essentially an individualist, he found the prevailing doctrine of collective decision-making in the ministry irksome in the extreme, never suffering fools gladly and having strong likes and dislikes amongst his colleagues. Still those of us who were closest to him found it exhilarating to see him crash through the gears of the official machine and single-handed send it off at top speed. There would be chaos if every senior officer acted in that way; but there is little risk of that in modern times. Large, impressive, courageous, he could achieve what seemed impossible. He was immensely well-read, a chess player, a broadcaster in Round Britain Quiz, a yachtsman, a gardener, a delightful host and always able to illuminate any situation with a witty and absolutely apt phrase. He was generous in personal matters. Above all he had a capacious understanding for the whole public scene. I owe a lot to him. A man of this sort does not waste effort on courting popularity and inevitably has many detractors.

One cannot think of Ronald Green without thinking also of his colleague, friend and neighbour James Aitken, an architect and planner trained at the School of Art in his native Edinburgh. James was the artist *par excellence,* perceptive in all things visual and musical. It was an education to travel with him as he would stop and draw attention to a building, a doorway, an old man, a pretty girl; or sketch a caricature on a menu-card; or compose a parody to be sung at the final session of some conference. The office was never again as interesting and as colourful a place after James died. Many people outside the service will concur with that remark for he had an extraordinary number of friends and professional colleagues whom he somehow attracted to his room at Stormont. In its day this was a form of communication and participation, bringing many people from the business, professional and artistic world into easy and fruitful relationship with government.

The Ulster countryside owes a lot to Dick Rogers, a quiet, modest and unassuming man who devoted much of his private life and the best years of his office career to the protection and improvement of the beautiful hills, valleys and fields of this Province. Many of us were lifelong admirers of his culture, his knowledge, his good humour and his steadfastness in the face of real adversity. Each time I see a street or a square in some Ulster town named after some local councillor I wish I could name some whole range of mountains and valleys 'Dick Rogers Land' and I know for sure that many would acclaim the title. It is customary to hold a little ceremony when a colleague retires and to hand over some gift, but we are not at our best on these occasions and the speeches too often remain stilted and self-conscious. When Dick was retiring in the early 1970s he struck a note which immediately obtained a genuine response from the company of his colleagues: 'Come to think of it, my forty-seven years roughly corresponds with the notorious Fifty Years of Misrule. In all that time I was never asked to do (nor was it suggested to me directly or indirectly that I should do) anything dishonourable or anything which I or any self-respecting official would consider unworthy.' It is a rule in the service, and a wise one, that a man is better not to be engaged officially in the administration of any function in which he has a close personal interest, even of a purely charitable, voluntary and non-commercial nature. This often strikes the observer as an odd rule, for he may well imagine that the official will do his job better if he has direct knowledge of the subject matter. The trouble is that he will not only have knowledge but also personal sympathies, particular attachments and so on that are liable to involve him emotionally and to render him less impartial than he ought to be; and, even if he behaves impeccably, are sure to make him seem less impartial in the eyes of other people with rival connections. The keen amateur archaeologist in charge of grants for archaeology; the enthusiastic opera-goer with a say in grants to opera—these are the situations that the service tries to avoid. But the rule can be successfully ignored at times. Dick Rogers for example served for many years on the administration of laws and finances dealing with the protection of the countryside after having spent a lifetime as an enthusiastic voluntary worker in the preservation of the countryside, the youth hostels, the National Trust and other similar endeavours. The experiment worked well. Maybe the service is too stuffy and too sensitive on such matters.

Has personal charm a place in official life? If there was one man in the service who made no enemies it was R F R Dunbar, the Dubliner of infinite charm, patience, good-humour and, yes, timelessness.

Has grit a place? The first Ulsterman ever to become head of the Ulster civil service was Cecil Bateman, a man who taught us all how to get things done by sheer commonsense, hard work and tenacity. Practical and humane, Cecil assumed no pose, put on no airs and graces but simply clenched his teeth and pushed his business along. It is little wonder that he was invited to join several business concerns when he retired, and was a boon to them.

Does hard work not compensate for a lot of other shortcomings? It does and it doesn't. Although it may sound ungrateful to say so, there is such a fault as being over-zealous in a good cause. The hardest worker I met in the service was E H Jones, with whom I shared a room at the thrilling stage of the post-war reconstruction in 1946–48. He worked enormously long hours, his work was real work with no pretence, and his output was prodigious. He was utterly searching and comprehensive in everything he put his hand to. After researching the needs of blood transfusion as a part of the newly emerging health service he made a submission to the Ministry of Finance in the form of a letter running to 127 paragraphs, number 127 stating (sincerely but unnecessarily), 'If however there is any further information required . . .' When we reached ten o'clock one night I threw down my pen and declared that I would catch the last bus, leaving the office at 10.20; he declined to come with me, declaring 'I haven't managed to get much done today; do you mind if I stay a bit longer?' Later when he became secretary to the Northern Ireland Hospitals Authority, we parted on the street late one evening after a prize distribution ceremony for student nurses, with the plaintive cry from Eric Jones: 'I must go back to the office now. I always use the peace and quiet to clear up some things.' It was admittedly hard work like this that gave the Hospitals Authority a flying start over English Regional Boards on 5 July, 1948.

In an indirect way one of the most influential men in our departmental life over many years was our senior solicitor George Hamilton. In a complex department with many specialities and with much legislation a solicitor actually working day by day alongside the administrators can be of immense value in keeping busy and over-anxious officials on the rails; we certainly insisted on having Hamilton in the closest contact with us in the various branches. It was from him that most of us learned our respect for the law and the judicial processes, the importance of a cold impartial scrutiny, the demands of natural justice, the value of well-chosen words, the unique obligations imposed on a public department by anything in the nature of a quasi-judicial function, such as the granting or withholding of a vesting order for compulsory acquisition of land or the determination of a planning appeal. His knowledge of the law affecting public bodies was, and is, outstanding and many a private practitioner has beaten a path to his office door in search of discreet advice.

Is it possible for one man to influence a whole course of events in public affairs? That is precisely the achievement of George Scott Robertson during the 1920s, 1930s and 1940s. A Scotsman educated at Durham University, he came to the Queen's University of Belfast in 1921 as lecturer in agricultural chemistry, became professor in 1924, and then Dean of the Faculty as it was developing its dual role as university faculty and also research and advisory service to the ministry. In 1928 he moved over into administration and in 1933 he became permanent secretary (after an extraordinary episode in which the outgoing permanent secretary tried to secure the appointment of a succcessor of his own choosing—only to find that the staff would not have him). A subsequent permanent secretary, speaking at the university in 1972 (and speaking with inner knowledge) when delivering the George Scott Robertson Memorial Lecture, was able to declare: 'As an administrator Scott Robertson is remembered as a man who got things done'. No higher praise in the eyes of the civil servant; and the tribute may have carried just a tinge of envy when the ability of one official 'to get things done' is viewed from the more complex and frustrating administrative scene of the 1970s. However, here was a man who both knew what to do and how to do it. It was not a case of a mystic vision or blinding revelation. It was a case of asking 'What are the assets of agriculture in Ulster? What are its shortcomings? What needs to be done?' and then of setting about it. The founding of the Agricultural Research Institute at Hillsborough, County Down; the variety of marketing schemes that both raised the standard and made the fullest use of local produce; the organisation of food production during the war—these and other practical achievements testify to the insight, understanding and energy of one official. Such a man is not always the easiest of colleagues, he may have scant regard for the problems of other departments (as I found), his methods will not be universally acclaimed, he will have little time or patience for a weak minister, but he gets things done.

Is there a useful place for a man with a rare combination of talents? One town planner stands out in the service on account of his unusual qualities. In Cecil Newman we had not only a planner, but a great many other things as well: a mapper, a calligrapher, a photographer, an aerial photographer, a rifle-shot, a guitarist, a folk singer, a linguist—I need go no further. An evening looking at a selection of coloured slides of superb quality combining views of unspoilt countryside (taken by helicopter on a sparkling Sunday morning) with pictures of sheer vandalism committed by those vandals in the various public utility services —a memorable experience not matched anywhere I have been.

And on the other hand, is there room for a man with no remarkable talents? When the department once had to issue some press statement about Caldwell Hoey, those responsible for preparing it wanted to omit all references to particular experience or past appointments and instead to write quite simply 'He is a good civil servant. That is his achievement.' I was moved by that tribute and subscribed to it in the case of this consistently fair, humane, practical and totally unpretentious administrator.

Most good offices can boast one or two literary men. We certainly had our writers, our poets and our historians. One who had the gift for language, for expression and for repartee in a high degree was our Newry colleague, Paddy Shea, who became head of the Ministry of Education. He wrote successfully for broadcasting and must have contributed something special to life and work in his department.

We have been fortunate in our parliamentary draftsmen, that is to say the lawyers who advise departments on constitutional problems and who prepare new government legislation on their instructions. I referred to Arthur Quekett, and the great importance of the post, in an earlier chapter. He was succeeded by Jack Caldwell, a delightfully fresh and uninhibited man who pretended he was no lawyer but only a sort of carpenter who could knock together a few clauses to make up a bill. He was a pleasure to work with, ready, helpful and generous.

His successor—Bill Leitch—was a powerful man in every way, an able lawyer, indeed a muscular lawyer, a combatant, a courageous fighter for causes dear to his constitutional ideals, a man who never let the bone go with the dog. Nothing and no one overawed him. I was present in the Palace of Westminster when he forcefully debated the constitution with the Lord Chancellor of the day; and many of us have been witnesses when he went out of his way repeatedly to educate the British Home Office in the verities of Irish law and Irish legal practices—a sadly necessary, if uphill task, as he saw it. Here was a draftsman of really colossal ability. In the course of a consultation we would ask, on behalf of the department, for some new point to be included in the bill he was drafting for us, whereupon he would lean back in his chair, puff his pipe and dictate off the cuff an intricate clause which not only did what we wanted but also struck a blow for some worthy legal cause he had been seeking to promote. Such a clause seldom needed correction or improvement when we later saw it in typescript. It was not that I was ever in much of a position to learn from those legal skills, but rather that I always came away from our consultations encouraged and emboldened to fight harder for the things that were worthwhile in public life.

If I were to come any closer to the present day I should find myself getting too far in amongst my personal friends and recent colleagues and that is something I do not wish to do. I prefer to go back again over the years and recall the skills and contributions of some officers in the more junior ranks who gave top-class service without becoming known. I keep thinking again and again how true of Ulster are the words which Tolstoy slipped into an appreciation he was writing of a story by Chekhov: 'The best of all as the unknown always are'. I seize this opportunity to place something on record about men and women whose names would otherwise go unrecorded in history and to emphasise again the variety of men.

When I set foot in the factories branch in 1937, the working arrangements there were controlled by Bob Maltman, a clerk of ability, energy and (that other quality in good clerks) the knack of knowing where every document was, of finding it and of turning up with it at the right moment. He was a disciplinarian in the essential drills of filing papers, recording information and instilling respect for official records. There were times when we suspected that he arranged matters so that he personally could be seen to be the indispensable man, but no matter. He illustrated the contention that administration can better be learned on the job than in any training school.

Trade union organisation is strong in the civil service here, and though it seldom receives publicity it nevertheless is an effective force in the negotiation of terms and conditions. I received my

induction through Joe Patton, one of the early radical thinkers
and a man both skilled in rational argument and strong in his
human sympathies.

Although I have written earlier that few women have been
appointed to the higher ranks, it is a fact that some have been
extremely influential in particular positions. Two stand out.

Rachel Best was the person who masterminded the personnel
work of the Ministry of Development throughout the great years
of the 1960s. By a combination of commonsense, human interest
and a disarming frankness and directness of approach this excellent
woman made it her business to get to know everyone in the department—uniformed messengers, temporary clerks, professional
heads and so on—as well as their personal strengths and weaknesses, with the result that we probably had fewer unhappy misfits
than any comparable office. An official of Glenavon football club
in Lurgan, she was always on the lookout for energetic young
people who might be pining away in the prison-house that is the
office. She set herself the particular aim of spotting the keen and
able young entrants, giving them opportunities and bringing
them on in a manner that would gladden the heart of every head-
master and headmistress persuaded into recommending the service
as a career.

Eileen Lyons was another of our women staff who greatly influenced the office. The immaculate private secretary, she not only
kept the minister's accommodation and arrangements in perfect
order but established the highest degree of efficiency that we ever
achieved in day-to-day and minute-to-minute service to the minister. Our papers had to be absolutely complete, accurate, capable
of standing up to any criticism, and it seemed to us that the dead-
line for submission was always yesterday. Was it a coincidence, a
fortunate or unfortunate arrangement, that Eileen Lyons served
for most of her spell in the private office as private secretary to
Dame Dehra Parker, a most distinguished minister but hardly
the most consistent of human beings?

Let me conclude this catalogue by jotting down a few more
names of colleagues who stand out clearly in totally different ways.
Bill McClintock achieved the rare feat of serving for forty-nine
years, having gone from his home in Tandragee at the age of
sixteen to the customs service in the London docks at the height
of the first world war. Jack Donaldson was the craftiest of operators and was responsible for coining the useful aphorism 'If a bad
mistake is made on a file, look out, for there is sure to be a
second'. William Henderson (theosophist or Rosicrucian or was

it anthroposophist?) after an office life of, shall we say, relaxed contemplation handed over his job to me at one stage with the remark 'We who have borne the burden and heat of the day . . .' A P FitzGerald (I have got the spelling exactly as he would have wished) studious, urbane and analytical, enshrined himself for me in the characteristic phrase with which he always helped his exposition of a subject along: 'At this point I ask myself the question . . .' I am being petty here and I know that our colleague Norman Dugdale has enshrined the man much more suitably in his poem:

> Died as he lived, an apostate; was burned
>   without the benefit of clergy.
> Flowers, music, prayers one Saturday—a few
>   Colleagues at hand, to do their duty.
>
> And making cumbrous jokes about his name
>   And family's heritage and pride
> That brooked no compromise. It struck me then
>   He meant it all. Lived as he died
>
> In scorn of pliant men who'd rather
>   Bend than break: gave what was due
> In honour forty years, took nothing back
>   Except the means of holding to
>
> His passion for astronomy.

Billy Stewart came from Ballyclare. And here I might interpolate an interpretation of Ulster society from the sociologists at the Queen's University to the effect that it is essentially a derivative or ascriptive society, in the sense that everyone likes to know where everyone else comes from, what their background is, where their origins lie and so on. This is true of the Northern Ireland civil service too and I believe it is one of the influences which has kept it human and prevented it from becoming a bureaucracy. Officers are known to one another by name, not by branch or designation. (Significantly perhaps it was in the former Ministry of Home Affairs that the only attempt was made to address officers as PH or PM.) The common practice has always been to say that you are going to see Noel Cox in Finance rather than AS2 or AS (Misc) or whatever. Not only is the name used but often also a description that will help to place the man—'the Foyle man' or 'the man from Mallow' or 'the fellow who came to us from the Farmers' Union'. I am sure this is all to the good.

Billy Stewart came from Ballyclare.

Billy was an example of the man who used whatever talents he had to the fullest extent. He explored every dark corner and there were no fuzzy edges to his thinking. He had the great ability to get the best out of every part of the machinery of the service: registry, accounts, stationery office, ordnance survey, valuation office, registry of deeds and a score of other offices were all made to operate at maximum usefulness to our department. He managed to set aside a few minutes every day to instruct his staff about the wider implications of their work. On top of everything else he ran the civil service choir. He died, as too many of our people have done, from a heart attack in his fifties. Let me leave it at that.

Chapter 26

SOURCES

It will be plain by now that the sources on which I have relied have been quite simply my experience as an ordinary person born and brought up in the Province and as an official working in its public service. That being so, it would be pointless to try to document and support every memory and every impression gained over a lifetime. What is more, given the personal style in which these chapters have been written, it would interrupt the flow of the narrative to insert detailed references in the text or to be-spatter the pages with tedious footnotes referring to acts of parliament, Blue Books and so on. I ask the reader to accept my word and, if he wishes to go more closely into any particular point, to turn to the relevant publications which I now try to summarise.

The most convenient reflection of public affairs in Ulster since 1921 is probably to be found in the columns of Hansard, the official report of every word spoken in the House of Commons and the Senate and later in the Assembly of 1973–74. Constructive or destructive, positive or negative, the debate is on record; ministers pronounce, opposition attack and backbenchers plead or press or obstruct. Even if debates were not always well informed nor speeches well researched the pages of Hansard do record in handy form the flow of business and the spirit of the times. And the speeches of ministers introducing bills or motions held a mirror to the thinking behind that business. For an understanding of the spirit of the times few publications are more revealing than the debates of the Commons in their first session running from 7 June till 14 December 1921. This slight volume reveals a state of outside events pressing on ministers that bears a depressing resemblance to the state of events of the 1970s.

The acts of parliament are then the second main source—both the public and general acts and the local and private acts. Even closer to the problems of administration are the annual volumes of statutory rules, orders and regulations, the subordinate instruments made by departments under powers conferred on them by the statutes.

Since that field is obviously too vast for anyone to try to study comprehensively it may be helpful to draw attention here to a few acts which illustrate what can be done by a subordinate parliament to legislate independently in order to cope with a local problem in a realistic and economical way:

The Ministries of Northern Ireland Act (NI) 1921, setting up the new ministries as corporate bodies and laying down the ground rules in brief convenient form

Section 22 and the second schedule to the Local Government Act (NI) 1934, providing a fair and effective procedure for the compulsory acquisition of land in the form of the vesting order which has proved in many cases superior to the corresponding provisions for compulsory purchase orders in Great Britain

The Great Northern Railway Act (NI) 1953, dealing with cross-border arrangements

The Flags and Emblems Act (NI) 1954, dealing in plain terms with a problem which had been causing constant trouble and embarrassment on the streets of Ulster. Unfortunately, this problem remains and is a salutary example of the type of problem which no legislation can eradicate

The New Universities (Acquisition of Land) Act (NI) 1966, empowering local authorities to acquire land and make it over to any new university

The Agricultural Trust Act (NI) 1966 setting up a new body to undertake pioneering work

Various acts permitting and regulating the use of public roads for motor-car and motor-cycle racing in 1922, 1932, 1950 and 1952. Here was a subject in which the general public was greatly interested, which represented a lucrative form of tourist revenue but which of course raised fundamental questions concerning freedom to use the Queen's highways. Section 1 of the Road Traffic Act (NI) 1968 embodies the special form of legislation on the breathalyser test which Home Affairs insisted on holding back for a year until they had perfected it, despite enormous local pressure the previous year to 'follow England' with a less good test

The Resettlement Services Act (NI) 1971 provided in three short sections for a system of mobility grants as inducements to people to move from Belfast out to planned growth centres. A remarkable example of a short simple act of parliament directed at helping to solve a profound economic, social and human problem

The Payments for Debt (Emergency Provisions) Act (NI) 1971, creating entirely new and unpalatable law to deal with one of the most intractable problems in modern society, namely the deliberate withholding of rent, rates and gas and electricity payments.

These are just a few examples of many acts of parliament promoted to meet special local situations. All are short and clear. The British Royal Commission on the Constitution (Kilbrandon), interested in this question of the effective use made by the Stormont parliament of its devolved powers of legislation (confronted with the repeated accusation that Stormont merely rubber-stamped Westminister legislation), records that out of a total of 190 acts passed in a selected period of five years thirty-six closely followed Westminster statutes, seventy-six were peculiar to Northern Ireland, sixty-two fell somewhere in between while sixteen were of an essential, technical nature such as appropriation acts and consolidated fund acts. This small sample suggests—insofar as it is possible to count such matters—that there may have been something like a thousand measures either peculiar to Northern Ireland or substantially adapted to the special needs of the region between 1921 and 1972.

By far the most useful quarry for extracting facts and figures is without question the *Ulster Year Book,* of which about sixteen issues have now appeared, starting with 1926, 1929, 1932, 1935 and 1938. Each issue is packed full of reliable information and for the researcher there is the additional value attaching to the simple fact that the information was compiled contemporaneously with the events as they unfolded, and unwittingly reveals the atmosphere of the years in which it was recorded. I am looking as I write at a crude, hand-drawn graph in the 1926 issue which shows the percentage of unemployment wavering around the twenty per cent line and never dropping below fifteen. The 1929 issue records, without comment, a gentle but steady decline in the cost of living year by year. Neither the fact that the *Ulster Year Book* follows the same familiar layout time after time nor the prevalence of conventional photographs of royalty ought to be allowed to deter anyone wishing to trace the history of different aspects of public affairs. It would be helpful if every country had as clear and handy a record.

Most of the ministries and departments have published annual reports on the discharge of their statutory functions.

Another great source lies in the multitude of blue books, white papers and green papers published over the years. These are usefully noted in the bibliographies contained within each issue of the *Ulster Year Book*.

The last ten years or so have seen the emergence of a new form of presenting not only information but also departmental ideas and proposals: the Regional and Area Plan. The planned growth of hospitals for example was explained in the Hospital Plan 1966–75 (Command 497). Another good example was in the realm of forestry when *Forestry in Northern Ireland* (Command 550) in 1970 set out the plans of the Ministry of Agriculture for the future of this constructive and attractive industry. In the more general field of regional physical planning there was the Matthew report (Command 451) in 1963, published again in two volumes with handsome photographs and maps in 1964. The Wilson economic plan (Command 479) followed in 1965 and then came the Development Programme 1970–75 (no Command number but accompanied by a government white paper, Command 547, setting out an analysis of both physical and economic problems, along with proposals for dealing with them. These documents reached far down into the physical and economic activities of all departments. At the level of distinctive areas within Northern Ireland, a series of some fifteen illustrated Area Plans has appeared since 1963. Two of the more attractive were *Ulster Lakeland* in 1963 and *Mourne* in 1970, both of them capable of bearing comparison with similar work anywhere.

The references in the preceding paragraph, being of course highly selective, are intended only to illustrate some of the wealth of published material concerning the practical administration of the various departments and have to be read along with the comprehensive bibliographies included (under subject headings) in the *Ulster Year Book. A Catalogue and Breviate of [Stormont] Parliamentary Papers* by Arthur Maltby provides a helpful service to researchers in this particular field. It really was a labour of love for a librarian not only to read but also to summarise carefully such a wide range of admittedly dreary blue books of long ago.

Another fund of information is in the *Digest of Statistics* published half-yearly; over forty issues have now appeared.

Turning to published sources independent of government there is understandably little that has any bearing on the internal work of administration. The closest point is reached in the publication by Magee University College, Londonderry, of a series of papers read there during the session 1966–67. As several of the speakers were engaged in public work themselves, their findings and expositions are of considerable help to an understanding of the administrative situation. One of the most succinct and at the same time penetrating surveys of public affairs since 1921 was written by Martin Wallace in his *Northern Ireland: 50 years of Self-Government.* Hugh Shearman's *Northern Ireland 1921–71* is closer to the Unionist political position but remains a readable account of public affairs and has a wealth of valuable photographs. There is a huge amount of information (much of it surprising, and some of it liable to force one to reconsider one's most cherished myths) in Richard Rose's monumental work *Governing without Consensus.* I have looked again at some of the published material critical of the Northern Ireland situation to see whether it sheds any light on administrative problems here, but without result. Conor Cruise O'Brien's *States of Ireland,* Garret FitzGerald's *Towards a New Ireland,* Bernadette Devlin's *The Price of my Soul,* Rosemary Harris's *Prejudice and Tolerance in Ulster*—none help in this respect. John Darby comes closer to administrative problems in his book *Conflict in Northern Ireland* and includes a massive bibliography; but he does not manage to throw any light on the adminstrative process itself.

More than the servants of most other governments, Stormont officials are accustomed to see tendentious public statements made about government work on which they have been professionally engaged, statements that are often wholly wrong in fact or that they know (as few other people know) to be wildly misdirected. These form part of a constant flood of anti-Ulster propaganda, and the problem is to distinguish genuine political criticism from sheer distortion. It is none of their business to attempt to correct those statements; they can only hope that ministers will publish corrections or else they must sadly watch them pass into accepted mythology. As I certainly have no wish now to reopen old wounds, or to enter into any form of political controversy. I will simply pick as a small, obscure and harmless example a reference by Professor F S L Lyons in his learned, eight-hundred-page history of *Ireland Since the Famine.* In a footnote to page 751 he goes out of his way to summarise the history of local government reform in Northern Ireland from 1967 onwards. The impression conveyed is wholly derogatory. Yet the writer is obviously a scholar and he is presumably seeking to produce an objective piece of work. Looked at through my eyes, and I had a part in all the main stages of this reform, the five lines of print contain five errors—one concerning a date, two being misguided slants that bear no relation to the facts, and two being serious and relevant omissions.

James Callaghan in his book *A House Divided* gives an account of several important meetings at which Stormont as well as Whitehall officials were present in Stormont Castle in 1969. It was from decisions taken at those meetings that many of the events of the subsequent years in Ulster flowed, so that *A House Divided* is another relevant source-book. *Ulster Under Home Rule,* a collection of essays edited by Tom Wilson and published by Oxford University Press in 1955 analyses and tries to assess the achievements in various fields. R J Lawrence comes much closer to the problems of administration in his scholarly and well documented work *The Government of Northern Ireland: Public Finance and Public Services* 1921–64, published by Oxford University Press in 1965. A scientific survey worth recording is *Belfast in its Regional Setting,* prepared by local scholars in readiness for the visit to Belfast in 1952 of the British Association for the Advancement of Science.

But still most of the literature is by people, however learned and well-informed, who lacked the inside knowledge and understanding that come from working year in year out as a slave attending the machine. When therefore in the spring of 1950 the *Irish Times* published a series of thirteen articles by G C Duggan CB, OBE, LLD (former principal assistant secretary in the Ministry of Finance and former comptroller and auditor-general, by that time retired and living in the Irish Republic), and carrying the title *Northern Ireland—Success or Failure?*, one fell on them eagerly. They created a small sensation at the time and there were some hard words spoken about 'biting the hand that fed him' and so on. I have recently re-read the Duggan articles. They seem tame today. It is true that the whole tone is slightly deprecatory and the sense of humour mildly sardonic. He heads each article with a literary quotation and the one which graces article 11 on the Senate runs:

> We thought her dying when she slept
> And sleeping when she died
>
> (Thomas Hood)

which can hardly have been expected to please everyone. To my mind the only error he committed (and it was an egregious error by any standard) was to quote what Lord Craigavon said to him in 1937 in the course of a private conversation in his study at Stormont Castle. It was a conversation, without witnesses, between prime minister and senior official in a totally privileged and con-

fidential setting. As the subject was the extremely sensitive one of
the border and the prime minister's views on its permanence or
otherwise, few officials or ministers anywhere in the British parliamentary system would agree, even in the much more permissive
climate of today, that Duggan was right to record it. I make no
comment on the decision of the *Irish Times* to publish it. Despite
his candour on this one topic, Duggan does not tell us much about
administrative life, contenting himself rather with observations
and reminiscences of the public scene as well as extensive quota-
tions from debates in parliament. He could have served posterity
a great deal better if he had offered a comparison between administrative work in London, Dublin and Belfast (for he was one of a
tiny number who had the experience of working in all three systems) or if he had explained why it took from 1921 till 1938 or so
for the Ministry of Finance to reach an acceptable financial settlement with the British Treasury.

Going back still further, we find the pre-1922 Irish administration in Dublin well recorded and documented. The major work is
without question R B McDowell's book *The Irish Administration
1801–1914*. Everything is here: constitution, politics, personalities
and human interest as well as a detached appraisal of the development of the administration itself, board by board, office by office,
inspector by inspector. The second piece of obligatory reading, and
a most amusing one, is Sir Henry Robinson's *Memories Wise and
Otherwise*. My copy has the added benefit of having been anno-
tated in the margins by an anonymous colleague of Robinson's
(and eventually of mine) who took a much more pedestrian view
of the Irish scene and could not allow Robinson to tell any of his
countless anecdotes about experiences with local bodies and personalities without adding 'Pure invention' or 'I don't believe this
happened' or 'He would never have said this about the man if he
had still been alive' or 'How utterly insincere', a salutary gloss for
anyone else writing his memoirs! His most telling annotation
runs 'He (Robinson) represents the Irish people as ignorant idiots
or rogues', for it is indeed surprising how far Robinson lets himself go in telling anecdotes of the Somerville and Ross type in the
course of recording really important experiences and giving us
some penetrating insight into the workings of the government system.

The mention of one other source may encourage the researcher
dismayed by the paucity of good official records surviving in Ireland after the disastrous fire at the Public Record Office in Dublin
in 1922. Let him turn to any old copy of *Thom's Directory*, an

ordinary commercial street directory published by Alexander Thom and Co Ltd of Dublin. The copy to which I have access is for the year 1917 and contains 2 250 pages crammed, in small type, with an astonishing amount of useful information bearing directly on some of the matters I have been trying to deal with here.

Incidentally the *Belfast Street Directory* is not to be despised as a source-book. Year by year the compilers include some sixty pages of detailed and reliable information about government departments, local boards, voluntary bodies and so on, thus not only providing a handy book of current reference but also contributing substantially to the material of social and administrative history.

In writing a memoir of this sort one of the less obvious difficulties lies hidden in the blending of public affairs with personal experiences and the matching of official sources with personal impressions. How far should personal impressions be allowed to colour the official record of events and how far should the personal element be suppressed? For the dutiful civil servant this poses special problems. The best models are to be found in the memoirs of retired members of the diplomatic service and in three of them in particular—Duff Cooper's *Old Men Forget,* William Strang's *Home and Abroad,* and Ivone Kirkpatrick's *The Inner Circle* (London). Another memoir of the same kind is by Stephen Tallents, *Man and Boy* (London). Unfortunately his account stopped in 1920, tantalisingly short of the period when he served as private secretary to the Lord Lieutenant of Ireland. Tallents was present with him at the opening of the first parliament in Belfast in 1921 and his impressions of the occasion would have been interesting, for he wrote with verve.

In the search for first-hand accounts of life in a government office one could keep on ransacking at random the pages of English literature until one finds oneself reading Samuel Pepys or, even further back, that well-known civil servant who saw through the foibles and pretences of his colleagues, warning us

> No-wher so bisy a man he ther nas,
> And yet he seemed bisier than he was.
>   Chaucer (*Man of Law*)

One of the most important sources of all to be acknowledged here is the experience and judgment of several of my colleagues who saw the manuscript of this work and were good enough to offer their detailed, written criticisms. Sincere thanks are due to them for their trouble and their candour. In line with the tradition of the service they will remain anonymous and their satisfaction will resemble the satisfaction which they derive each time they look at a published blue book or white paper and recognise points included, or left out, on their advice—or points retained despite their best efforts. My colleagues will equally recognise in these chapters points included at their request, gaps where points have been deleted, and still other places where points have been foolishly and stubbornly retained despite their best endeavours. It may be of added interest to record that out of about two hundred and forty criticisms and comments made on the manuscript only about twenty coincided; all the remainder were totally disparate. This can be taken as a measure not only of the hasty and superficial quality of my writing but also of the wide spread of attitudes and outlooks amongst even half a dozen senior civil servants.

Chapter 27

CONCLUSION

In this part, part III, I am drawing the threads together—first in human terms, then in terms of source material and now, most important of all, in relation to the society we serve. The civil service is only a small part of the wider public service. It represents an even smaller proportion of the gainfully occupied population as a whole. About three thousand strong in the 1930s, the non-manual, non-industrial civil service had risen in the 1970s to around fourteen thousand. It took a further leap to nineteen thousand in 1974 as a result of the reorganisation of local government when it absorbed many officials who had been previously employed by local councils. To see those figures in perspective it helps to recall that the total gainfully occupied population of the region is close on six hundred thousand.

But at nineteen thousand the civil service seems quite big enough to those working in it. Opinions naturally differ but a fair balance of view within the service would be in favour of future reduction rather than expansion. The qualities that were so admired and valued in the past—informality, intimacy, knowing one's colleagues, easy access, minimum need for conveying information by paper, general responsiveness—those qualities are being severely tested now by the sheer growth of the service. Whether it will continue to grow and whether there is any prospect of reducing the numbers depends entirely on the demands made upon the service. First there is the demand in the sense of the acts passed by parliament creating new functions of the state that have to be carried out, paid for and enforced. Second there is the demand made by politicians and the public for answerability, for reporting, for consultation, for public participation and so on. Let us be clear that both these demands result in the growth of officialdom. The problem is therefore, to an extent, quantitative but it is also qualitative. It is the quality of the administration that counts. In that context

I am acutely aware of the task I have here to convey a fair picture and (remembering the power that the service wields for good or ill and the duties that go with that power) I earnestly ask whether I have conveyed too favourable a view of the service.

Too favourable a view of the service? Taken chapter by chapter or paragraph by paragraph, what has been said in the book about the service could well be open to argument and to modification in detail, much of it is oversimplified for such a complex, changing subject, much of it could do with the insertion of qualifying phrases. Like any body of people we have our weaker brethren and—what is more to the point—each of us has within himself the human frailties that reveal themselves from time to time in the feebler and sillier aspects of government and bureaucracy.

I openly confess that I always see the tumbler as half-full while my neighbour sees the same tumbler as half-empty. There is no use pretending to be other than I am. I have therefore recorded the development of the service as I have seen it, some of its achievements and failures, some of the principles on which it works as well as some of the personalities who have helped to make it. Knowing at first-hand, and in the intimacy of confidential government activity, the hard work, steadfastness and impartiality of hundreds of staff around me I simply do not see the essence of the Northern Ireland civil service in any other light nor am I capable of writing an account of the service that stresses its blemishes and shortcomings at the risk of undervaluing those excellent qualities.

I believe that the service has served the Ulster public well for fifty-six years. It has been a steadying influence in a turbulent, unsettled and contentious society. No matter what form of political settlement emerges, a local civil administration of some kind will be an asset to the incoming political authorities, whether they sit in London, Dublin, Belfast or elsewhere. It would be unwise for quite a time to come to try to govern without one.

Looking more deeply into the structure of government from 1921 to 1977, it is clear that the administrators have occupied a more vulnerable position than their counterparts in Great Britain and even than those in the Republic. This has arisen naturally and indeed inevitably from the sheer facts of the situation.

For a long time most of the Northern Ireland ministers were frankly part-time ministers. They were certainly paid only as such. Many of them had to keep a foot in their business or professional firms in order to earn a livelihood. The restrictions on maintaining outside means of livelihood came only in the 1960s. Besides, ministers were forced by circumstances to adopt certain priorities. First

came the responsibility of warding off the enemies of the state, as
they saw them, internal as well as external, a concern which has
obviously occupied the minds of ministers right from the Sinn
Féin campaign in 1921 until the present day. Second came the task
of coping with pressure groups. Elsewhere in this book there have
been references to the easy access which local interests have to
ministers; one can get to see a minister at Stormont within a matter
of hours. But the obverse of that coin is the sheer pressure which
such interests can then exert, and the time and energy which
ministers must put into dealing with it. (Scotland and Wales would
do well to bear this in mind as proposals for devolution take shape.)
Then there has always been the disproportionately large element
of public relations work that has been thought essential. Appearances at public functions, speaking at the multitude of regional
societies in the business, farming, social and professional circles,
interpreting departments to the public and the public to departments—these duties have occupied much time and attention. In all
those circumstances it was inevitable that a heavier load of departmental responsibility should fall on senior officials than is the case
in most countries and that they should be exposed to pressures of
every kind, public as well as private.

It is necessary to go even further and ask the question: Is the
service to the public too good? This may seem an extraordinary
question to pose until one takes account of the series of results of
the first objective and statutory investigations into Northern Ireland departmental administration ever to be carried out, namely
the published reports of the Parliamentary Commissioner for Administration, commonly known as the Ombudsman. Not only do
these give the administration a clean bill of health, as one would
expect, but they record the high degree of care and concern taken
by departments for the interests of the humblest private citizen.
But even those parliamentary reports do not tell the full story. For
two years—1969 to 1971—the Commissioner for United Kingdom
administration and the Commissioner for Northern Ireland administration were one and the same man, Sir Edmund Compton.
He was thus in a literally unique position to compare the standard
of administration in Northern Ireland with that in the rest of the
United Kingdom. Here is an extract from his report for 1970, published 26 January 1971, reference H.C. 2076:

9.   My 33 completed investigations have covered a wide range
of Government Departments and activities, so that my case-
work over the first 18 months since my Office began to operate,

is in fact a scrutiny by sample of the detailed working and attitudes of 8 out of 10 of the bodies subject to my investigation, including all the principal Ministries. As a result of this experience I think it fair to say the quality of administrative performance in the Northern Ireland Ministries compares well with my experience of Government Departments in the United Kingdom. Indeed, the individual citizen frequently gets a better service from a Northern Ireland Ministry than he would get from a United Kingdom Department in similar circumstances, owing to the easier access to central Government that is both feasible and customary in a territory of the size of Northern Ireland. This readiness of access may indeed be criticised by some, from the standpoint of the general body of citizens, as detrimental to the efficiency and economical working of the apparatus of government. Be that as it may, it is all to the good from the standpoint of particular citizens doing business with the Ministries, and I have noticed the advantage taken of it by many of the complainants whose cases I have investigated.

And facing a press conference reported in the *Belfast Telegraph* on 27 January 1971 he said he had found high quality of administration in the central (i.e. Stormont) government—almost to a fault. An individual here received noticeably higher consideration than those in any other part of the United Kingdom. From the point of view of efficiency it was almost too high; for the citizen it was all to the good. There was not one incident of culpable action by any organ of central government.

I am proud to have belonged to such a service.

No matter how high the quality of the service nor how meticulous the attention given to individual matters, these still do not reflect the full extent of the contribution to society. When the analogy is used of an instrument of public policy, it is important to understand that the instrument is no mere tool or implement. A better analogy might be of the service as a motor car with, seated at the driving wheel, the political Minister of the day, a car that is capable of developing considerable power and momentum. A less happy analogy is one which looks on the service as a kind of welfare organisation endlessly conveying benefits on an ever-widening scale and constantly enlarging its patronage. Rather than adopt any of those analogies it is best to regard the service as a body of trained and impartial men and women concerned with converting public policies into practical effect; it is of the nature of such policies that they should be constantly changing and evolving.

Although this book has been largely concerned with the past it is the future that matters for the men, women and children of the Province and it is reasonable to predict that the service will have a large part to play in shaping the future. The three problems that beset Ulster, constitutional instability, political violence and economic weakness will have to be faced by whatever government is in charge and wherever that government sits, be it in Belfast, London or Dublin. In the very process of working towards a new and better state of affairs the Northern Ireland service will have a contribution to make, for its administrators both live and work in the area and they have the practical experience of operating the system in good times and ill, under peace, war, terrorism and insurrection, under the former parliament, direct rule, the power-sharing executive and direct rule again. Few others anywhere in the British Isles have had the benefit of that experience and have endured to such an extent the conflicting emotions of private feeling and public duty.

The assumptions commonly made about the political situation in the future are perhaps three: some measure of devolved government; power-sharing in a cabinet; and continuing religious division resulting in the alienation of many catholics from whatever system is created. It is by no means necessary to adopt those assumptions and a more hopeful prospect emerges if the many alternative possibilities are looked at objectively and in turn.

Within the primary matter of the future constitutional status there are a great many possibilities ranging from total integration into the United Kingdom, through devolution, federalism, independence, redrawing the border and cantonisation to a merger of some kind with the Republic of Ireland. The administrator sees all those possibilities as workable solutions, at a price in each case. It is the price, in all its many facets, that needs to be assessed, clarified and made known to the public if a sound judgment rather than an emotional stampede is to take place.

In the same way power-sharing or the distribution of seats, by whatever means, in a regional cabinet is far from being the only way of achieving political stability. Before such fragile devices are considered several basic requirements have to be met in the form of recognition of the state, acceptance of its laws and a deeply felt willingness to make the system work, whoever is in political charge. From that situation there flows a long series of honourable and dignified forms of participation and partnership at the many places

where power in a democratic, regional administration resides,
ranging from the representative of the monarch, the privy council,
a council of state, an elected assembly, a second chamber of that
assembly to its committee structures, the way in which it reaches
its decisions, its various offices of dignity and influence and on to
the innumerable statutory boards, local authorities and other parts
of the whole public process. Once more the administrator sees all
of those as the realities of the situation, the substance of power
rather than the shadow.

Again, the reputed division of the community into two irrecon-
cilable religious factions does not strike the practical administrators
as nearly so complete or so daunting. Being realists, administrators
are well aware of the conflict in society; but being realists they are
just as aware of the cohesion that exists in the everyday affairs
which they handle. In particular the talk of the catholic population being alienated from the system of government and administration seems to them to be dangerously exaggerated. Every day
the administrator sees the practical cooperation of protestant and
catholic in the statutory boards and, with some limitations, in the
local authorities. He is impressed by the cohesion in the hospital
and health service, and by the admirably practical way in which,
contrary to popular report, the catholic schools cooperate happily
with the various organs of the state. Child care, industrial training,
manpower services, the economic council, the police authority, the
huge field of social security cash benefits, the arts council, the
tourist board and countless other state services attract the ready
cooperation of protestant and catholic alike, in the sense both of
managing them and of benefiting from them.

I have dealt much more fully with these possibilities for participation in a new system of government in another work being published by Political and Economic Planning in London. I have
therefore been confining myself here to suggesting that the administrator sees the issues in less colourful and less pronounced terms
than the politician or the journalist, and believes that he can discern various ways ahead to which ordinary people could readily
subscribe.

Given that the two great needs of the Province still are to resolve the fundamental question of national allegiance and to embrace the politics of consensus and accommodation, then the
administrator would suggest from his experience that no one
vaunted formula can be guaranteed to provide a solution and that
it is a cruel deceit to proclaim that it will. How often in the past

have attractive solutions turned to ashes in our mouths. Progress must be gradual and many approaches tried.

Looking back over the administrative history of the last two or three hundred years, there is ground for saying that the Ulster problem may well have to be accepted, however reluctantly, as one of those problems to which there is no solution. It may be sadly necessary for Ulster, Britain and Ireland to live with the problem unsolved just as Belgium has to live with an insoluble language problem, Holland with a deepseated confessional problem and the whole world, indeed, with the harsh separation into communism and non-communism that holds absolutely no promise of a solution within foreseeable time.

It is all the more important in that situation to have our public services supervised and controlled by elected politicians of the highest quality. One of the regrets of administrators in Northern Ireland down the years since 1921 has been the tendency for so many able people of standing in business and professional life to eschew politics and, after perhaps paying a nominal cash subscription to a political party, to draw their skirts away. Each time administrators heard critics denigrate the ministers with whom they worked, or pour scorn on the quality of the Commons or Senate whose debates they sat through, the feelings uppermost in their minds were of regret that those superior and clever critics did not enter politics, offer themselves for election and show how much better they could have discharged the immensely difficult task of managing the public affairs of the Province.

To make good that shortfall is one of the pressing tasks of today, made even more pressing by the new tendency discernible amongst some of the most earnest citizens in the peace movement (and many other organs of reconciliation) to resign themselves to the thought that the politicians have let down the community and that party politics offers no way forward. A well-meaning but dangerously vague concept of community action is offered as a replacement. Potentially more dangerous still is the astonishing new growth of community associations, some with dubious connections but nevertheless intent on imposing their will on housing, roads, redevelopment, community halls, libraries and so on to the virtual exclusion of elected politicians and of rational argument, financial considerations, ordered priorities and other realities of public administration. The alternative to elected representative government can only be anarchy or tyranny in the long run.

Even if elected politicians were to achieve a constitutional and political settlement and even if violence were to end, the task of governing the Province, of restructuring industry, of reducing unemployment and of raising the standard of living would be an exacting one. The long years of reported violence have tended to conceal the equally corrosive influences of lawlessness, of rejection of authority, of rent and rate strike, of imprisonment of young people alongside dedicated terrorists and of children growing up in the atmosphere of those influences. Service to the government and to the community in that task and in that situation will make at least as heavy demands on the civil service as have the years of instability and violence. Measures will have to be taken to prepare the service; but even before those are contemplated some strategic decisions are needed.

If the constitutional future leans towards integration with Britain then the balance of argument is in favour of doing away with the Northern Ireland service as a separate entity and merging it with the British. If there is to be some form of union with the Republic of Ireland, then steps would have to be taken to combine with the Dublin service. If the future lies with devolution or federalism then the retention of the Northern Ireland service as a separate and distinct crown service should be the undoubted starting-point in the interests of total loyalty to the new regime and of total control by that regime.

Given that starting point as the restated position, much could be done to equip the Northern service for the harder work ahead. The immediate need will be to rebuild morale and to infuse departments with more of the savour, zest and sense of satisfaction they used to display. Much could be done by shortening lines of communication, by bringing detailed decision-making closer to the scene of the action and by throwing overboard some of the excessive deck cargo of well-meaning but inhibiting arrangements for control and supervision. Interchange of staff with the British service could be greatly extended; it could well be the rule that every promising young administrator spend a year in Whitehall and that young Whitehall officers spend a year in Northern Ireland (or for that matter in any of the regions). The present extremely limited opportunities for service in the institutions of the European Communities or in the United Kingdom delegation to the European Community might be extended with benefit. More contact, and above all more open and recognised contact, with officers in the Dublin departments would undoubtedly be beneficial. Within the Province some further opening out of experience would be helpful. Subject to preserving the essential and most valuable qualities of the generalist administrator, with his impartiality and detachment, the service, in cooperation with industry, commerce and the trade unions, could do much to arrange short-term exchanges of staff. On a different level the service needs to be constantly refreshed by the promotion of younger men and women and, even more important, by the giving of responsibility at an earlier age and at lower ranks if real contact is to be maintained with the rising generation in the Province. Another need is to strengthen the all-too-tenuous working links between the service and the two universities and the Ulster College. In other words, great though the contribution of the service can be in helping create new structures and in making them work, the energies and abilities of a much wider circle of people will be needed to get the best out of the undoubted qualities of the Ulster people, to arrest the emigration of so many of the more energetic young men and women and to rebuild a settled and prosperous society. Those aims are justified not only in terms of the internal needs of Ulster but also in terms of enlarging the contribution which Ulster can in so many ways make to Ireland, Britain and the world.

Appendix I

GENERAL SERVICE GRADES IN THE NORTHERN IRELAND CIVIL SERVICE

SECRETARY, or Permanent Secretary: the chief permanent official in a ministry or department. Formerly the Permanent Secretary of Finance was also Head of the Civil Service but the latter has now a separate and higher position.

DEPUTY SECRETARY: originally one officer who deputised for the Secretary in his absence but now a recognised grade since 1970.

SENIOR ASSISTANT SECRETARY: much in use (instead of Deputy Secretary grade) from 1958 till 1970. Less in use now. Some top professional positions are graded at this level.

ASSISTANT SECRETARY: the first, that is the lowest, grade recognised by law as competent to commit the corporate ministry or department. Also in common practice the lowest grade normally authorised to advise the minister on policy. One of the grades that have operated throughout the history of the service since 1921 unchanged in title or authority.

SENIOR PRINCIPAL: a modern development used, in the main, for posts controlling a large bloc of executive work.

PRINCIPAL: again, one of the key grades right since 1921; generally head of a branch; much of the internal day-to-day administration turns on this grade.

DEPUTY PRINCIPAL: a grade peculiar to the Northern Ireland Civil Service since the 1920s, carrying effective administrative and executive responsibility. It is at this grade that the two streams of promotion meet—from the clerical and executive grades on the one hand, and on the other from the university entrants to the Administration Trainee grade. A Principal might therefore have two Deputy Principals in his Branch—an officer of 50 with thirty-two years' service and a young graduate of 25 with perhaps only three. Either might suceed the Principal when his post fell vacant.

ASSISTANT PRINCIPAL: the 'cadet' grade for university honours graduate entry from the 1920s till 1972. Known as A.P. and regarded as the golden road.

ADMINISTRATION TRAINEE: the modern replacement for the A.P. and a more descriptive title as this is essentially a 'training' grade. The young graduate will spend part of his time on in-service training courses; part of it as secretary to a committee or private secretary to a permanent secretary or minister; and part of it with more experienced colleagues 'learning on the job.' Many honours graduates of course nowadays enter the Service at the Executive level, a reflection of the broader educational opportunities now open.

These are the grades available to a Permanent Secretary in the grading and paying of his administrative staff. It should not be thought that all those grades necessarily operate in the hierarchy of day-to-day authority or in career advancement. Both the command structure and the career ladder are simpler in practice. In addition to these administrative grades there are the executive and clerical grades, where the greater numbers of staff are engaged, and where the greater part of the day-to-day work is discharged.

Appendix II

THE AUTHOR'S CAREER AS SEEN IN CIVIL SERVICE TERMS

1936   Sat British First Division Civil Service Commission examinations and failed.
1937   Sat British examinations again and qualified for several home and foreign services. Opted for the Northern Ireland Civil Service.
1937   Entered the Northern Ireland Ministry of Labour as an Assistant Principal.

1938   Seconded to the Northern Ireland Council of Social Service on its foundation and acted as its first secretary.

1938   Recalled to Ministry and appointed Private Secretary to the Parliamentary Secretary.

1940   Transferred to the new Ministry of Public Security and appointed Private Secretary to the Minister immediately after Dunkirk.

1940   Promoted Deputy Principal.

1942   Appointed Private Secretary to a Minister again.

1943   Appointed Private Secretary to another incoming Minister.

1944   Transferred to the new Ministry of Health and Local Government.

1945   Promoted Principal.

1946   Appointed Principal of a Special Branch to concentrate on post-war reconstruction legislation—tuberculosis, health and welfare services.

1954   Sent to Imperial Defence College, London for a course in home, commonwealth and foreign affairs.

1954   Promoted Assistant Secretary in the Ministry of Health and Local Government.

1958   Promoted Senior Assistant Secretary.

1963   Promoted to the grade of Permanent Secretary in the position of Second Secretary.

1964   Transferred to the new Ministry of Development as Second Secretary.

1971   Appointed Permanent Secretary of the Ministry of Development.

1974   Appointed Permanent Secretary of the new Department of Housing, Local Government and Planning.

1975   Appointed Chief Adviser to the Chairman of the Constitutional Convention.

1976   **Retired.**

INDEX